Microsoft Access 97 Exam Cram

The Cram Sheet

This Cram Sheet contains the distilled, key tasks in Microsoft Access 97. Review this information last thing before you enter the test room, paying special attention to those areas where you feel you need the most review. If you transfer any of the tasks from this sheet onto a blank piece of paper before beginning the exam, you can refer to it while taking the test.

DATABASE DESIGN

1. Design databases using reverse engineering; start with the output and work your way back to the objects that must be in place for the output to be created.

2. Tables are the fundamental objects in Access.

3. Queries require tables.

4. Bound forms require queries or tables.

5. Unbound forms are application interface objects.

6. Macros automate repetitive tasks.

7. Modules make macros and other actions more efficient.

8. Objects can be opened or designed starting from the Database window.

9. Third normal form is required for an efficient relational database.

10. The Relationships window displays, creates, and edits relationships, and is accessible via the Relationships button.

11. In a relational database, tables are linked via the primary key in the parent table and the same key (now called the foreign key) in the child table.

12. Tables linked in a parent-child relationship are said to have a one-to-many relationship.

TABLE DESIGN AND MANIPULATION

13. The first field in a new table is often a primary key field; you can set primary key status using the Primary Key button.

14. The primary key often has a data type of AutoNumber.

15. Data type can be set in the Data Type column using the drop-down list.

16. Text fields cannot be added, subtracted, or otherwise manipulated.

17. Further formatting of the data type can be performed in the Field Properties portion of the Table Design screen.

18. Lookup fields can be created using the Lookup tab of the Field Properties section.

19. The Bound Column property of a Lookup field dictates what data is inserted into the receiving table.

20. Default values, input masks, and validation rules can be set in the Field Properties section.

21. Indexing as well as the requirement for data (Required) can be set in the Field Properties section.

22. Fields should have individual values (such as city) rather than composite values (such as city-state-zip).

23. One-field tables often serve as lookup lists.

24. Values that can be calculated from existing values do not have fields, but are derived later in queries, forms, and reports.

DATASHEETS

25. Resize a datasheet to fit fields by choosing Format|ColumnWidth|Best Fit.

26. Rename fields by double-clicking on the field header and then editing the name.

27. Filter records by selecting data and then clicking on the Filter By Selection button.

28. Sort records by clicking on the Sort button (either Ascending or Descending).

29. Sort multiple columns of data by clicking on one column and then shift-clicking on others.

30. Sort data in different orders by choosing Records|Filter|Advanced Filter/Sort from the menu bar.

31. Apply filters by clicking on the Apply Filter button.

QUERY DESIGN

32. Add tables to an existing query by choosing Query|Show Tables from the menu bar or by clicking on the Show Tables button.

33. Add fields to a query by clicking on and then dragging the fields from the table.

34. Join tables in a query by clicking on and then dragging primary key fields from the parent table to the child table.

35. Change join types by right-clicking on join lines and then editing the join.

36. Remove tables from an existing query by selecting them and then pressing Delete.

USING QUERIES

37. Add search and retrieval criteria to a query by entering an example in the Criteria row.

38. Search for one value or another by entering data in the Or row.

39. Search for an approximate value by using wild cards along with the data you enter: the asterisk (*) for any value and the question mark (?) for an individual character.

40. Create new fields or calculated fields by going to a blank field column, typing the name of the new field followed by a colon (NewField:), and then entering the expression.

41. Use totals (Sum, Count, and so on) in a query by choosing View|Totals from the menu bar or by clicking on the Totals button and then selecting the type of total you wish to use from the drop-down list in the Totals row.

42. View and change SQL in a query by choosing View|SQL View from the menu bar.

43. Change the function of a query by choosing Query from the menu bar or by clicking on the Query Type button and then selecting the type of query you wish to change to (Crosstab, Make-Table, Append, Update, and so on).

FORM DESIGN

44. Add controls and graphic elements to a form with the Toolbox, accessible via the Toolbox button or from the menu bar (View|Toolbox).

45. Change the properties of a control by right-clicking on the control and then opening the properties sheet.

46. Use the shortcut menu to change frequently modified properties (such as color and special effects).

47. Adjust control sizing and spacing with the Align and Size choices on the shortcut menu.

48. Make design easier by enabling the grid in Design mode (choose View|Grid from the menu bar).

49. Change tab order using the Tab Order function from the shortcut menu.

50. Go from the properties of one control to those of another (when a properties sheet is already open) by clicking on the other control.

51. Display the properties of an invisible or hard-to-select control or object by using the object selector drop-down list on the Form/Report Formatting toolbar and then clicking on the Properties button.

Microsoft

ACCESS 97

MICROSOFT
OFFICE
USER
SPECIALIST

David Mercer

Microsoft Access 97 Exam Cram

Limits Of Liability And Disclaimer Of Warranty

Trademarks

The Coriolis Group, LLC
14455 N. Hayden Road, Suite 220
Scottsdale, Arizona 85260

602/483-0192
FAX 602/483-0193
http://www.coriolis.com

Library of Congress Cataloging-in-Publication Data
    Mercer, David (David Steuart)
        Microsoft Access 97 exam cram / by David Mercer.
        p.   cm.
    Includes index.
    ISBN 1-57610-223-8
    1. Microsoft Access (Computer file).   2. Database management.   I. Title.
QA76.9.D3M448   1999
005.75'65--dc21   98-29401
                                                            CIP

Printed in the United States of America
10 9 8 7 6 5 4 3 2 1

Publisher
Keith Weiskamp

Acquisitions Editor
Shari Jo Hehr

Marketing Specialist
Cynthia Caldwell

Project Editor
Michelle Stroup

Technical Reviewer
George Sparks

Production Coordinator
Kim Eoff

Cover Design
Jody Winkler

Layout Design
April Nielsen

CD-ROM Developer
Robert Clarfield

14455 North Hayden, Suite 220 • Scottsdale, Arizona 85260

The Smartest Way To Get Certified ™

Thank you for purchasing one of our innovative certification study guides, just one of the many members of the Coriolis family of certification products.

Certification Insider Press™ was created in late 1997 by The Coriolis Group to help professionals like you obtain certification and advance your career. Achieving certification involves a major commitment and a great deal of hard work. To help you reach your goals, we've listened to others like you, and we've designed our entire product line around you and the way you like to study, learn, and master challenging subjects. Our approach is *The Smartest Way To Get Certified.*

In less than a year, Coriolis has published over one million copies of our highly popular *Exam Cram, Exam Prep,* and *On Site* guides. Our *Exam Cram* books, specifically written to help you pass an exam, are the number one certification self-study guides in the industry. They are the perfect complement to any study plan you have, as well as to the rest of the Certification Insider Press series: *Exam Prep,* comprehensive study guides designed to help you thoroughly learn and master certification topics, and *On Site,* guides that really show you how to apply your skills and knowledge on the job.

Our commitment to you is to ensure that all of the certification study guides we develop help you save time and frustration. Each one provides unique study tips and techniques, memory joggers, custom quizzes, insight about test taking, practical problems to solve, real-world examples, and much more.

We'd like to hear from you. Help us continue to provide the very best certification study materials possible. Write us or email us at **craminfo@coriolis.com** and let us know how our books have helped you study, or tell us about new features that you'd like us to add. If you send us a story about how an *Exam Cram, Exam Prep,* or *On Site* book has helped you, and we use it in one of our books, we'll send you an official Coriolis shirt for your efforts.

Good luck with your certification exam and your career. Thank you for allowing us to help you achieve your goals.

Keith Weiskamp
Publisher, Certification Insider Press

To my wife JoAnn, and the kids, Mike and Charlene. It's been a long road, but we're finally there. I love you.

❧

About The Author

Having worked in an industrial facility for more than 20 years, Dave Mercer is a veteran database user. Large mainframe databases still contain the basic data that tracks production, expenditures, and payroll, and users are still wrestling information out of them daily. But since 1981—when Dave first used an Apple computer to solve a production problem—he became convinced that there must be a better way. He now uses Microsoft Access to design database solutions from his desktop for himself and others, professionally and for fun.

Dave has a Bachelor of Science degree in Business Administration, has enrolled in many computer and database programming courses, and has pursued continuing education in Microsoft Office applications. His work experience includes industrial engineering, professional instructing, and database design. Dave recently co-authored the *Access 2000 Developer's Black Book* (published by the Coriolis Group) with Lars Klander. Dave is a certified Access 97 Expert.

Dave operates AFC Computer Services in Spring Valley, California, where he lives with his wife JoAnn. You can reach him at **mercer@e4free.com**.

Acknowledgments

Thanks to Shari Jo Hehr, Michelle Stroup, Kim Eoff, Paula Kmetz, and everyone on the Coriolis staff for all your help, understanding and patience while we waited for the Access exam to be released, and thanks to my agent, David Fugate, for finding a project so well suited to my talents. Thanks also to Gabriel Wizard, Elisabeth Parker, and the other *Exam Cram* authors whose support, advice and goodwill gave me the moral support I needed to get through this.

Contents At A Glance

Table Of Contents

Introduction

Welcome to *Microsoft Access 97 Exam Cram*. This book aims to help you get ready to take—and pass—the Microsoft Access 97 Expert exam. In this introduction, I introduce the Microsoft Office User Specialist program in general and talk about how the *Exam Cram* series can help you prepare for the Microsoft Office User Specialist exams.

Exam Cram books help you understand and appreciate the subjects and skills you need to pass Microsoft Office User Specialist exams. The books are aimed strictly at test preparation and review. They do not teach you everything you need to know about an application. Instead, I (the author) present and dissect the questions and problems that you're likely to encounter on a test. I've worked from Microsoft's proficiency guidelines, the exams, and third-party test preparation tools. My aim is to bring together as much information as possible about the Microsoft Office User Specialist exams.

Nevertheless, to completely prepare yourself for any Microsoft test, I recommend that you begin your studies with some classroom training or that you pick up and read one of the many study guides available. I recommend *Exam Preps* from Certification Insider Press—a complete learning and test preparation system when used in conjunction with the *Exam Cram* you have in hand. *Exam Preps* feature a practice environment that simulates the application you are learning on the companion CD. If you choose another study guide, I strongly recommend that you install, configure, and fool around with the software or environment that you'll be tested on, because nothing beats hands-on experience and familiarity when it comes to understanding the questions you're likely to encounter on a certification test. Book learning is essential, but hands-on experience is the best teacher of all. The tests are designed to validate your skill level for a specific Microsoft Office application. They accomplish this by testing you on real-world problems within the application on which you are being tested. The Microsoft Office User Specialist certification sets you apart from candidates with whom you are competing for job openings in all areas of business and industry. It proves to a potential employer that you have the skills that are in demand.

The Microsoft Office User Specialist program currently offers certification for Word, Excel, PowerPoint, and Access. Exams are available for Word and Excel in '95 versions, Word 97, Excel 97, and PowerPoint 97, and Access 97.

FrontPage, Outlook, and Office Integration Expert will follow over the next several months.

There are two certification skill levels for Word and Excel: Proficient and Expert. Only the Expert level is offered for all other applications at this time. Proficient Specialists are able to perform a wide range of daily tasks. Expert Specialists are able to handle more complex tasks in addition to the daily tasks.

The most prestigious certification is that of the Microsoft Office Expert. In order to obtain the Microsoft Office Expert certification, users must obtain Expert Specialist status on all five core Office 97 applications and then pass the Office 97 Integration exam. Passing this exam guarantees that you are not only skilled in each application, but also that you possess integration skills between the Office 97 applications. For more specifics about the MOUS program, see Table 1.

Table 1 Microsoft Office User Specialist Program*

Application	Proficiency Level	Expert Level
Microsoft Word 97	Proves your ability to handle a wide range of everyday tasks. This exam will not qualify for Office Integration Expert.	Proves your ability to do all everyday tasks, plus more complex assignments.
Microsoft Excel 97	Proves your ability to handle a wide range of everyday tasks. This exam will not qualify you for Office Integration Expert.	Proves your ability to do all everyday tasks, plus more complex assignments.
Microsoft Access 97	There will be no Proficiency exam.	Proves your ability to do all everyday tasks, plus more complex assignments.
Microsoft Outlook 97	There will be no Proficiency exam.	Proves your ability to do all everyday tasks, plus more complex assignments.
Microsoft PowerPoint 97	There will be no Proficiency exam.	Proves your ability to do all everyday tasks, plus more complex assignments.
Microsoft Office Integration	There will be no Proficiency exam.	Has attained Expert status in each of the 5 core Office 97 applications. Demonstrates an ability to synthesize the various applications within the Office Suite.

* The **Microsoft Office User Specialist** program will be expanded to include Microsoft applications outside the Office Suite, such as Microsoft FrontPage 97 and Microsoft Project.

Proficiency and Expert level tests are also available for Microsoft Word 7 and Microsoft Excel 7 (Office 95).

Taking A Certification Exam

All Microsoft Office User Specialist exams are offered by Authorized Client Testing (ACT) Centers. Although exams are currently available only in English, exams in Japanese and other languages will be offered as soon as courseware exists. Each computer-based exam costs between $50.00 and $100.00, and if you do not pass, you may retest for an additional $50.00 or more each time. Although most centers require that you pre-register, you may be able to walk in and test. Don't be afraid to ask. You may register by calling 800-933-4493, or contact a local ACT Center directly. If you dial the 800 number, you will be asked for your ZIP code. You will then be given the contact information for one or more centers located near you. Each ACT Center has policies that cover canceling an appointment, missing a scheduled appointment, and arriving late (e.g., you may not be able to get a refund for a missed appointment). Be sure to find out about your responsibilities and your options. Visit one of these Web sites for more information about the program, the exams, and what people are saying about their test experience before you schedule your exam: **www.officecert.com** or **www.microsoft.com/office/train_cert**.

All exams are timed; you will have one hour or less for each one. The tests measure productivity and efficiency; that means that both speed and accuracy are important in order to pass! You will be asked to perform approximately 40 tasks within about 60 minutes.

Be sure to arrive early enough to complete the registration that you began on the phone. Many centers require you to appear within a specific time interval before the test begins. For example, you might have to arrive 30 minutes prior to your test appointment time. When you call to schedule your exam, ask when you need to be there. You must provide two valid forms of identification at the test center. The tests are monitored and you may not use any test aids (books, notes, etc.). A blank sheet of paper and pencil or a wipe-off board and marker will be provided on which you can take notes. If there is a task with which you are unfamiliar or one that will take more time than you feel you have to complete it, answer it anyway. You have to answer the questions in the order in which they appear. You must complete all parts of a question if you are to receive credit for any of it. Office Help screens are available to you, but you won't have time to use them *and* complete the exam within the time allowed. You must surrender the paper or wipe-off board on which your notes are written when you leave the test room.

Test results are shown on the computer screen when the exam ends, so you will know immediately if you passed or failed. On most exams, you will pass if you perform all but two tasks correctly, so there's not much room for error. If you do not pass, the screen will display a wide range of skill areas that you need to practice before you attempt to take the test again.

Tracking MOUS Status

If you pass your exam, a certificate will be sent to you by mail within one to two weeks. Exam results are reported only to you and to Microsoft. If you pass the Access Expert level exam, your certificate will affirm that you are a "Microsoft Access 97 Expert Specialist." You will have the proof you need to substantiate the level of expertise you include on your resume.

How To Prepare For An Exam

At a minimum, preparing for an Access 97 test requires that you obtain and study additional materials. I highly recommend the *Microsoft Access 97 Exam Prep*, also from Certification Insider Press. This comprehensive, Microsoft-approved study guide provides step-by-step coverage of all of the topics included on the exam. There's a lot of practice, too—end-of-chapter review questions and projects in the book, plus the award winning Access 97 tutorial simulator on the companion CD-ROM. This interactive tutorial guides you every step of the way through all of the Access 97 basics and then tests your skill mastery. The CD-ROM also includes the practice documents you'll need in order to perform all of the exercises in the book, saving you hours of valuable study time.

If you can't find the *Microsoft Access 97 Exam Prep* on the shelf at your favorite bookstore, please visit our Web site at www.certificationinsider.com or ask your local bookstore to order a copy for you.

If you know that you need more practice or if you like to study by using a variety of resources, then please refer to the "Need to Know More" sections at the end of each chapter. These Web sites also offer suggestions for further study: **www.officecert.com** or **www.microsoft.com/office/train_cert**.

About This Book

Each topical *Exam Cram* chapter follows a similar structure, along with graphical cues about especially important or useful material. Here's the structure of a typical chapter:

➤ **Opening hotlists** Each chapter begins with lists of the terms and skills that you must learn and understand before you can be fully conversant with the chapter's subject matter.

➤ **Tasks** Within the body of each chapter you'll find a series of tasks to complete that are related to the topics.

➤ **Study Alerts** We will highlight information helpful for the test using a special Study Alert layout, like this:

This is what a Study Alert looks like. Normally, a Study Alert stresses concepts, terms, or activities that will most likely appear in one or more certification test questions. For that reason, we think any information found offset in Study Alert format is worthy of special attentiveness on your part. Indeed, most of the facts appearing in The Cram Sheet (inside the front cover of this book) appear as Study Alerts within the text.

We have also provided tips that will help build a better foundation of knowledge about the Office application on which you'll test. Although the information may not be on the exam, it is highly relevant and will help you become a better test taker.

 This is how tips are formatted. Keep your eyes open for these, and you'll become a test guru in no time.

You will also find items called "Hold That Skill." Consider these as necessary skills you should practice over and over again until you can do them without thinking. They are essential for you to pass the exam.

HOLD That Skill!

Look to Hold That Skill as something for you to practice so you can ace the test.

➤ **Practice Exercises** This section presents a series of mock test exercises and solutions.

➤ **Details and resources** Every chapter ends with a section titled "Need To Know More?" That section provides direct pointers to Microsoft and third-party resources that offer further details on the chapter's subject. In addition, this section tries to rate the quality and thoroughness of the topic's coverage by each resource. If you find a resource you like in this collection, use it, but don't feel compelled to use all the resources. On the other hand, I recommend only those resources that I use on a regular basis, so none of my recommendations will be a waste of your time or money.

The bulk of the book follows this chapter structure slavishly, but there are a few other elements to point out: the sample test and the answer key to the sample test that appears in Chapters 17 and 18, and a reasonably exhaustive glossary of terms. Finally, look for The Cram Sheet, which appears inside the front cover of this *Exam Cram* book. It is a valuable tool that represents a condensed and compiled collection of facts, figures, and tips that we think you should memorize before taking the test. Because you can dump this information out of your head and onto a piece of paper before answering any exam questions, you can master this information by brute force—you need to re-member it only long enough to write it down when you walk into the test room. You might even want to look at it in the car or in the lobby of the testing center just before you walk in to take the test.

How To Use This Book

This book is designed to be read in sequence and the tasks and skills practice questions allow you to build on what you've learned. We encourage you to do yourself a favor and go for a complete review. However, if you already know Access 97 and are just brushing up before the exam or if you have taken the exam and failed, you can take the practice exam at the end of the book to reveal any skill weaknesses you need to work on. You can then focus on practicing the skills that you need to work on (the one challenge in this approach is that the practice documents that are provided on the companion diskette may build on earlier practice questions).

We'd like to hear from you! If you have comments about this book, email them directly to me at mercer@e4free.com.

Thanks, and enjoy the book!

Microsoft Office User Specialist Tests

Terms you'll need to understand:

√   Exercise

√   Task

√   Testing strategy

√   Testing environment

√   Careful reading

√   Process of elimination

Skills you'll need to master:

√   Preparing to take a Microsoft Office User Specialist exam

√   Practicing (to make perfect)

√   Making the best use of the testing software

√   Budgeting your time

√   Working under pressure

√   Guessing (as a last resort)

You've probably taken literally hundreds of tests in your life by now: multiple-choice, essay questions, fill-ins, and the kind where you have to show your work. Microsoft Office User Specialist (MSOUS) tests focus on accomplishing real-world requirements through the use of preconstructed documents and tasks. In each task, you must complete several steps (a step-by-step progression to fulfilling the objectives of the exercise). You've probably already performed many of these tasks during your training or day-to-day work, so your job is to learn how they are formatted for the test.

The concept behind testing is that if you pass, you know the material and are proficient at it. However, as we all know, some folks are better test-takers than others. This leads to the notion that someone who is very good at doing the actual work could still fail the test, whereas someone who is only mediocre could pass the exam with flying colors.

In fact, even the most carefully designed test cannot perfectly predict on-the-job performance. Be that as it may, most people would agree that a well-constructed test is better than no test at all. What other objective measure can employers use to tell the difference between those who claim they're knowledgeable and those who really are? Therefore, it's up to you to learn the skills and strategies you need to do well on the test.

Understanding the exam-taking particulars (how much time to spend on questions, the setting you'll be in, and so on) and the testing software will help you concentrate on the material rather than on the environment. Likewise, mastering a few basic test-taking skills should help you recognize (and hopefully overcome) the tricks and traps you're bound to find in the Microsoft test exercises.

For the Access 97 test, trick questions take the form of an ordinary question that you can't answer without knowing a hidden fact. For instance, one question might ask you to "make the Switchboard form open upon database startup." One way to make something occur when the database first starts is to create a macro named Autoexec. Access 97 is programmed to automatically run a macro named Autoexec (if it exists) when the database first starts. Any commands in the macro, such as opening the Switchboard form, are then executed, but there are no clues in the task that reference macros or an Autoexec macro.

In this chapter, we'll explain the testing environment and software, as well as describe some proven test-taking strategies you can use to your advantage. The entire Exam Cram team has compiled this information based on the many MOUS and other Microsoft certification exams we have taken ourselves. We've also drawn on the advice of our friends and colleagues, some of whom have taken quite a number of Microsoft tests themselves.

The Testing Situation

When you arrive at the center where you scheduled your test (see the introduction for more information on how to find a test center near you), you'll need to sign in with a test coordinator. He or she will ask you to produce two forms of identification, one of which must be a photo ID. Once you've signed in and your time slot arrives, you'll be asked to deposit any books, bags, or other items you brought with you, and you'll be escorted into a closed room. Typically, that room will be furnished with anywhere from one to half a dozen computers, and each workstation will be separated from the others by dividers designed to keep you from seeing what's happening on someone else's computer.

You'll be furnished with a pen or pencil and a blank sheet of paper, or in some cases, an erasable plastic sheet and an erasable felt-tip pen. You'll be allowed to write down any information you want, and you can write stuff on both sides of the page. We suggest that you memorize as much of the material that appears on The Cram Sheet (inside the front cover of this book) as possible and then write that information down on the blank sheet as soon as you sit down in front of the test machine. You'll be able to refer to it anytime you like during the test, but you'll have to surrender the sheet when you leave the room.

 You can use several techniques to memorize important facts and figures for the exam. One is to associate a list of facts with an easily remembered phrase. For instance, Microsoft Access 97 supports nine data types: Text, Memo, Number, Data/Time, Currency, AutoNumber, Yes/No, OLE Object, and Hyperlink. To recall these, you could make up a phrase such as: The Maximum Number of Data/Types Currently Allowed Yields/No Objective Hype. It's corny, but it works!

Most test rooms are designed to permit the test coordinator to monitor the room, to prevent test-takers from talking to one another, and to observe anything out of the ordinary that might go on. The test coordinator will have preloaded the Microsoft certification test you've signed up for (for those of you reading this book, that's Microsoft Access 97 Expert), and you'll be permitted to start as soon as you're seated in front of the machine.

Note: At the time the Access 97 test was released, the introduction sheet still labeled the test "Evaluation only." However, a Microsoft tech rep I spoke to said that this was just some old beta text that hadn't yet been removed, so don't worry if you see that on your test at startup.

All Microsoft Office User Specialist exams have a time limit (for example, the Access 97 test allows 85 minutes total time, with 60 minutes of actual working time). The Microsoft Access 97 Expert exam consists of 48 tasks, with approximately 6 short steps each, randomly selected from a pool of exercises. You're permitted to take up to 85 minutes to complete the exam. You should bring a watch, because there is no on-screen clock, just a counter that lets you know what task you're on. All the Microsoft Office User Specialist exams have a passing percentage (it's 70 percent for Access 97 Expert). The system will calculate your score and let you know right away (at the end of the test) whether you've passed or failed, but it takes four to six weeks to get your certificate in the mail. You can, however, ask the administrator to do a screen print if you'd like instant proof.

Make sure to have the test administrator write down the test number when you begin the test. Your test results can be verified later if you have the test number.

All Microsoft Office User Specialist exams are computer generated and use a task and steps format. Each task consists of perhaps three to seven steps, each task being a one- or two-sentence instruction that must be followed before the next task can be started. The tasks are specific to the exercise and guide you through a progressively more complex application.

Although this might sound easy, the exercises are constructed not just to check your mastery of basic facts and figures about Microsoft Access 97, but they also require you to evaluate one or more sets of circumstances or requirements. There will probably be several technically correct ways to accomplish the objective, but you need to use the most efficient method, or the best or most effective solution to a problem. To get an idea of what Microsoft considers the best method for doing a task, try consulting the Help system within Access 97. Remember, you'll have to practice this before the test, because there won't be enough time to consult Help during the test, at least not more than two or three times.

In any case, taking the test is quite an adventure, and it involves real thinking. This book will show you what to expect and how to deal with the problems, puzzles, and predicaments you're likely to find on the test.

Test Layout And Design

The Microsoft Office User Specialist exam consists of 48 exercises composed of as many as 7 tasks each. The tasks in each exercise are sometimes preceded by a short explanation of the situation. It will be basically enough information to give you a feel for the context in which the tasks are to be performed and the desired objective. The tasks tell you what to do (and which preloaded files to use) but not how.

In order to give you the ability to learn, review, and practice all at the same time, the chapters in this book are interspersed with explanations of each topic as well as sample tasks that include much additional detail about the subject. At the end of each chapter is a set of practice tasks and steps, followed by explanations of the correct method and desired results (described in numbered steps).

A sample task and steps are depicted in Exercise 1. As with many of the exercises in this book, this exercise is designed to be similar in scope to actual test exercises, but more extensive. We've made it that way because we don't know every question that might be asked, but we want to cover all the bases. Actual exam tasks will be about as hard but somewhat shorter.

Our sample exercise requires you to build a simple database with a preloaded selection of data, then construct a data entry form, a query, and a report from the tables. Following the exercise is a brief summary of each technique you need to use for performing the tasks. And by the way, don't get confused about an "exercise" versus a "task." Microsoft calls them tasks, but we refer to our samples as exercises because they are intended to give you a little Access workout.

Exercise 1   Create a new database and common objects.

You work for a small company that has just gotten large enough to convert its employee records from an Excel spreadsheet to an Access 97 database format. The spreadsheet information is in the form of rows and columns of data, and there are now 15 employees, 3 of whom have the last name Smith. Using the data file EmployeeData.dat, build a database named Employees.

Create a new database in Access. Save it as Employees.

Create the tables required for the data in EmployeeData.dat.

Save the tables, naming them Employees and Paychecks.

Create a form for data entry in the Employees table. Use the Form Wizard defaults.

Save the form, naming it EmployeesDataEntry.

Create a query based on the Paychecks table. Use the Query Wizard defaults.

> Construct the query so that only Employees named Smith ppear.
>
> Save the query as EmployeesSmith.
>
> Create a report based on EmployeesSmith. Use the Report Wizard defaults.
>
> Save the report as SmithPaychecks, then Preview it.

The correct way to create the database is to start a new database in Access 97, name it Employees, and then review the data in the data file EmployeeData.dat, before building the required tables. In order to complete the first and second tasks, you must be familiar with how to create a new database, as well as how to efficiently format fields for tables based on existing data.

For Tasks 3, 5, 8, and 10, you must be familiar with saving your work. For Tasks 4, 6, and 9, you must understand how to use the Form, Query, and Report wizards. You must also be familiar with how tables are joined (notice that the tasks don't come out and tell you specifically that this must be done, but it definitely has to happen for the exercise to be correctly completed). In addition, in Task 7, you must understand how to properly set query criteria within a query.

This sample exercise corresponds closely to those you'll see on the Microsoft Office User Specialist Access 97 test (except that the actual exercises are shorter). To correctly complete the tasks during the test, you would read the instructions, perform each task in order according to the instructions, and indicate when you are done. The only difference between the Microsoft Office User Specialist exam and this exercise is that you don't get to see the answers after the real exercises.

For each exercise, the tasks may have one or more correct solutions. However, as far as we can tell (Microsoft won't comment), the exercise is scored as wrong unless you choose the *best* solution. In other words, a technically correct but less than optimum answer does not result in partial credit when the test is scored. In addition, if you make the wrong choice when you solve the first task, it will lead you in the wrong direction on the following tasks, because each task may build upon previous tasks.

 Some of the questions ask you to find or save documents, so you'll have to know how to find your way around the hard drive.

Using Microsoft's Test Software Effectively

One of the first things to check for when you begin your testing experience is to make sure everything is working properly. Is the monitor large enough to use easily? Does the software seem to be functioning smoothly, and are all the required controls present? A rather large horizontal bar that contains the Next, Instructions, and Quit buttons will occupy the bottom of your screen. When the test starts, the instructions will first appear in large type, in a large box in the center of the screen. When you click on the box, the instructions will appear in smaller type in the bar at the bottom of the screen, so you can see all the database objects. If you want to make them appear in the center of the screen again, simply click on the Instructions button.

If anything unusual is occurring or something doesn't seem right, make sure the test administrator is aware of it. Because the program is still quite new, software glitches have been known to happen.

 If a Quit button displays outside the bottom bar during the test, do not click on it. It stops the test, and there is no warning dialog box or other option to cancel the Quit command.

Make sure you are familiar with how to navigate using the mouse or the keyboard throughout the application. When the test starts, the application will be present on your screen as well as on the task list (for each exercise currently underway). Also, be familiar with the menu choices for using tools such as Find and Go To. With Microsoft Office User Specialist exams, speed counts.

If there are any data files you need to complete an exercise, they will be provided. Occasionally, you will be asked to enter data, create a table, and so on, but the application should contain most of the objects and data required.

A well-known test-taking principle is to read over the entire test from start to finish first, but to work out only those exercises that you feel absolutely sure of on the first pass. This way, you quickly complete all the easy ones, picking up clues to the harder ones (and giving yourself more time to think about them). On subsequent passes, you can dive right into the more complex exercises, knowing how many you have and with a better understanding of how to solve them.

Unfortunately, the Microsoft Office User Specialist exam software makes this approach impossible. You are forced to accomplish each exercise in order, with no option for skipping and then returning to difficult exercises later. Be prepared to carefully read and perform each task in order, and take the time to ensure you're not making mistakes as you go.

When you first sit down at the workstation, you should see a series of opening messages on your screen. After reading each message, click on the Next button until you are finally ready to start the test. A warning box is displayed (read it, and click on OK), then the test starts. The test timer (which doesn't appear on screen) starts when you click on the Start Test button.

Keep working on the exercises and tasks until you are completely finished or until you run out of time. Towards the end, if there are still unsolved tasks, you'll want to zip through them and guess. No answer guarantees no credit for a task; a guess has at least a chance of being correct. This strategy works only because Microsoft counts blank answers and incorrect answers as equally wrong.

At the very end of your test period, you're better off guessing than leaving tasks blank or unsolved.

Taking Testing Seriously

The most important advice we can give you about taking any Microsoft exam is this: Read each exercise carefully! Some exercises are deliberately ambiguous, some use double negatives, and others use terminology in incredibly precise ways. We've taken numerous practice exams and real exams, and on nearly every test, we've gotten at least one task wrong because we didn't read it closely or carefully enough.

Here are some suggestions on how to deal with the tendency to jump to an answer too quickly:

➤ Make sure you read every word in the task. If you find yourself jumping ahead impatiently, go back and start over.

➤ As you read, try to restate the task in your own terms. If you can do this, you should be able to perform the task much more easily.

➤ When returning to the start of a task after your initial read-through, reread every word again—otherwise, the mind falls quickly into a rut. Sometimes seeing a task afresh after turning your attention elsewhere lets you see something you missed before, but the strong tendency is to see what you've seen before. Try to avoid that tendency at all costs.

➤ If you read through a task more than twice, forget the task for a moment, and try to write down, in one phrase, the exact point you don't understand about the task or what appears to be missing. If you chew on the subject for a while, your subconscious might provide the details that are lacking, or you might notice a "trick" that points to the right solution.

Above all, try to deal with each exercise by thinking through what you know about the Microsoft Office application utilities, characteristics, behaviors, facts, and figures involved. By reviewing what you know (and what you've written down on your information sheet), you'll often recall or understand things sufficiently to determine the best solution to the task.

Exercise-Handling Strategies

Based on the tests we've taken, a couple of interesting trends in the solutions have become apparent. Many of the exercises have only a single correct solution, but usually, the text of each task will seem to suggest several workable methods. Unless the correct solution leaps out at you (and if it does, reread the task to look for a trick—sometimes those are the ones you're most likely to get wrong), begin the process of arriving at the correct solution by eliminating those methods that are obviously incorrect.

To identify a solution that is incorrect, you must be aware of each requirement for a given scenario. If you need to use awkward data types, strange calculations, too many extra fields or tables, or nonexistent functions, there's a good chance you're on the wrong track. If you've done your homework for an exam, no invalid or unwieldy methods should be necessary to complete a task. As long as you are sure what's right, it's easy to eliminate what's wrong.

Numerous tasks assume that the default behavior of a particular Office application is in effect. It's essential, therefore, to know and understand the default settings for Microsoft Office applications. Knowing the defaults and understanding what they mean will help you untangle many complex situations.

Likewise, when dealing with tasks that require multiple steps, you must know and perform all the correct steps to get credit. This, too, qualifies as an example of why careful reading is so important.

As you work your way through the test, a counter that Microsoft thankfully provides will come in handy—the number of tasks completed and tasks outstanding. Budget your time by making sure that you've completed one-fourth of the tasks one-quarter of the way through the test period (or between 10 and 12 tasks in the first 12 to 15 minutes). Check again three-quarters of the way through (you should have answered between 30 and 36 tasks in the first 40 to 45 minutes).

If you're not through with the test after 50 minutes of working time, use the last 10 minutes to guess your way through the remaining tasks. Remember, guesses are potentially more valuable than blank answers, because blanks are always wrong, but a guess might turn out to be right. If you haven't a clue about any of the remaining tasks, use whatever solutions come to mind, even if you're pretty sure they're wrong. The goal is to submit a test for scoring that has a solution for every task. By the way, it appears to us that only a small number of wrong choices can cause you to fail the test, so be careful.

Strategies For Success

The two most important factors in passing the test are a thorough understanding of the material and extensive practice. As the saying goes, practice makes perfect, and practicing the demonstration of knowledge on simulated exams is just the ticket. If you study the materials in this book carefully and review all of the practice exercises and tasks at the end of each chapter, you shouldn't have any trouble identifying those areas where you need additional preparation and practice.

Next, follow up by reading some or all of the materials recommended in the "Need To Know More?" section at the end of each chapter. The idea is to become familiar enough with the concepts and situations you find in the sample exercises and tasks to be able to reason your way through similar situations on a real exam. If you know the material and have practiced extensively, you have every right to be confident that you can pass the test.

After you've worked your way through the book, take the practice test in Chapter 17. This will provide a reality check and additional help in identifying areas that you need to work on more. Make sure you follow up and review materials related to the questions you miss before scheduling a real test. Only when you've covered all the ground and feel comfortable with the whole scope of the practice test should you take a real test.

 If you take Chapter 17's practice test and don't score at least 75 percent correct, you'll want to practice further. At a minimum, check to see if the Personal Exam Prep (PEP) tests and the self-assessment tests are available at the Microsoft Training And Certification Web site's download page (its location appears in the next section). If you're more ambitious or better funded, you might want to purchase a practice test from a third-party vendor, although none was yet available at press time. Also, free practice tests are available at www.mous.net, but as of this writing, they don't include practice Access 97 exams.

Armed with the information in this book, and with the determination to augment your knowledge, you should be able to pass the Microsoft Office User Specialist exam. Considering that the fee for taking the test (pass or fail) each time may be from $50 to $100 (probably $60), it's definitely worth the effort to work hard at preparation. If you prepare seriously, the exam should go flaw-lessly. Good luck!

Need To Know More?

We've distilled all the best Microsoft Office User Specialist for Access 97 Expert exam information into this book. If you want to delve into greater detail, the Microsoft Corporation itself is an excellent source of information. Because its products and technologies—and the tests that go with them—change frequently, the most up-to-date place to go for exam-related information is online.

If you haven't already visited the Microsoft Training And Certification pages, do so right now. Also, check out the Microsoft User Specialist page at www.mous.net (see Figure 1.1). Another Web site devoted exclusively to Microsoft Office User Specialist certification is http://officecert.com (no "www" in the URL). Also, New Horizons, a Microsoft Independent Courseware Vendor with offices around the country, maintains a succinct Web site that details the Microsoft Office User Specialist program; visit www.newhorizons.com.

Note: The Microsoft Training And Certification pages might not be at the preceding URL by the time you read this, or they may have been replaced by something new and different, because things change regularly

Figure 1.1   The Microsoft User Specialist Page offers practice exams, how-tos, and more.

on the Microsoft site. Should this happen, please read the section titled
"Coping With Change On The Web," later in this chapter.

The menu options in the left column of the home page point to the most important sources of information in the Microsoft Training And Certification pages. Here's what to check out:

➤ **Train_Cert product summaries/by product and technology** Use this to jump to product-based summaries of all classroom education materials, training materials, study guides, and other information for specific products. Under the heading of Microsoft Windows/Access 97, you'll find an entire page of information about MOUS for Access 97 training and certification. This tells you a lot about your training and preparation options, and it mentions all the tests that relate to Access 97.

➤ **Technical certification/search** This pulls up a search tool that lets you list all Microsoft courses, exams, and training providers. You can find information about any course offered by Microsoft, all exams pertinent to any Microsoft certification (MCPS, MCSE, MCT, MOUS, and so on), and the exams that cover a particular product. It also provides links and phone numbers for Microsoft Independent Courseware Vendors (ICVs). This tool is quite useful not only to review the options, but also to obtain specific test preparation information, because each exam has its own associated preparation guide. For this test, be sure to grab the one for Microsoft Access 97 Expert.

➤ **Downloads** Here, you'll find a list of the files and practice tests that Microsoft makes available to the public. These include several items worth downloading, especially the Certification Update, the PEP tests, various assessment exams, and a general Exam Study Guide. At press time, Microsoft still had not provided these aids for the Office User Specialist courses, but hopefully they will be there by the time you read this. Try to make time to peruse these materials before taking your first test.

Of course, these are just the high points of what's available on the Microsoft Training And Certification pages. As you browse through them—and we strongly recommend that you do—you'll probably find other resources we didn't mention here that are every bit as interesting and compelling.

Coping With Change On The Web

Sooner or later, all the specifics we've shared with you about the Microsoft Training And Certification pages, and all the other Web-based resources we mention throughout the rest of this book, will go stale or be replaced by newer information. In some cases, the URLs you find here might lead you to their replacements; in other cases, the URLs will go nowhere, leaving you with the dreaded "404 File not found" error message.

When that happens, please don't give up! There's always a way to find what you want on the Web—if you're willing to invest some time and energy. To begin with, most large or complex Web sites—and Microsoft's qualifies on both counts—offer a search engine. Looking back at Figure 1.1, you'll see that a Search button appears along the top edge of the page. As long as you can get to the site itself (and we're pretty sure that it will stay at www.microsoft.com for a long while yet), you can use this tool to help you find what you need.

The more particular or focused you can make a search request, the more likely it is that the results will include information you can use. For instance, you can search the string "training and certification" to produce a lot of data about the subject in general. However, if you're looking for the Proficiency Guidelines for the Access 97 Exam, then the search phrase "MOUS for Access 97" will be more likely to get you there quickly.

Likewise, if you want to find the Training And Certification downloads, try a search string with Boolean operators (AND, OR, NOR, and so on), such as this one:

```
training and certification AND download page
```

Finally, don't be afraid to use general search tools, such as www.infoseek.com, www.altavista.com, www.webcrawler.com, and www.excite.com to search for related information. Even though Microsoft offers the best information about its certification exams online, plenty of third-party sources of information, training, and assistance in this area do not have to follow the corporate line (like Microsoft does). Essentially, if you can't find something where the book says it is, start looking around. If worst comes to worst, you can always email us! We just might have a clue.

Access 97 Overview

. . . .

Terms you'll need to understand:

√ Architecture

√ System requirements

√ Installation

√ Configuration

√ Data control

√ Relational database

√ Database application

√ Object oriented

√ Grayed out

Skills you'll need to master:

√ Determining system requirements

√ Installing Access 97

√ Starting Access 97

√ Configuring Access 97 toolbars

Access 97 is an object-oriented, event-driven, programmable, relational database software package. It gives you the flexibility to build applications for your own use as well as applications that are transportable and networkable for many users. You can also create applications that run independent of Access 97. This chapter reviews the architecture of Access 97, the various modes it runs in, and how you can set up all the components to work together.

First and foremost, Access 97 is a database program. Let's start by defining a *database*: a collection of data organized for a specific purpose. Any set of data can be a database: your Rolodex, papers piled on your desk, the *Yellow Pages*. For our purposes, when we refer to a database, we mean the fields, records, tables, and other objects created as a single file in a database program.

Next, let's define *relational database*: a database that allows you to create relationships between records in different tables using data that is common to records in both tables.

For instance, if you have five customer records, each with an individual customer's name, address, and phone number, you wouldn't want to type that data in again each time one of them orders a product. Using the relational database structure, you can create a relationship between the customer table and the order table by using a customer ID number to link orders to customers. Technically, a database application of this type is called a Relational Database Management System (RDBMS).

Finally, we come to object oriented and event driven. *Object oriented* means that each fundamental thing in Access 97 is considered to be its own separate object (such as a table, field, button, report, and so on). Objects exist within a hierarchy and have names. Each object can have its own properties, such as:

➤ Size

➤ Coloring

➤ Data types

➤ Format

Objects can also have their own events that can affect them (such as lighting up when you move the mouse over them), and actions they can take when triggered by an event (such as displaying an error message or accepting some data). Such objects are said to be *event driven*.

Access 97 is programmable; right-clicking an object gives you access to its properties and events. Using Visual Basic for Applications (VBA), you can insert programming code to perform many functions. VBA is a close relative of Microsoft's popular Visual Basic, a powerful yet easy-to-use programming language with roots in the historical Basic programming language. Using an object's name (and perhaps the names of the parent objects), you can access, control, and affect the properties and data of that object.

System Requirements And Installation

You can find the system requirements and installation instructions on the box and in the documentation that comes with your software, whether you've bought Microsoft Office 97 or just Access 97. The term *system requirements* refers to the computer hardware and operating system that must be present in order to run Access 97; typically, they are described both as minimum and recommended. The system upon which you'll be taking the exam will have at least the following:

➤ PC computer with a 486 or higher processor

➤ Microsoft Windows 95 or Windows NT 3.51 Service Pack 5 or later

➤ 12MB of RAM with Windows 95 and 98; 16MB of RAM with Windows NT

➤ 28MB through 60MB of available hard-disk space; 40MB of space with a Typical installation, depending upon the configuration

➤ CD-ROM drive (although the Access 97 package comes with a coupon for ordering 3.5-inch disks)

➤ Video adapter with VGA or higher resolution

➤ Mouse

Other items that will come in handy are:

➤ 14.4Kbps or higher modem

➤ Sound card and multimedia software components

➤ Internet access

The term *installation instructions* refers to the documentation about installation options for Access 97. Access 97 can be installed in Typical, Custom, or Portable installations. Keep in mind that you can further customize the setup of Access 97 during configuration. For the exam, your system should have had Access 97 installed using the Typical installation.

Starting Access 97

Starting Access 97 is as easy as clicking on the Start button on your desktop, finding MS Office, locating Microsoft Access 97, and releasing the mouse button (for example, click on Start|Programs|Microsoft Access). Or, you can put an Access 97 shortcut on your toolbar and just give it one click to start.

When the program starts, you'll see a mostly blank screen with only a few menu choices available. The startup dialog box lets you create a new database or open an existing one. With either option, you see a Database window immediately. Access 97 relies heavily on the Database window as the primary interface for just about everything else the program does.

Configuring Access 97

After you have installed and started Access 97, you may want to modify the default settings so the program will run as you desire. Prior to creating a new, blank database, the only options you can change are the toolbar settings.

You can quickly open these dialog boxes and reset the default toolbars (if the defaults have been changed). You can also quickly add additional toolbars to the display if you prefer to work using some other configuration.

Although the machine on which you take your test should be set up with all toolbar options in the default condition, it is important to know what these options are, how to check them, and how to change them. As a matter of fact, it would be a good idea to check them before starting the test, just so there are no surprises. Task 1 runs through opening toolbars and checking their settings, and Figures 2.1 and 2.2 show the associated dialog boxes (Customize and Toolbar).

Task 1   Opening the Customize dialog box.

1. Choose View|Toolbars|Customize from the menu.

2. The Customize dialog box opens (see Figure 2.1), showing three tabs: Toolbars, Commands, and Options.

3. The Toolbars tab should be selected.

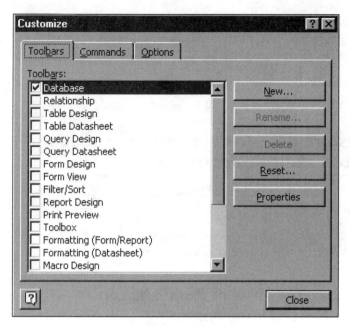

Figure 2.1   The Customize dialog box.

Task 2   Reviewing the Customize dialog box's settings.

1. Scroll down the Toolbars selection box.

2. The only toolbars checked should be Database and Menu Bar. Note that you can select each existing toolbar without checking the box next to it.

3. Checking the box causes the toolbar to display in Access.

4. Selecting the toolbar allows the function buttons (New, Rename, Delete, Reset, and Properties) in the dialog box to become active for that toolbar.

Task 3   Opening the Toolbar Properties dialog box.

1. With the Database toolbar selected, click on the Properties button. The Toolbar Properties dialog box opens (see Figure 2.2).

2. Selected Toolbar allows you to select any other existing toolbar for a change of properties. Toolbar Properties allows you to change docking options as well as customize, resize, move, and show/hide the toolbar.

3. Note that, because this toolbar is built in, some of your options are grayed out (unselectable).

Task 4　Restoring the Toolbar Properties dialog box to the default settings.

1. At the bottom of the Toolbar Properties dialog box, there is a button labeled "Restore Defaults."

2. If you suspect the defaults have been changed, press this button to restore the defaults to their original state.

Task 5　Closing the Toolbar Properties and Customize dialog boxes.

1. Click on the Close button on the Toolbar Properties dialog box.

2. Close the Customize dialog box as well by clicking on Close.

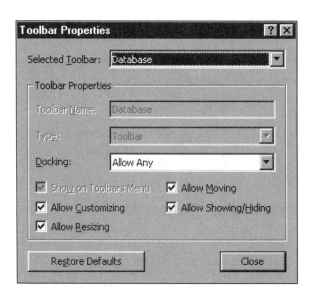

Figure 2.2　The Toolbar Properties dialog box.

The Database and Menu Bar toolbars are the default toolbars. Other toolbars, however, may come in handy during the various exercises and tasks that comprise the test. Read through each exercise and task carefully once the test begins, noting the requirements. If you spot a task that you can perform more easily with a particular toolbar displayed, make sure to open it during that portion of the test.

Major Components Of Access 97

Access 97 lets you create any database you can conceive of, but all databases use the same major components:

➤ **Tables** Store data using fields and records

➤ **Queries** Search, retrieve, modify, and create data in tables

➤ **Forms** Provide an interface for entering, editing, and finding data in tables

➤ **Reports** Present selected sets of data in an attractive format

➤ **Macros** Automate routine tasks

➤ **Modules** Program functions that can be executed within the database

Each of the preceding components is an object within Access 97. You build these objects when constructing a database application, and you establish relationships between them as well. Microsoft Access 97 makes it easy to build applications by providing wizards that automate many routine construction tasks. If you have the expertise and wish to do so, you can also hand-code queries in Structured Query Language (SQL). You can build objects from scratch as well.

How Access 97 Works

Tables form the basis of any database application in Access 97 (or any database application at all, for that matter). Upon starting the program, your first order of business is to start a new database using either the Microsoft Access dialog box or the File|New command on the menu bar.

A new database is similar to a new document or spreadsheet; it's like a clean sheet of paper, ready to be filled with the structures and data that make up your database application. Generally, after planning and designing the inputs, structure, and outputs of your application, you will use the powerful tools provided within Access 97 to:

➤ Build tables to contain data and make relationships between them

➤ Create forms and queries to enter, review, select, or modify data

➤ Build reports to output data

➤ Create macros and modules to control the flow and capabilities of your application

➤ Enter data

Of course, these activities will probably occur in one form or another throughout the construction process, as you build objects and functions, and then refine and debug them.

When your application is complete, you can place security restrictions on it, and even distribute it as a runtime version (meaning it can be run without Access 97 installed on the user's machine). For all practical purposes, you can build database programs that are basically just like any other software program on your local computer store's shelf.

Microsoft Access 97 is a powerful, fully functional database program as well as a database application development package. Access 97 is object oriented and event driven, and you can assemble tables, forms, queries, reports, macros, and modules into secure, distributable applications. You can code queries using SQL, and you can program modules using Microsoft's VBA. Using module code, you can call Windows Application Programming Interface (API) routines, extending your application beyond Access 97.

Access 97 requires significant resources to be available to run, including a 486 or higher CPU, 12MB through 16MB of RAM (depending upon the operating system, Windows 95 or Windows NT, you run), and around 40MB of hard drive space. The program also benefits from standard components and resources, such as a mouse, CD-ROM, sound card, modem, Internet access, and multimedia player programs.

You can configure the toolbars displayed by the program (in the absence of any open databases), and you can create new toolbars for macros and programmed functions (modules). Access 97 works by allowing you to build, customize, and program the fundamental objects in a database application, and powerful tools built into Access 97 (such as the Form, Query, Report, and Macro wizards) make the construction process simple and straightforward.

Practice Exercises

Exercise 1

> You have just been assigned to build a database application using Microsoft Access 97. An IT person finished loading Microsoft Access 97 the previous evening, and you want to check the default toolbar settings. Complete the following tasks to open and check the toolbar settings:
>
> Start Microsoft Access.
>
> View the toolbar list.
>
> View the Database toolbar properties.
>
> Close the toolbar dialog boxes.

Answer To Exercise 1

You can start Microsoft Access by clicking on the shortcut or Start|Programs|Microsoft Access. Note that Access 97 should already be started when you take the test.

To view the toolbar list, click on View|Toolbars|Customize.

To view the Database toolbar properties, click on the Database toolbar to select it (actually, it should already be selected by default); then, click on the Properties button.

Close the dialog boxes after you're through by clicking on the Close buttons.

Need To Know More?

 Klander, Lars and Dave Mercer. *Access 2000 Developer's Black Book,* Coriolis, Scottsdale, AZ, 1999. ISBN 1-57610-349-8. Chapter 21 provides an overview of the installation and setup of Access 2000.

 Viescas, John L. *Running Microsoft Access 97*, Microsoft Press, Redmond, WA, 1997. ISBN 1-57231-323-4. Chapters 1 and 2 provide detailed descriptions of the fundamentals and uses of Microsoft Access 97.

 www.e4free.com
The Access Overview page provides plenty of data about how Access works as well as configuration and installation issues.

Introduction
To Access 97

· ·

Terms you'll need to understand:

√   Tabular

√   Design mode

√   Toolbar

√   Menu bar

√   Navigation

√   Configuration

Skills you'll need to master:

√   Understanding databases

√   Opening and closing databases

√   Using the Access 97 Database toolbar

√   Using the Access 97 menu bar

√   Working with Access 97 operating modes

√   Selecting objects and setting properties

√   Using the Access 97 Help system

Obviously, Access 97 is a database program, a software application that allows you to store, manipulate, and display information in ways many people seem to find quite useful. But what is a database? Why is it so useful? And how does an expert like yourself interact with the program successfully? The secret to your success with Access 97 (and any other well-designed program, for that matter) is familiarity with the interface; that is, being able to find the screens, dialog boxes, menu choices, and commands that will make the program do your bidding.

Understanding Databases

Simply put, a database is a collection of information related to a particular subject, stored as tabular records. Tabular records consist of individual items of data (name, address, phone number, and so on) arranged in rows.

Rows are a useful way of organizing information, because all items of data on each row are directly related. For instance, if you see my name followed by a telephone number in a row of data, you can correctly assume the phone number is mine, and vice versa.

The containers that hold the individual items of data in a row are called *fields* and are analogous to cells in a spreadsheet. Fields can be various data types (such as Text, Number, Date, and so on) with each data type possessing its own unique characteristics.

A database program, such as Access 97, provides the tools and functionality to assemble fields into rows, rows into tables, and tables into relationships, thus forming a relational database (we'll examine the qualities of a relational database in more depth in Chapter 10).

Access 97 Operating Modes

Designing database applications with Access 97 represents only part of what the program can do; it can also run Access 97 applications efficiently. As a default administrator of the database program and all database applications within it, you can design, create, test, and debug database applications during the development process. Then, you can publish production versions for users and still completely control usage or future design changes.

Whenever you create a new object, you do so in Design mode. Clicking on the New button on the Database window automatically begins the design process for whatever object you are creating. The type of object that you create depends upon which tab of the Database window is selected at the time. For instance, if the Form tab is selected when you click on the New button, a blank form is opened in Design view. You can also create a new object of any type using the New Object button on the Database toolbar.

In order to run a database application, you typically open the first form (although you can specify a form to open at startup whenever you open a given database). Any objects that are opened are in Run (or Normal) view; the user cannot alter them unless Design mode is activated. You can make it impossible for a user to make design changes, which you would typically do for an application you wish to distribute to other users.

Because you are prompted to save or confirm before exiting any object in a database, there's no need to save before exiting the program itself, if everything else is closed. Simply click on the window's Exit button, and the program closes.

Opening And Closing Access 97 Databases

We covered starting Access 97 in Chapter 2, so let's create a new database. Making a new database or opening and closing an existing database application is easy; simply start the program and choose File|New from the menu bar, or select the database you'd like to open from the startup window. The Microsoft Access dialog box, shown in Figure 3.1, offers you these choices:

➤ Create A New Database (using a Blank Database or using the Database Wizard)

Figure 3.1 The startup window with Open An Existing Database selected.

➤ Open An Existing Database (existing databases are listed in the dialog box)

Configuring An Access 97 Database

In Chapter 2, you learned how to configure toolbars in Access 97, because no other configuration options exist when no databases are open. For specific database applications, Access 97 contains quite a few configuration options on 10 dialog box tabs (click Tools|Options to reach them), listed here:

➤ **View** Show (or hide) the status bar, the Startup dialog box, hidden objects, and system objects. Show (or hide) in macro design the Names column and/or the Conditions column.

➤ **General** Set print margins, the default database folder, and a new database sort order. Enable (or disable) feedback using sound.

➤ **Hyperlinks** Set hyperlink appearance (colors, underlining, and so forth), the path to an HTML template document, data source information, and Active Server Pages (ASP) output.

➤ **Edit/Find** Set the default Find/Replace behavior and Filter By Form defaults. Enable (or disable) confirmations for record changes, document deletions, and action queries.

➤ **Keyboard** Set the action taken when you press Enter (don't move, move to next field, or move to next record). Set arrow key behavior (next field, or next character). Set the behavior after you enter the next field (select entire field, go to start of field, or go to end of field). Enable (or disable) the cursor's stopping at the first/last field.

➤ **Datasheet** Set default colors for the font, background, and gridlines. Set the default font face, weight, and size. Enable (or disable) bold and italics. Set the default Gridlines Showing, the default Column Width, and the default Cell Effect. Enable (or disable) Show Animations.

➤ **Tables/Queries** Set default field sizes (text and number) and the default field type. Set the default AutoIndex on Import/Create. Enable (or disable) query design options. Set run permissions.

➤ **Forms/Reports** Set the selection behavior as well as the path to Form and Report templates. Enable (or disable) Always Use Event Procedures.

➤ **Module** Set code colors for the text area, foreground, background, and indicator. Enable (or disable) coding options and window settings. Set the font face, font size, and tab width.

➤ **Advanced** Set the default record locking and the default Open mode. Enable (or disable) DDE operations. Set variables for OLE/DDE Timeout (Sec), Number Of Update Retries, ODBC Refresh Interval (Sec), Refresh Interval (Sec), and Update Retry Interval (Msec). For the current (open and selected) database only, set command-line arguments, conditional-compilation arguments, and the project name. Set error-trapping options.

These settings are meaningful in the context in which you ordinarily use them. For instance, it would be appropriate to adjust the print margins for the entire program if you know you'll be using those margins for nearly all of your work. Likewise, when you are printing a particular report or form, you can adjust the print margins from the menu one time only.

Navigating Access 97: Toolbars And Menus

Like all Windows programs, Access 97 uses the familiar window style of Windows 95 (as shown previously in Figure 3.1). From the top, here is what you see: the title bar with minimize, maximize, and exit buttons on the right; the menu bar with File, Edit, View, Insert, Tools, Window, and Help choices; and the Database toolbar.

Table 3.1 shows the Database toolbar buttons and the corresponding menu bar choices that accomplish certain actions. Use this table to guide you as you perform Tasks 1, 2, and 3, and Practice Exercise 1.

Twenty-two toolbars are available in Access 97. You will see most of them at one point or another when you are engaged in using or designing a database application. We will examine each toolbar button and menu bar choice in detail as we progress through this book. We assume you know your way around the Windows 95 interface fairly well, so work your way through the toolbar during Tasks 1, 2, and 3.

 Although Microsoft hasn't formally notified us about this, it's our guess that Microsoft would rather you use the toolbar buttons than the keyboard equivalents, and the technique you choose may affect your score.

Table 3.1 The Database toolbar and corresponding menu bar choices.	
Database Toolbar Button	**Menu Bar Choice**
New Database	File|New Database
Open Database	File|Open Database
Save	File|Save
Print	File|Print
Print Preview	File|Print Preview
Spelling	Tools|Spelling
Cut	Edit|Cut
Copy	Edit|Copy
Paste	Edit|Paste
Format Painter	No menu bar equivalent
Undo	Edit|Undo
Office Links	Tools|Office Links
Analyze	Tools|Analyze
Large Icons	View|Large Icons
Small Icons	View|Small Icons
List	View|List
Details	View|Details
Code	View|Code
Properties	View|Properties
Relationships	Tools|Relationships
New Object: AutoForm	New (from the Database window)
Office Assistant	Help|Microsoft Access Help

Task 1   Displaying the ToolTip for each button on the toolbar.

1. Place the arrow over each button.

2. Note that some functions are grayed out. This is because Access 97 is context sensitive, meaning some functions will not be available (and in fact, the menu bars and toolbars change) depending on whether you have opened or are designing particular objects.

Task 2   *Reviewing menu equivalents for each button.*

1. Open the menu bar for the each of the same functions.

2. Note again that some of the menu choices are grayed out. Also, note that many menu functions have keyboard equivalents.

Task 3   *Reviewing additional buttons on toolbar buttons.*

1. On the New Object: AutoForm button, click on the small down arrow next to the button. A short list of additional buttons appears.

2. Standard objects that can be built in Access 97 are on the list, making it the toolbar form of a drop-down menu.

3. Click on any location to close the list.

HOLD That Skill!

While performing the exercises in this book, you should consciously practice using toolbar buttons to speed up your actions. For example, I have a habit of using the menu bar choice File|Save to save objects following design. Before taking the test, I practiced using toolbar buttons exclusively to break the habit. A friend of mine, who is extremely well versed in Microsoft Word, failed her first Word MOUS exam because (she feels) she used keyboard equivalents rather than buttons. It may not seem fair (after all, if you can get the job done more quickly with your preferred technique, what difference does it make?), but that appears to be what Microsoft values.

Objects And Properties

As we mentioned in Chapter 2, fields contain data, rows contain fields, tables contain rows, and databases contain tables. However, databases also contain other objects, such as reports, queries, forms, macros, modules, and controls. The term *object* has a specific meaning in the context of databases (as well as in many other application programs and programming languages).

Being an object specifically means that something can be addressed directly via its name, and that its data and its properties can be modified when it's called by its name. For instance, suppose you want to use a command button to open a form. Enter the name of the form in the button's OnClick event, and thereafter, anytime that button is clicked on, the form opens.

You can access properties by right-clicking on the object and choosing properties from the shortcut menu that appears. Like toolbars and menu bars, shortcut menus appear with choices that are appropriate for the object and context in which they are being displayed.

Getting Help

Help is only a click away in Access 97. Clicking on the menu bar Help choice opens a submenu that offers several interesting options:

➤ **Microsoft Access Help** Starts the Office Assistant, an automated Help function that leads you either to the answers you seek or through the menu choices required to effect the action you wish to perform.

➤ **Contents And Index** Opens the more traditional Help listings, which allow you to choose from a list of thousands of Help topics, organized alphabetically.

➤ **What's This?** Adds a Help function to the cursor. When you click on the next button or the menu choice, an in-depth explanation is displayed.

➤ **Microsoft On The Web** Displays a list of useful Microsoft-sponsored Web sites, such as Product News, Developer Forum, and Frequently Asked Questions.

➤ **About Microsoft Access** Displays the program title, version number, registered owner, copyright notice, and license warnings. In addition, you can display in-depth system and technical support information by clicking on the System Info and Tech Support buttons. Most Windows programs have a similar "About" choice.

Designing effective database applications requires that you understand the capabilities and strengths of databases as opposed to what you can do with other tools for manipulating data, such as spreadsheets. Databases contain data in tables, relating each field to the others and allowing relations across tables (via the primary key field) as well. For manipulating large amounts of data that represent multiple data sources, no other tool will do.

Using a modern database program, such as Access 97, requires that you understand its user interface and its operating modes. We've covered how to start it; navigate through the menus, dialog boxes, objects, and properties; get help;

and open and close a database (the fundamental object that contains all other objects related to a particular database).

Your next task is to plan and create an actual database with a table and fields, enter some data, and then exercise your skills using the datasheet. Although many database applications use forms instead, the datasheet has many of the same capabilities as a form and is easier to use for administrative purposes. We will address this subject in Chapter 4.

Practice Exercises

Exercise 1

> You have just started a new project, and time is of the essence. You want to review database toolbar buttons to boost your speed.
>
> Open a sample database (Northwind is fine).
>
> Display the function tags for each button on the database toolbar.
>
> Leave the database open for the next exercise.

Answer To Exercise 1

Click on the Open button or use the File|Open menu command. Locate the database you want, select it, and click on Open.

To make function tags appear, place the cursor over each button.

> *Note: This exercise is very simple, but it is worth doing to remind yourself of the available toolbar buttons. To use the tools on the toolbar correctly, place the cursor over the button and click on it to activate it. Non-active buttons are grayed out, but their function tags still appear.*

Exercise 2

> You need to find out the details of one of the tables in a sample database. You decide to check the properties.
>
> Open the Properties dialog box of one of the tables in the sample database.

Answer To Exercise 2

Right-click on one of the tables in the sample database from the Database window to cause the shortcut menu to appear.

To cause the Properties dialog box to appear, click on Properties from the shortcut menu.

Note: *This exercise is also very simple, but it is worth doing because it is a powerful feature that is used extensively throughout all Microsoft applications, not just Access 97. Just about anything you want to do when constructing Office 97 applications can be accomplished or is affected by object properties accessible via the right click.*

Exercise 3

You need to find out more about how to use the toolbar, and you're in a hurry.

Use Help to find out more about the Tables tab of the database window.

Answer To Exercise 3

To use Help effectively to find out about the Tables tab, choose Help|What's This?, then click on the Tables tab. A tip will appear that explains the function of the tab.

Need To Know More?

 Klander, Lars and Dave Mercer. *Access 2000 Developer's Black Book*, Coriolis, Scottsdale, AZ, 1999. ISBN 1-57610-349-8. Chapters 21 provides an overview of the usage of Access 2000.

 Viescas, John L. *Running Microsoft Access 97*, Microsoft Press, Redmond, WA, 1997. ISBN 1-57231-323-4. Chapter 3 provides a guided tour of Microsoft Access 97.

 www.e4free.com

The Access Navigation page has more information about how to get around in Access.

Creating Databases

Terms you'll need to understand:

- √ Reverse engineering
- √ Database window
- √ Field properties
- √ Primary key
- √ Indexed field
- √ Focus
- √ Data type
- √ Datasheet
- √ Dynaset
- √ Logical AND
- √ Logical OR

Skills you'll need to master:

- √ Planning your database
- √ Creating tables and fields
- √ Entering, modifying, and deleting data
- √ Formatting the datasheet
- √ Filtering and sorting data in tables
- √ Modifying field layout
- √ Navigating the table
- √ Modifying the presentation of a database
- √ Sorting data on multiple fields
- √ Adding filters (selection and form)

Before you actually start creating the components (or objects) of your database, you will plan it. Because the final functions of a database depend so heavily upon the components you create—and because modifying the database later can mean tons of extra work—good planning is essential to the database-creation process.

Tables, forms, queries, reports, macros, and modules are all database objects. The final functions the database performs are enabled using database objects, in the same way that the engine, transmission, and wheels on your car enable you to move down the road.

Planning Your Database

Reverse engineering is a phrase you may have heard in the popular media. It refers to evaluating the end product and determining the steps taken to create it. You will do something similar when building and planning your database.

The first step is to decide what the end product should be. For instance, you may want a report that shows how much an employee should be paid for a given pay period and then prints out a check.

Task 1   Identify functions the database will perform.

1. Ask yourself, managers, and clients what the required outputs will be.

2. Differentiate between outputs and capabilities (reports as opposed to data-entry forms, for instance).

3. Typical database functions include data entry, data storage, data retrieval, data reporting, and data maintenance.

 Unless the database is a classroom or research exercise, the database must support some process, such as sales transactions, tracking shipments, marketing surveys, and so on.

Task 2   Grouping functions into database objects.

1. Printed matter requires a report; reports are based on queries or tables. Informational outputs (displayed on the screen) may require only a query or form.

2. Data storage requires tables; data entry requires a table or a form.

3. Determine whether your report requires you to create a query or other database objects.

Task 3   *Identifying database objects that require other database objects.*

1. Reports usually require queries or tables (or both).

2. Queries require tables (or other queries).

3. Forms frequently (but not always) require tables.

Next, ask yourself, what data does the report depend upon? Let's list the elements for a check-printing report:

➤ **Employee ID** To make sure we have the right person

➤ **Employee name** To print on the check

➤ **Pay period** To calculate the pay

➤ **Pay per period** To calculate the pay

➤ **Pay date** To initiate the check

➤ **Withholding rules** To take care of Uncle Sam

Task 4   *Identifying the data required for each object.*

1. Mailing lists require names and addresses in a particular sort order.

2. Paychecks require pay numbers, employee names, SSNs, salaries, and pay dates.

3. Sales reports require item numbers, sales transactions, and sales dates.

Task 5   *Determining data types for each object.*

1. Names, addresses, and phone numbers use text fields.

2. Numbers use number and currency fields.

3. Dates use date fields.

4. Evaluate each kind of data you intend to enter and determine the proper data type. Remember that numbers can be calculated upon (added, subtracted, multiplied, and divided), but text cannot.

We now know some of the items of data we need in a database that is designed to compute pay and print a check. Although the basic reverse-engineering process can be quite a bit more complicated than this, we will use it along almost every step of the way.

Creating Tables And Fields

After planning your database, the next step is to make a database and create tables. For this lesson, we'll build an actual table so that we have something to explore with (rather than use the built-in samples that come with Access 97).

Table creation involves two parts: building the table structure and filling it with data. Before you start building your table, you need a database to put it in, so create a blank database and name it "test".

Creating A New Database

To create your new database, click on File|New Database to open the New dialog box and then click on OK (the Blank Database icon is selected by default). Next, name the database "test.mdb" and then click on Create to finish the process. You should see something similar to Figure 4.1 on your screen.

Creating a new table in Access 97 involves choosing the type of design tool (see Figure 4.2) and building the table structure. Building the table structure consists of naming and structuring fields (as in Figure 4.3).

 Keep in mind that field names cannot start with an empty space.

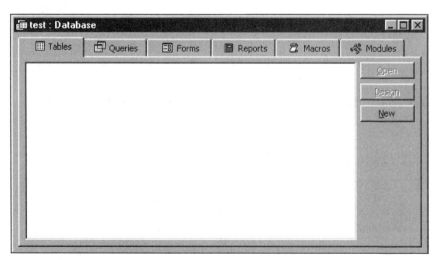

Figure 4.1   The Database window with the Tables tab selected.

Table structure can be thought of as:

➤ **Field order** Primary Key, Name, Address, Phone, and so on.

➤ **Field names** ID, Name, Address, Phone, Zip Code, and so on.

➤ **Data types** Number, Text, Date, Memo, and so on.

➤ **Type formats** Currency, Integer, and so on.

➤ **Field properties** Size, Format, Decimal Places, and so on.

 You can enter field descriptions to the right of Data Type, but they are not necessary.

Task 6   *Creating a new table.*

1. Make sure Tables is the selected tab in the Database window.

2. Click on New. The New Table dialog box opens.

3. Select Design view, and click on OK.

4. Type "Employee Number" in the first Field Name box. Press Tab.

5. Click on the down-arrow, and select Number as the Data Type. Field Size defaults to Long Integer.

Figure 4.2   The New Table dialog box with Design View selected.

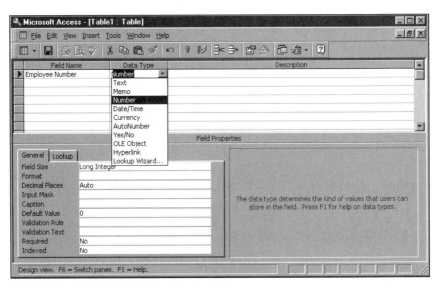

Figure 4.3   A new table in Design View.

Task 7   Setting the data type for the second, third, and fourth fields.

1. Type "Employee Name" in the second Field Name box. Press Tab. Data Type defaults to Text; Field Size defaults to 50 characters.

2. Type "Employee Street Address" in the third Field Name box. Press Tab. Data Type defaults to Text; Field Size defaults to 50 characters.

3. Type "Employee Pay Per Hour" in the fourth Field Name box. Press Tab.

4. Click on the down-arrow, and select Number as the Data Type. Field Size defaults to Long Integer.

5. Click on Field Size, click on the down-arrow, and select Integer.

Relational databases require some special fields (such as primary key fields, as shown in Figure 4.4) to function properly. In addition, you can use some other methods (normalization, optimization, and so on) to make your database perform well.

Field Name	Data Type
Employee Number	Number

Figure 4.4   The primary key icon.

Task 8   *Modifying field formats and saving the table.*

1. Make the first field a primary key by clicking on the gray box to the left of the first field to select it. Click on the Primary Key button.

2. Make the first field a required field by clicking on the Required box (on the lower half of the screen). Click on the down-arrow, and select Yes.

3. Change the fourth field's format to Currency by clicking on the Data Type box and selecting Currency.

4. On the General tab at the bottom, next to Decimal Places, the format specifies *Auto*. Click on that box and then select 2.

5. Save the table by choosing File|Save As/Export from the menu bar. The Save As dialog box opens.

6. Type "Employees" (the file name you are assigning), and click on OK.

7. Close the table by clicking on the Exit button on the Table window.

HOLD That Skill!

A *primary key* field is frequently the first field in a table. It has two purposes: to uniquely identify each record from all other records in the table, and to allow records from one table to be related to records in another table. You cannot create a relational database without it. Access 97 includes functions for automatically creating primary key fields. The first time you save a new table, Access 97 asks you if you'd like a primary key.

Indexed fields can be located anywhere in the table (primary key fields are actually a form of index field). Their purpose is to generate special information that the database uses to speed up searches on that field.

Keep in mind that you should use index fields only where they are required, because generating the extra information can slow down overall database function, depending on the number of records the table contains. It's a trade-off between fast searches and somewhat slower overall performance.

You set field properties in the Field Properties section (in the lower half) of the Design View window. The right-hand side contains helpful tips and cautions; the left-hand side shows the properties that you can set. There are two tabs on the left-hand side: General and Lookup (refer back to Figure 4.3).

On the General tab, field properties you can set include the length of the field; format; whether the field is required or indexed; and other properties, depending upon the data type you've chosen. The Lookup tab gives you access to lookup properties; we'll discuss table lookup in Chapter 11.

Entering, Modifying, And Deleting Data

In this section, you will enter, modify, and delete data directly inside the table, in Datasheet view (as shown in Figure 4.5). Tables are where you store all data, and data is the critical element that makes a database valuable.

Task 9   Opening a table in Datasheet View.

1. In the Database window, select Employees on the Tables tab.

2. Click on Open. The table opens in Datasheet view.

Each item of data goes in its own field, and each field has certain properties that limit the data type, size, and values it can have. Access 97 makes sure you follow those rules as you enter data and prompts you when you err.

Moving from record to record and field to field is simply a matter of using the arrow keys, Enter, or Tab. Starting a new record is as easy as pressing Tab from the last field of the current record.

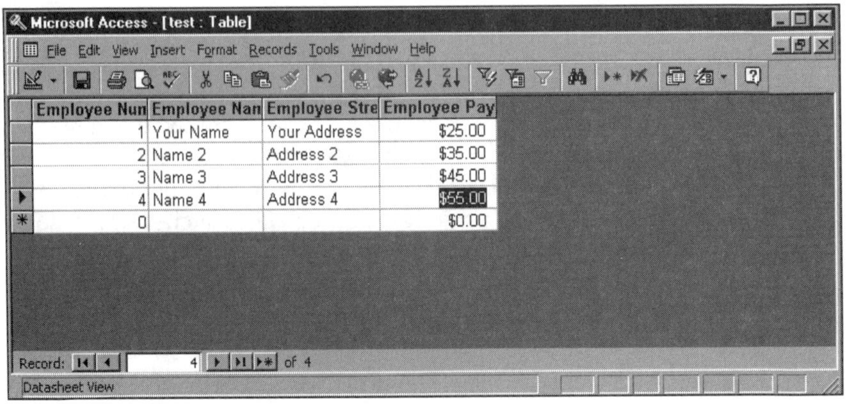

Figure 4.5   The table in Datasheet view.

Task 10 *Entering data and moving around the datasheet.*

1. The cursor will be in the first field of the first record. Enter "1", and press Tab.

2. Enter your name, and press Tab.

3. Enter your address, and press Tab.

4. Finally, enter your pay per hour (make it a round figure, like 15, 20, 25, 30, and so on). Press Tab or Enter to move to a new record.

5. Enter fictitious data for three more employees using the same method.

6. To move up the datasheet, click on the first field of the second record or use the arrow key.

 As soon as you've begun entering data in a record, you'll notice that Access 97 creates an empty record below it. This record isn't part of your table; it's just a placeholder.

As you travel to various records, the record cursor (an arrow pointing to the right) moves with you in the gray box to the left of the records.

Simply opening a table allows you to create new records, edit (or modify) existing records, or delete existing records. There is no need to use a Save function, as you would with an ordinary file; moving from one record to the next, moving to a new record, or exiting the Table view automatically updates the table with all the changes you've made.

Task 11 *Deleting a record and closing the table.*

1. Select any record by clicking on the gray box to the left of the record (where the arrow cursor is), then delete it by pressing Delete.

2. You'll be prompted to confirm the deletion.

3. To close the table, click on the Exit button in the Table window.

 Data is automatically updated in the table whenever you move to another record or exit the table. The only exceptions are with the Cut and Delete functions. When you want to cut a value from a field or delete the current record, a dialog box prompts you to confirm that you really want to do so.

Navigating The Table

Once your table has data in it, you'll want to find and use the data. In Datasheet View, you can use the Find function to find records with a specific value in a particular field. You can also go directly to the first record, a particular record number, or the last record using the record-navigation tools located at the bottom of the Datasheet window.

Task 12   Navigating among records.

1. In the Database window, select Employees, and click on OK.

2. At the bottom of the datasheet, click on the Last-Record button. You'll go to the last record in the set.

3. To go to the first record in the set, click on the First-Record button.

4. If you want to go to a particular record, double-click on the record-number box to select it. Then, type a number for the record you wish to go to, and press Enter. You'll go to that record.

HOLD That Skill!

Notice as you navigate around, the record you're on is selected (or highlighted). In database terms, this is where the *focus* is. Focus is an important database concept, because your keystrokes affect the object that has the focus on it.

The Find function (see Figure 4.6) searches through the table from beginning to end, and when you use the Find First button, the first record with the value you enter appears on your screen. To find the next record with the same value, use the Find Next button.

 When you're asked to find data within a record using the Find function, make sure to select All in the Search field. The data may be hidden, making it difficult to locate manually.

Task 13   Using the Find and Find Next functions.

1. Find a record by searching on the Name field. Start by clicking on the Name field, then click on the Find button (or choose Edit|Find).

2. In the Find In Field dialog box, enter the name you are searching for, and click on the Find First button.

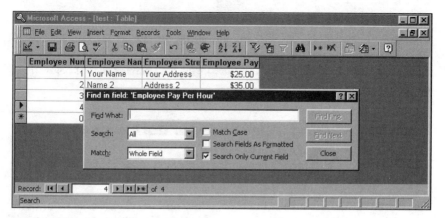

Figure 4.6 The Find In Field dialog box.

3. Click on the Find Next button. Doing so moves you to the next record that contains the same name, or, if no more cases are found, you get a dialog box to that effect.

4. Close the table.

Unless you disable (deselect) Search Only Current Field, the Find First function searches for your entered value only in the field on which you clicked, so make sure you click on the correct field before starting your search.

The Find Next function searches below the record you're in till it gets to the end of the database. Then, it prompts you before it starts over again at the top of the database.

HOLD That Skill!

Wildcards can be substituted for an exact value when you're not sure what the value might be, or when you want several values to be found. Wildcards work by letting you specify a broad placeholder for a specific value. For instance, Access 97 lets you use three wildcards:

➤ **Asterisk (*)** Substitutes for any character or group of characters

➤ **Question mark (?)** Substitutes for any single character

➤ **Pound (or number) sign (#)** Substitutes for any single-digit number

Formatting The Datasheet

Now that you've experimented with entering, modifying, and searching your data using the datasheet, it's time to make the datasheet easier to use.

You can modify several aspects of the datasheet. You can make rows thicker or thinner and fields wider or narrower, have columns appear in a different order, and choose to have data in each field display a certain way. For instance, if you want all data in the table to be colored red, you can change the font color in the datasheet to red.

Task 14   Making fields wider or narrower as well as changing row height.

1. In the Database window, select Employees and click on OK.

2. Place the cursor between the field names on the column headers until it turns into a cross, and move it to the right or left. The field gets wider or narrower.

3. Place the cursor between rows along the left side (in the gray boxes) until it becomes a cross, and move it up or down. Rows become thicker or thinner.

 You can even change the name of the column header (the field name). Just keep in mind that doing so changes the field name in the table as well, and changing the field name can affect many other objects that use field names.

Task 15   Setting field sizes and automatically sizing columns.

1. Place the cursor on the column heading. Click on the right mouse button. A shortcut menu appears.

2. You can now select the exact width of the column in characters, or use the Best Fit button to have Access 97 size it for you.

3. Double-click on the right side of a column heading. The column size is fitted to the existing data.

Access 97 allows you to change fonts and colors for readability. Figure 4.7 shows the Cells Effects dialog box, and Figure 4.8 shows the Font dialog box. You can access both of these from the menu bar under Format.

Task 16   Changing the format of the datasheet.

1. Choose Format|Cells to practice changing cell background colors or adding special effects such as Raised or Sunken cells.

2. Choose Format|Font to practice changing the table's font.

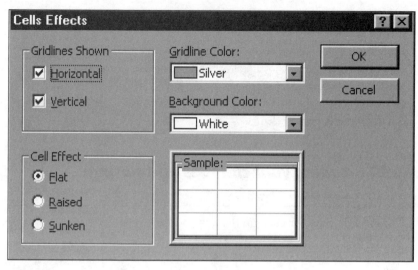

Figure 4.7   The Cells Effects dialog box.

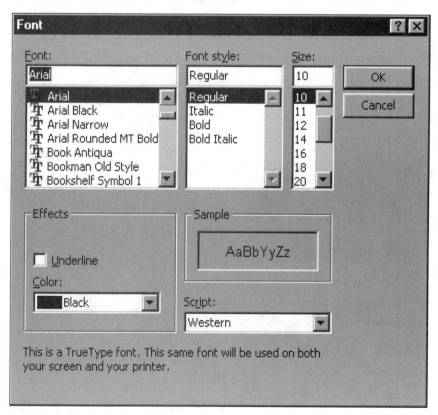

Figure 4.8   The Font dialog box.

HOLD That Skill!

Remember that changes you make to the datasheet affect the display of all data in the table, but do not affect the underlying data or the data display in any other view (such as in a form or a report). Also, if you want the datasheet for a table to be displayed the same way every time you open the table, you can save your datasheet changes.

Task 17   Saving your changes and closing the datasheet.

1. Choose File|Save (or click on the Save button).

2. Exit the Datasheet window.

Filtering And Sorting Tables

When viewing your records in a datasheet, you may want to view only certain records in a certain order. Selecting sets of records is accomplished by *filtering*. Specifying the order is called *sorting*.

These functions are similar to basic query functions, but easier to perform rapidly in the Datasheet view. The Sort buttons (shown in Figure 4.9) and the Filter buttons (shown in Figure 4.10) are located on the Database toolbar for easy access. They can be very effective tools for managing your data.

Figure 4.9   The Sort buttons.

Figure 4.10   The Filter buttons.

Task 18   *Sorting on a field: ascending or descending.*

1. In the Database window, select Employees, and click on OK.

2. Click on the field you want to sort on.

3. Click on the Sort Ascending or Sort Descending button, or choose Records|Sort|Sort Ascending (or Sort Descending).

Sorting orders the displayed records from highest to lowest or lowest to highest. In numbers, 0 is lowest, so a sort in 0, 1, 2, 3, 4 order is called ascending. Descending order is the opposite.

In alphabetical entries, A to Z is ascending (Z to A is descending). No distinction is made between uppercase and lowercase.

Task 19   *Sorting on multiple fields.*

1. Select the fields you wish to sort on by clicking on them above the column name.

2. Use Shift+click to select multiple columns.

3. Click on the Sort button, either ascending or descending. The fields are sorted starting at the leftmost item and proceeding to the right.

Filters select records for viewing based on conditions. That is, you enter criteria by which the filter decides to either display (include) a record or exclude it. The resulting set of records is called a *recordset*.

One way to apply criteria is to select from existing data within a field the information that you'd like to filter. For instance, if you're looking for all names beginning with Smith (including Smith, Smithson, Smithsonian, and so on), select "Smith" in the Employee Name field, and apply the filter (you'll see the word *filtered* appear next to the Record buttons).

Task 20   *Filtering and excluding records by selection.*

1. Click on the field you wish to filter by.

2. Select (by clicking on and dragging) the portion of the entered data that represents your filter criterion.

3. Click on the Apply Filter button.

4. Click on the field you wish to filter by.

5. Select the portion of the entered data that represents your filter criterion.

6. Choose Records|Filter|Filter Excluding Selection.

HOLD That Skill!

You can access filter functions using the menu bar, the Database toolbar or by right-clicking on the field of interest. Right clicking causes a shortcut menu with all filter tools available to appear.

When you use the Filter By Form function, a grid that has fields in it appears, as shown in Figure 4.11. The values you enter in the fields control the filter, and, if you enter values in several fields, the filter displays only records that have the first value *and* the second value, and so on. This aspect of filters is called a *Logical AND*.

Task 21   Filtering records by one or more criteria.

1. Click on the Filter By Form button.

2. Enter the data you wish to filter for in the field to be filtered upon.

3. Click on the Apply Filter button.

4. Choose Records|Filter|Advanced Filter/Sort.

5. Drag down to the filtering grid the fields you wish to filter by (see Figure 4.11).

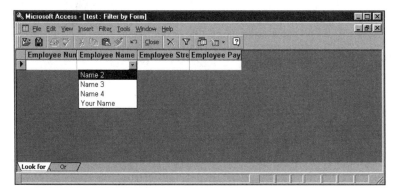

Figure 4.11   Creating a Logical AND filter.

6. Enter your Logical AND criteria below the field names you've chosen.

 When you enter data in a field, only enter the exact text you're looking for. Access 97 puts quotation marks around it for you. If you put criteria entries in more than one field, you automatically create a Logical AND.

Using the Advanced Filter/Sort function gives you a basic query layout. You can enter data in several field grids (labeled "Criteria" and "Or," as shown in Figure 4.12) when creating filters. By doing this, you can set values in the Criteria grid (the Logical AND), but values in the Or grid make the filter search for either the values in the first row *or* values in the second row. This is called a *Logical OR*.

Task 22   *Filtering records using several grids (Logical OR).*

1. Choose Records|Filter|Advanced Filter/Sort.

2. Drag down to the filter grid the fields you wish to filter by.

3. Enter your criteria below the field names you've chosen, and enter Or criteria beneath that (see Figure 4.12).

4. Click on the Apply Filter button.

 When you enter data in a field's Criteria and Or rows, the filter selects records using your entry in the first row *or* your entry in the second row. You can combine ANDs and ORs in the same filter.

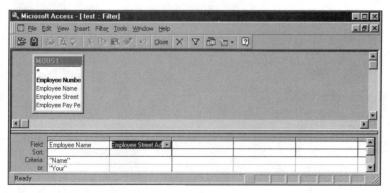

Figure 4.12   Creating a Logical OR filter.

Task 23 Saving a filter as a query, removing a filter, and closing a datasheet.

1. In the Advanced Filter/Sort window, choose File|Save (or click on the Save button).

2. Name the file with the query name of your choice. It appears on the Queries tab in the Database window.

3. Exit the Filter window, and click on the Remove Filter button.

4. Click on the Save button, then exit the Table window.

 The filter that is currently active is saved with the table; however, you must reapply the filter each time you open the table. The only way to save a complex filter is as a query.

As we've discussed, planning your database is the first step in creating it, followed by building tables and filling them with data. Data is the critical element of a database; tables, datasheets, and the other elements are just structures for storing and manipulating the data.

Tables themselves are the basic object within your database for storing data; as with a spreadsheet in Datasheet View, you can enter, sort, and filter data at will. The datasheet is merely a specialized kind of form. We will cover forms in Chapter 5.

Practice Exercises

Exercise 1

You've been assigned to build a database for inventorying training materials. Gather the data you need, and begin building your
database.

Determine the subjects to be tracked (training materials, such as
videos, books, and so on).

Determine the fields required (Material ID, Material Name, Material Stock Number, Amount In Stock, Refill Date, and Supplier).

Create a database named Training Materials.

Create a table, and build the correct fields.

Set the field data types.

Set Material ID as the primary key.

Save the table.

Answer To Exercise 1

To figure out which subjects to track, you'll need to do some brainstorming by
yourself or with your managers or customers. Remember that you can track
concepts (such as monthly sales) as well as actual things (such as people or
computers). In the case of monthly sales, you might need to make a table for
orders, because each individual order contains a dollar amount of sales, and if
you add them up for a month, you'll get monthly sales. In the case of people or
computers, you can simply make a table for each.

To figure out what fields are required, make a list of each detail you want to
know about the subject to be tracked. For example, for a person, you might
want to keep track of his or her birth date if you think you might need to
calculate the person's age at some point.

To create a database, click on File|New, click on OK in the New dialog box,
and then name the database.

To create a table and fields in your new database, click on the New button in
the Database window (the Table tab should be selected by default), and enter
the field names. Set their data types by clicking on the Data Type area and
clicking on the down-arrow.

Select the field you want to set, and click on the Primary Key button on the Table Design toolbar.

Click on the Save button to save the table.

Exercise 2

You've built a database and table. Now, navigate it using the Find and Find Next functions, modify the datasheet to make it more readable, apply filters, and save it.

Open the table in Datasheet mode.

Modify the datasheet to make the fields easier to read.

Enter some fictitious training materials data (about 10 records).

Practice finding records with the Find function.

Sort your records on one of the fields, ascending then descending.

Apply a filter to find only one of the records you've entered.

Close the table.

Answer To Exercise 2

To open the table in Datasheet mode, click on the Open button in the Database window (the Tables tab should be selected as well as the table you've created).

To modify the fields in the datasheet, place the cursor between the cells at the top of the table, and move it when it turns into a black crosshair icon.

Click on the binoculars (Find) icon on the Table Datasheet toolbar.

Put the focus in the field you want to sort, and click on the Sort Ascending or Sort Descending button on the Database toolbar.

To apply a filter, select something in one of your fields that you want to filter for, then click on the Filter By Selection button.

Click on the Exit button.

Exercise 3

You need to reorder the fields in your table.

Change the order of fields to Employee Number, Employee Pay Per Hour, and Employee Street Address.

Answer To Exercise 3

To change field order in a table, click on the gray box left of the field, then click and drag the field to its new position.

Need To Know More?

 Klander, Lars and Dave Mercer. *Access 2000 Developer's Black Book*, Coriolis, Scottsdale, AZ, 1999. ISBN 1-57610-349-8. Chapters 1 through 9 comprise the basics of correctly designing and building databases.

 Litwin, Paul, Ken Getz, and Mike Gilbert. *Access 97 Developer's Handbook*, Sybex Inc., San Francisco, CA, 1997. ISBN 0-7821-1941-7. Chapter 1 contains a brief description of what's new in Access 97.

 Viescas, John L. *Running Microsoft Access 97*, Microsoft Press, Redmond, WA, 1997. ISBN 1-57231-323-4. Chapters 1 and 2 provide detailed descriptions of the fundamentals and uses of Microsoft Access 97.

 www.e4free.com

The Access Table And Datasheet page has more information about how to create tables and modify datasheets.

Form Design

Terms you'll need to understand:

√ Properties sheet

√ Handles

√ Bound, unbound, and calculated

√ Controls

√ Display attributes

√ Form views

√ Default values

Skills you'll need to master:

√ Working with forms

√ Improving forms navigation

√ Creating eye-pleasing form layouts

√ Changing the display attributes and default values of controls

√ Navigating forms, finding records, and entering and editing data

√ Printing forms

Forms are useful for efficiently entering, editing, and displaying data. You might ask yourself why forms are even necessary—because datasheets can fulfill many of the same functions.

To answer the question: Forms allow many additional options for displaying fields, displaying the results of calculations upon those fields, and displaying graphical cues. Using forms should reduce data-entry errors and enhance the interface between the user and the database.

Creating A Simple Form

You may have noticed a tab on the Database window labeled Forms; its prominence should give you some idea of the relative importance of forms to Access 97. From this tab, you can open existing forms for data entry and editing, open forms in Design view (so that you can modify the form itself), or create new forms.

When creating a form—much like when creating a table, query, or report—you just select the Forms tab and then click on the New button. A dialog box with several options for creating new forms appears:

➤ **Design View** Lets you build a form from scratch

➤ **Form Wizard** Builds the form to your specifications

➤ **AutoForm: Columnar** Builds a columnar form

➤ **AutoForm: Tabular** Builds a tabular form

➤ **AutoForm: Datasheet** Builds a datasheet-style form

➤ **Chart Wizard** Creates charts for your form

➤ **PivotTable Wizard** Creates a form with spreadsheet-like capabilities

In this chapter, we'll cover how to use Design view and the Form Wizard; later chapters cover the other options.

Forms come in two major types: bound and unbound. *Bound* means that your form is directly tied to data in a table or query. Think of a bound form as a *window* to the data in a particular table, allowing you to view, enter, edit, and delete table data as you choose. *Unbound* forms are just another part of your user interface; perhaps they contain buttons that open other bound forms for data entry or prewritten reports.

Let's assume you'll create a bound form first. Before beginning to create your form, it is wise to spend a couple minutes deciding the purpose of the form and the data it must contain. The form's purpose should tell you not only the particular fields to display but also how you want to arrange them, what calculations you may want to show, and what controls need to be available to the user. The data comes from the table or query it is bound to.

Task 1   Identifying the functions the form will offer the user.

1. Use a simple workflow diagram to pinpoint the tasks that the form will satisfy, such as creating a record of a new employee.

2. Use reverse engineering to determine what fields, calculations, and controls must be present.

3. Lay out a rough draft of the form on paper.

Task 2   Building a new form with the Form Wizard.

1. Click on New on the Forms tab of the Database window (you should already have your test database open). The New Form dialog box opens.

2. Select Form Wizard, and choose the Employees table from the drop-down box below. Next, click on the OK button.

3. On the first screen (shown in Figure 5.1), you can change tables if desired and select fields. Select Employee Number, Employee Name, Employee Street Address, and Employee Picture by clicking on the name of the field, then clicking on the single-arrow button (the one pointing to the right). The double-arrow buttons transfer all fields in the direction pointed to. Click on the Next button.

4. On the next screen, choose the Columnar layout style and then click on the Next button.

5. On the next screen, choose the graphic style Clouds and then click on the Next button.

6. On the final screen, you can enter a title for your form as well as choose to open it for data entry or modify it in Design view. The word *Employees* should already be entered as the title, so select Modify The Form's Design and then click on the Finish button. Your end result should look like Figure 5.2.

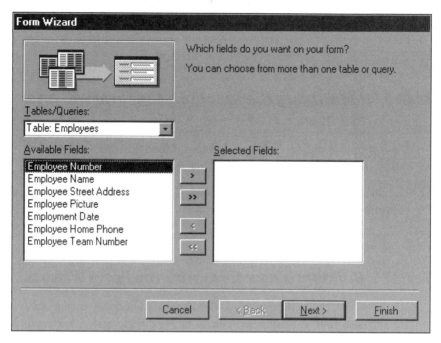

Figure 5.1   The first screen of the Form Wizard.

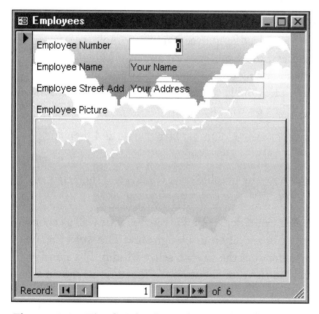

Figure 5.2   The finished Employees form.

Modifying Form Design

Now that you have a primitive form with the required fields on it, you can begin the process of arranging the fields, adding controls, and setting the tab order. Your objective, of course, is to provide users with exactly the data they need for the tasks they must perform—and you should do so in an eye-catching, attention-grabbing way. Namely, your job is to make their job *easy*.

Task 3   Modifying your form in Design view.

1. You chose to open your form for modification in Design view on the last screen of the Form Wizard, so your form should currently be open and ready for modification.

 Notice that the form has dots on it. This means Grid and Snap are active. Grid is a set of coordinates displayed as dots on the form, and Snap makes form controls *snap* to the *grid* coordinates. Together, they are convenient for lining up controls and giving your form a professional look.

2. Choose View|Properties from the menu bar. The Form properties sheet appears, as shown in Figure 5.3.

3. Notice the tabs on top. The All tab should be selected, and you can view all of the form's properties by scrolling down. If one of the other tabs is selected, you see a subset of the form's properties.

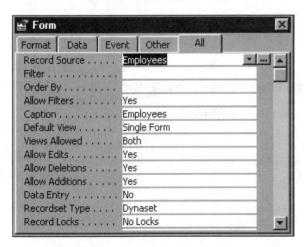

Figure 5.3   The Form properties sheet.

4. On the All tab, scroll down to the Picture property. Click on the text box and then click on the Build Button to the right. An Insert Picture dialog box opens.

5. Find the Access 97 folder named Bitmaps and the subfolder named Styles. Choose the file Globe.bmp as the source of your new background for the Employees form. Click on the OK button.

6. The new background style should immediately appear on your form in Design view without your having to close the properties sheet.

7. Click on the Exit button on the properties sheet to close it.

HOLD That Skill!

To manually set precise properties for the form and controls, select them and then right-click on them. A shortcut menu appears. If you select Properties, a dialog box displays each of the properties you can set (such as color, format, size, placement, transparency, and so on).

The Properties dialog box is the tool you use to access an object's properties when design is underway. You can open the Properties window by selecting the object and right-clicking on it, or selecting the object and choosing View|Properties from the shortcut menu. When you right-click on an object, the shortcut menu opens first.

Choose Properties from the shortcut menu to access all properties, or make your selection from the menu. Also, note that if you open the properties sheet for one object but click on another object, the properties sheet automatically displays the other object's properties.

Task 4   Changing the title of your form.

1. Right-click on the form (outside the form boundaries) to open the property sheet.

2. In the Caption text box, enter the title "My Employees".

3. Close the property sheet.

To display a form without any title, enter a blank space in the Caption text box.

Task 5   Modifying the form.

1. Maximize the form, then place the cursor at the right edge of the form. The cursor becomes a sizing cursor.

2. Drag the edge of the form to the right to make the form about two inches wider, then drag the bottom down to make the form about two inches longer (use the ruler on the top and left-hand sides to measure the form).

3. Click on View|Field List to cause the list of fields from the bound table (Employees) to appear.

4. Resize the Field List window so all the fields are visible, then click on and drag the Employment Date field onto the form. Notice that both the Label text box and the actual field itself are created automatically and linked to each other.

HOLD That Skill!

To select the control you wish to modify, click on it. If you use Shift+click, you can select multiple controls simultaneously; "drawing" a box around multiple controls with the cursor accomplishes the same task. You can simultaneously select more than one object by pressing Shift while selecting additional objects. If you need to give all your fields the same border treatment (Sunken, Raised, Shadowed, and so on), this method saves time. If the AutoResize property of the form is set to Yes, the form automatically resizes to display complete records. If you want the form to remain a fixed size, turn that property off (set it to No).

Task 6   Naming and saving your form.

1. Choose File|Save As/Export from the menu bar. A small dialog box opens.

2. Make sure Within The Current Database As New Name is selected. The name of your form (Employees) should be visible in the text box. You have the option of entering a new name for your form, although we won't change it.

3. Click on the OK button to save the form with the existing name.

Changing The Tab Order

By this time, you will probably be jumping from Design view to Form view to check your modifications. To make the process of entering data flow more smoothly for the person using the database, you can change the tab order. We will cover this topic here, even though you'll probably want to do it one more time after everything else is done.

Tab order means that whatever field is at the top of the list within the dialog box will be the first field or control upon which focus will be placed when the form is first opened (or the next record is opened).

When you complete your business with that field and hit Tab, the focus shifts to whatever field is next on the list, regardless of where on the form you have placed it. Use tab order to make it easy for users to perform their data entry or whatever task the form is being designed for.

Use the Auto Order button in the Tab Order dialog box, shown in Figure 5.4, to automatically create a left-to-right, top-to-bottom tab order. If you want to remove a control from Tab Order but still want to be able to select it, set its Tab Stop property to No.

Task 7   Changing the tab order.

1. Choose View|Tab Order from the menu bar. The Tab Order dialog box opens.

Figure 5.4   The Tab Order dialog box.

2. Select the Employment Date field by clicking on the small gray box to the left of it.

3. Click on it again, drag it up over the Employee Picture field, then let go. Click on the OK button to apply the new tab order.

4. Save the form, then check the new tab order by clicking on the Form View button and tabbing around your form.

5. Next, close the form.

HOLD That Skill!

You can set your tab order by clicking on Auto Order, but keep in mind that this will not always be the order you desire, especially if your fields have an odd configuration or if you need a customized order. Also, you can remove a control from the tab order entirely by changing its Tab Stop property from Yes to No.

Creating Controls On A Form

Microsoft Access 97 classifies everything you create on a form as a control. The three varieties of control are bound, unbound, and calculated, and their type dictates the way they are created. Bound controls have a direct effect on (and are affected by) fields in a table, unbound controls are independent of fields in a table, and calculated controls perform calculations that can be based on bound or unbound controls.

Figure 5.5   The Toolbox.

While in Design view, you may have noticed the Toolbox, shown in Figure 5.5, floating around; it is a toolbar that offers you the option to create bound, unbound, and calculated controls. From it, you can choose (from top-left to bottom-right) the following:

➤ **Select Objects** A tool that returns the ordinary arrow cursor

➤ **Control Wizards** A tool that turns on the Control Wizards

➤ **Label** A tool that creates an unbound control for descriptive labels

➤ **Text Box** A tool that creates a bound or unbound text box that either displays or accepts data

➤ **Option Group** A tool that creates option buttons, toggle buttons, or checkboxes in a group

➤ **Toggle Button** A tool that creates a toggle button that has two states: pressed and not pressed (Yes/No)

➤ **Option Button** A tool that creates a radio button that has two states: filled and unfilled (Yes/No)

➤ **Check Box** A tool that creates a radio button that has a check instead of a dot

➤ **Combo Box** A tool that creates a text box that allows you to choose from a drop-down list of values

➤ **List Box** A tool that creates a drop-down list that allows you to choose from a group of values

➤ **Command Button** A tool that creates a button to which you attach actions, such as opening a form

➤ **Image** A tool that creates a frame for an image

➤ **Unbound Object Frame** A tool that creates a frame for an unbound object, such as a logo

➤ **Bound Object Frame** A tool that creates a frame for objects in records in a table

➤ **Page Break** A tool that causes a page break to occur where it is placed on the form

➤ **Tab Control** A tool that creates tabbed areas for presenting controls more readably

➤ **Subform/Subreport** A tool that creates a frame for a subform or subreport

➤ **Line** A tool that builds a straight line when you click on and drag it

➤ **Rectangle** A tool that builds a rectangle when you click on and drag it

➤ **More Controls** Tools that offer HTML and ActiveX controls

We'll cover the more complex form controls in a later chapter. For now, let's put some of the simpler controls on our current form.

Task 8   Adding a simple form control.

1. Open and maximize the form in Design view.

2. Click on the Toolbox to turn off Control Wizards.

3. Select all controls on the form simultaneously by "drawing" a box around them with your mouse.

4. Move them as a group about an inch down the form (lengthen the form as necessary).

5. Click on the Label button on the Toolbox. This label will be like a descriptive heading for your form, so you should place it at the top of your form in the center.

6. Place the cursor on the form at the point where you want the top-left corner of your new control to begin. Drag the cursor to your new control's bottom-right corner and then let go. The new control now exists on your form and is ready for you to enter the label text.

7. Type the words "Employee Data Entry Form" and then deselect the control by clicking on the form. Note that if you fail to type anything, Access 97 automatically deletes the control.

Modifying Controls-Display Attributes

In my experience, no form ends up looking the way it's first intended to, despite the preplanning you may do. In fact, it's so easy to modify controls that sometimes the easiest way to create a form is to simply dump all the fields you might want onto the form and then weed them out and spruce them up.

As you proceed through the following tasks, note that one property of every form control is its *name*. By default, the name is either the name of the field it is bound to or the type of control it is, followed by a number (Text12, Line3, and so on). You can edit the name to make it easier to recall, and you can use the Select Object button on the Formatting (Form/Report) toolbar to select it by name (rather than having to search your entire form to find and click on it).

Task 9 Modifying simple form controls (labels and text boxes).

1. Select the Employee Picture field and its label by clicking on either the field or the label. Move the cursor near the edge of the Employee Picture field until it turns into a small hand (this indicates that you can now drag the entire control to any location on the form).

2. Click on and drag the Employee Picture field and label down about one inch.

3. Click on and drag the Employment Date field and label into the space between, letting the Snap place the field and label properly.

4. Select the Employee Name field by clicking on it. Small square boxes appear on each corner and at the centerlines between them. These are called *handles*, and you can use them to resize the fields. Resizing occurs when the cursor turns into a two-way arrow over the selection handles, just as movement occurs when the cursor turns into a little hand.

5. Right-click on the Employee Picture field to open the shortcut menu. Select Special Effect and then choose the Shadowed option (a small box with a shadow behind it). Another way to achieve this effect is to open the properties sheet for the Employee Picture field, scrolling down to Special Effects and selecting Shadowed.

6. You can manipulate the font of a selected control using word-processor-like settings on the second-level toolbar, such as Font, Size, Justification, Bold, and so on. Click on the label you created previously (Employee Data Entry Form), enlarge the font, and make it boldfaced.

Task 10 Changing the Format and Default Value properties of controls.

1. Open the property sheet of the Employment Date field. The Format is Short Date by default.

2. Click on the down-arrow and change Short Date to Medium Date.

3. At the Default Value property, click on the Build Button. When the Expression Builder opens, enter "= Now()".

4. Click on the OK button and then close the properties sheet.

Task 11   *Changing the default properties of new controls.*

1. Click on the Text Box control button in the Toolbox and then click on the Properties button on the Form Design toolbar. The properties sheet for that control opens.

2. Scroll to the Attached Label property, and change the value from Yes to No.

3. Test it by creating a new text box (or by adding another field from the Field List). No attached label appears. Don't forget to delete the extra text box.

Printing A Form

To take a look at your work, use the form for data entry or data display. To print it out, the form must be opened in Form view. The default Form view displays the form you've just created, but you can switch to Datasheet view based on your form as well. Unlike the table datasheet, the form datasheet shows only the fields you've included on your form.

Task 12   *Switching between views.*

1. Click on the View button's down-arrow on the Form Design toolbar.

2. In Form view, click on the View button's down-arrow, and select Datasheet view. The form datasheet appears.

3. If you want to return to Design view, click on the same button.

Task 13   *Printing a form.*

1. Switch to Form view.

2. In Form view, click on the Print button.

3. If you want to change the page setup or default printer, use the File|Print choice from the menu bar.

Forms are the primary means by which your users will view, enter, and delete data. Good form design can make these tasks easy by starting with a logical tab order; sizing, placing, and aligning form controls for maximum readability; and setting default values an ordinary user would expect.

Forms are useful for many of the functions a datasheet serves, such as navigating through a table, finding particular records, and sorting and filtering for unique sets of records. Their primary advantages are that they allow the use of specialized controls, they shield users from the table-like complexity that is exposed in a datasheet, and they can be printed with pleasing effect.

Using filters and sorting can yield answers to many common questions about the contents of a table or database, but specialized tools called *queries* have a much greater range of capabilities. Access 97 queries use a query-by-example method that can gather, sort, group, and calculate data. All you need to do is make a few simple choices. We'll cover queries in Chapter 6.

Practice Exercises

Exercise 1

> You have been asked to create a data-entry form for the Employ-
> ees table. The form should be connected to the Employees table
> and should contain the controls needed to enter all data in an
> effective manner.
>
> Determine the elements (fields and controls) required on the form.
>
> Create a form with the wizard, and add the required fields.
>
> Choose the International background for the form.
>
> Use the default name for the form.
>
> Save the form.

Answer To Exercise 1

Think about the process of entering data into the table. Do you need all the
fields or just a few? It depends on what you want the data-entry person to do at
that point in the process.

To create a form with the wizard, the Forms tab must be selected in the Database window. Click on the New button, and choose Form Wizard from the
dialog box. Next, you'll want to choose the Employees table, and add the fields
you need.

To choose the International background for the form, you need to wait until
you get to that screen of the wizard and then select International from among
your choices.

To accept the default name for the form, wait until you get to that screen (it
should be the last one) and simply accept the default.

Click on Finish on the last screen of the wizard to save the form.

Exercise 2

You've built a form with the wizard, but you've decided you want to change the layout to make it easier for data entry. You're going to modify the layout and change the arrangement of controls.

Open the form in Design view.

Change the font of each field to boldface.

Rearrange the position of the fields.

Save the form.

Print the result of your actions.

Answer To Exercise 2

To open the form in Design view, select the form, and click on the Design button.

Right-click on a control, and select Properties from the shortcut menu to change the font.

To reposition field controls, click on them, and position the cursor on them until it turns into a hand. Then, move the control until it's in the position you want.

Click on the Save button on the Form Design toolbar.

Click on the Print button on the Form Design toolbar to print the form.

Exercise 3

You notice data entry errors being made on your new form, so you decide to make your new form more graphically appealing.

Open the form in Design view.

Set the background of each text box to sunken.

Change the color of the background of each text box to light blue.

Save the form.

Answer To Exercise 3

Select the form in the Database window, and click on the Design button.

Right-click on a text box control, and choose Special Effect|Sunken from the shortcut menu.

Right-click on a text box control, and choose Fill/Back Color from the shortcut menu, then choose light blue from the palette.

Click on the Save button to save the form.

Need To Know More?

 Litwin, Paul, Ken Getz, and Mike Gilbert. *Access 97 Developer's Handbook*, Sybex Inc., San Francisco, CA, 1997. ISBN 0-7821-1941-7. Chapter 8 contains information about form design and layout.

 Viescas, John L. *Running Microsoft Access 97*, Microsoft Press, Redmond, WA, 1997. ISBN 1-57231-323-4. Chapters 12 and 13 provide information about building forms and modifying them.

 www.e4free.com
The Form design page has detailed information about changing the format of controls and designing forms.

6

Building Queries

Terms you'll need to understand:

√   Recordset

√   Select query

√   Action query

√   Append

√   Make-Table query

√   Criteria

√   Predicate clause

Skills you'll need to master:

√   Choosing query types

√   Retrieving data

√   Ordering data

√   Selecting data based on several criteria

√   Summarizing data in groups

√   Performing calculations on data

√   Printing the results

Typically, you don't just keep records on file forever, unchanging. Most database applications involve changing data frequently; customers come and go, prices change, inventory fluctuates, items become obsolete or marked down, and so on.

Imagine marking 15,000 items down by 25 percent for a blowout sale, *one at a time*, or addressing mailers to 700 high-volume customers from a pool of 100,000. Customized queries are the specialized tool you can use to automate such onerous tasks—and many other tasks in which selecting certain records is fundamental.

Understanding Query Types

Access 97 contains two major types of query:

➤ **Select query** Selects specific data for viewing

➤ **Action query** Performs actions (insert, update, and delete) with data

Select Queries

Select queries retrieve data in accordance with criteria you specify and then build a recordset (or table) of this information. You can browse, print, and update the data in the recordset. In addition, unlike datasheets, select queries can perform calculations on data as well as retrieve data from multiple tables. Thus, select queries can be sources of data for forms and reports.

Select queries come in the following varieties:

➤ **Simple Select** One table, one criterion specified

➤ **Multitable Select** Multiple tables joined via key fields

➤ **Logical AND** Several criteria specified on the first grid row

➤ **Logical OR** Criteria specified on the first and second (or more) rows

Action Queries

Action queries perform actions on chunks (or batches) of data. They automate tasks that would otherwise take a great deal of manual effort. They include:

➤ **Append query** Adds specific records in one or more tables to another table

➤ **Delete query** Deletes all specified records

➤ **Make-Table query** Creates a new table from specified records

➤ **Update query** Changes specified fields in specified records

Creating A Simple Query

Microsoft Access 97 makes it easy to build simple select queries; simply click on the New button when the Queries tab of the Database window is selected. You can specify a name for your query when you save it, and you can view the query's properties by clicking on the Properties button on the Query Design toolbar.

Task 1   Beginning a simple select query.

1. Open the test database that you created in Chapter 3. Click on the Queries tab of the Database window, then click on New. Design view is the default selection. Click on OK (clicking on the New Object button on the Query Design toolbar and selecting Query on the drop-down menu achieves the same result).

2. The Query Design View window opens, with the Show Table box on top. Select the Employees table from the list provided. Click on Add. A box that lists the fields in the Employees table appears in the upper half of the Design View window. Close the Show Table dialog box.

3. Click on and drag all the fields from the field listing to the top row of the grid below, starting in the field farthest to the left. Make sure the checkbox in the center of each field is checked (this means the field will display in the query output). A quick way to enter all the fields in the design grid is to double-click on the title bar of the field list, then drag all the fields to the design grid at once.

4. Enter one of the employee names in the Employee Name column, in the row next to the word Criteria. Run the query by clicking on the Run button on the Query Design toolbar.

5. Try running the query with a few variations on the name (first name only, first letter of last name, name in the Employee Number field, and so on). You should get an error message if you run the query with a name in the Employee Number field (mismatched data type). Reading the error messages can be helpful when you are designing or trouble-shooting queries.

6. Click on the Design View button on the Query Design toolbar to get back to Design view.

7. Click on File|Save. A Save As dialog box in which you can enter the name of your choice appears. Enter "Employees1", and click on OK.

Tables and queries must have different names. I like to use similar names for tables, queries, forms, and reports that show related data or have similar functions.

In Design view, you can change the properties of specific fields if you like. Fields in the query inherit the properties defined for the field in the table they come from. To override the inherited properties, simply click on the field in Design view, click on the Properties button on the Query Design toolbar, and then set the properties (see the Query Properties dialog box in Figure 6.1). For instance, if the table the field came from indicated that two decimal places should display—but you want no decimal places—set Decimal Places to zero in the Field Properties dialog box that opens. Changing this setting does not affect the underlying data nor the display of data in the table itself.

 You can format the query datasheet in much the same way as a table datasheet. You can change the font face and size; apply character formatting, such as bold, italics, underlining, and color; and modify the gridlines style and background color. In addition, to make the data easier to understand, you can apply numeric formatting to values in a datasheet.

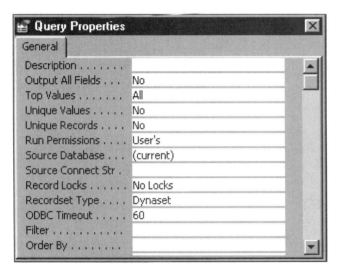

Figure 6.1   The Query Properties dialog box.

Specifying Various Criteria

When you run a Select query, you usually are searching for particular records from a table, meaning you want to specify criteria that the field values must match in order to be returned. To specify a particular name, enter the name in the Criteria row of the design grid, as we did in Task 1. You can specify just a part of the name, exclude some names, and so on by varying your Criteria row entries.

To specify dates, you need to surround the date you enter in the Criteria row with pound signs: #June 14, 1997#, for instance. Access 97 is comfortable with several variations of the date format, such as #6/14/97# or #14-Jun-97#. You can also use date and time functions to select records based on dates.

Task 2   Adding date criteria to the query.

1. Open the Employees1 query. In the Employment Date field's Criteria row, enter a date that will retrieve some (but not all) of the records you have entered (see Figure 6.2).

2. Run the query and see whether you get the results you expected.

3. If not, make sure that you have entered a date format Access 97 understands, and that you have put the pound sign (#) on both ends of the date.

4. Save the query.

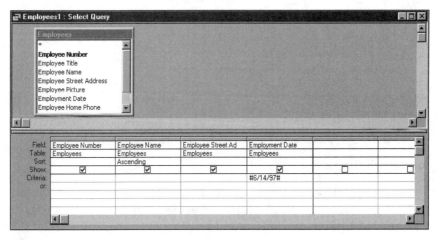

Figure 6.2   Specifying date criteria in the Employees1 query.

Sorting Data In A Query

Queries do not sort data by default. Because some tables may contain unsorted data, Access 97 queries include sorting functions. You can sort records by any field on the grid, and sorting occurs from left to right (the first field on the left is the major category, and each field after that is a subcategory to the one on its left).

HOLD That Skill!

Sorting on one field is easy enough to understand: All records in the table or recordset are sorted according to the alphanumeric order of the field being sorted upon. For example, a recordset containing country, state, and ZIP code would be sorted alphabetically by country if Country were the sort field (but the states and ZIP codes would still be jumbled).

Sorting on several fields can be more difficult to understand. Think of it like this: The first field sorted upon becomes the top category, and the next field becomes a subcategory of the first field, the third field becomes a subcategory of the second field, and so on. For instance, if the preceding example were sorted by country, then state, then ZIP code, the countries would be alphabetized into major groups first, then the states within each country's group of records would be alphabetized, then the ZIP codes would be sorted numerically within each state's group of records.

Task 3   Sorting by field in a query.

1. Open Employees1 in Design view.

2. Click on the Sort row of the query grid under Employee Name, then click on Ascending (see Figure 6.3).

3. Run the query, and examine the results. Click on the Design View button, and change the sort order to descending.

4. Run the query again, and examine the results.

5. Save the query.

To sort on fields in a particular order, you might have to rearrange them (remember that sorting produces categories from left to right along the grid). To rearrange the fields in the order you'd like, place the cursor at the top of the column. It turns into a little black arrow that points down. Click on it, and the entire column is selected. Click on and drag the column from right to left until you achieve the order you want. Then, sort away!

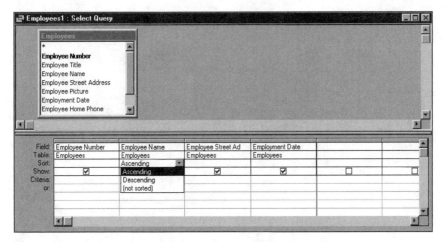

Figure 6.3   Choosing the sort order in the Employees1 query.

Creating A Query With Multiple Criteria (AND/OR)

Queries are actually questions you are asking of a table (or another query). If your table holds data about people, you may, for example, want to pull data on all the people over 30 with a college education. In this case, you tell the table to give you every record that meets the first criterion (over 30) AND the second criterion (college education). This is called a Logical AND, and you enter the specified criteria on the same row of the grid, as we discussed in more detail in Chapter 4.

Task 4   Creating an AND query.

1. For this task, to demonstrate how the query works, you'll have to open your Employees table and enter a few records with the same employee name but different pay amounts. Three or four records should be enough to illustrate the point.

2. Open the Employees1 query in Design view.

3. In the Criteria row of Employee Name, enter one of the employee names that occurs several times (see Figure 6.4).

4. In the Criteria row of Employment Date, enter a date that occurs only once.

5. Run the query. The query should return the employee record that has the name you specified and the date you specified.

6. Save the query.

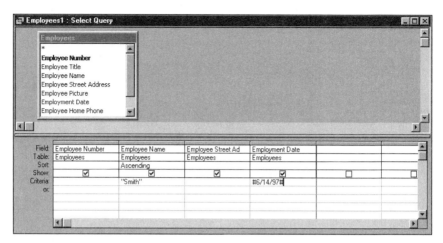

Figure 6.4 An AND query.

If, for some reason, you also want data about people over 45 without a college education, you tell the table to give you every record that meets the first set of criteria (over 30, college education) OR the second set of criteria (over 45, no college education). This is called a Logical OR, and you place the specified criteria in the Or row of the grid, as we discussed in greater detail in Chapter 4. You can add several Or rows if you desire.

Task 5 Creating an OR query.

1. Open the Employees1 query in Design view.

2. In the Criteria row of Employee Name, enter one of the employee names that occurs only once (see Figure 6.5).

3. In the Or row of the same column, enter another name that occurs only once.

4. Run the query. The query should return the employee records that have either the first name entered or the second name, but no others.

Using Predicate Clauses (Between, In, And Like)

Access 97 includes special operators that take some of the work out of defining queries. For instance, if you want to find all records where the value of one of the fields can range from 50 to 500, you can use the Between clause (Between 50 And 500) rather than entering ">=50 And <=500".

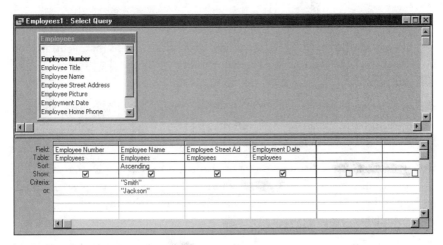

Figure 6.5 An OR query.

The In clause—In ("This", "That", "The Other")—causes the same effect as an Or statement. For instance, you could write the same statement like this: "This" Or "That" Or "The Other". Personally, I don't find the In statement any easier to remember or use, but it's there if it helps you.

The Like clause is quite useful, but it takes some practice to use it to its fullest extent. A simple Like clause (see Figure 6.6) may read: Like "M*". The search term is enclosed in quotation marks, and the asterisk after the M tells Access 97 to search—in the field with focus—for the letter capital M plus any number of other characters after that. Therefore, if you used this statement in the Name field, you'd get every record that started with a capital M.

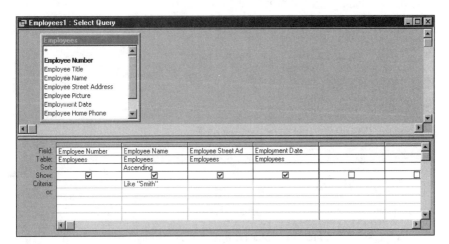

Figure 6.6 Using the Like predicate clause in a query.

You can use other wildcard characters to search for patterns with a Like clause:

➤ **The question mark (?)** Returns any single character in that position. For instance, "M?" returns any value beginning with capital M followed by one character.

➤ **The pound-sign character (#)** Returns a single numeric digit in that position. For instance, "M#" returns any value beginning with capital M followed by a number from zero through nine.

➤ **Brackets ([])** Indicates a range of characters in that single-character position. For instance, "M[a-z]" returns any value beginning with capital M followed by one character, which is allowed to be any alphabetic character from a through z.

➤ **The exclamation point inside brackets ([!])** Indicates that the characters following the exclamation point are exceptions. For example, "M[!0-9]" returns any value beginning with capital M followed by any character other than zero through nine.

Summarizing Grouped Data In A Query

When you run a query, sorting arranges records that are in a recordset into groups. Access 97 queries can summarize this grouped data for you using the summary functions. These include:

➤ **Group By** Groups all records by duplicated data in this field

➤ **Sum** Adds a group of numbers

➤ **Avg** Averages a group of numbers

➤ **Min** Finds the minimum value of a group

➤ **Max** Finds the maximum value of a group

➤ **Count** Counts the number of records in a group

➤ **StDev** Finds the standard deviation of a group of numbers

➤ **Var** Finds the variance of a group of numbers

➤ **First** Returns the first value in a column

➤ **Last** Returns the last value in a column

➤ **Expression** Creates a calculated field that includes a result from one of the other functions

➤ **Where** Uses data from ungrouped fields

When you want to use these summarization functions, the query undergoes a significant change in its character. You no longer see each record in the output, only the summarized records.

For instance, let's say that you'd like to know the average age of all your employees. To get the answer, simply use the Avg function on the Age field in a select query. If you'd like to know the average age of all employees in each division, use the Group By function in the Division field and the Avg function in the Age field. The ages of all employees in each group are averaged and displayed in the final output. In both of these cases, even though you are using all the records, only the groups and their totals are displayed in the output.

Task 6   *Grouping and summarizing query data.*

1. Open Employees1 in Design view. Click on the Totals button.

2. A row labeled Total appears as the third row down (after the Field and Table rows). If you click on this row, a drop-down box lists all the available functions (see Figure 6.7).

3. By default, Group By appears in the Total row of each field. Delete the Employee Number and Employee Pay Per Hour columns, and change the Total function for Employee Name to Count. Remove any criteria you have entered in the Criteria and Or rows of the Employee Name field.

4. Run the query. The query should return the number of employees in each group of names (two Smiths, three Jacksons, and so on).

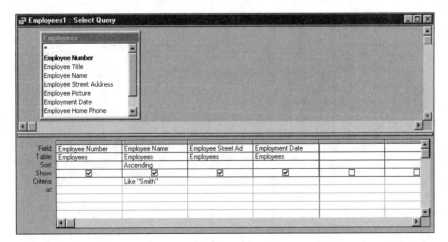

Figure 6.7   Choosing summarization functions in the Employees1 query.

Calculating With A Query

Select queries can result in more fields than they start with (more data than the underlying table contains). This is possible because you can create new fields using calculations, and you can name these new fields as you see fit. For instance, suppose you want to calculate a field that shows the gross profit for each item you sell, yet the underlying table shows only your cost and your sales price. Simply create a calculated field that subtracts your cost from the sales price, name it Gross Profit, and voilà! A Gross Profit field is automatically included when the query is run.

Task 7   Calculating with a query.

1. Open the Employees1 query in Design view.

2. In the top row of a blank column to the right of the existing columns, enter "SSTax:[Employee Pay Per Hour]*0.15". SSTax is the name of the new field, the colon separates it from the calculation, and the employee pay field name needs to have brackets—[]—around it (see Figure 6.8).

3. Run the query. A new field showing the hourly amount of Social Security tax you must pay for each employee appears.

4. Save the query.

 It's important to know how to create additional fields in a query. To create a newly named field, you must enter the name followed by a colon (name:) and then enter the calculation. And don't forget to put brackets around the field name if the field name contains spaces.

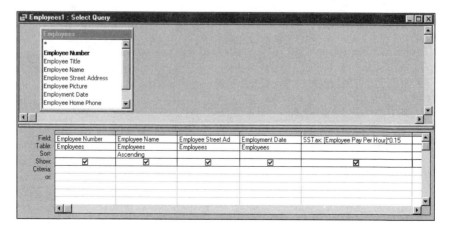

Figure 6.8   Creating a new, calculated field in the Employees1 query.

Task 8   Printing the result of a query.

1. Open the Employees1 query in Design view.

2. Run the query.

3. Click on the Print button. The query datasheet prints.

Queries can do much more than just "pull data," as demonstrated by the multiple query types Access 97 offers. Creating a simple query is a matter of opening a new query in the Design window, adding tables (or other queries), dragging fields in, entering criteria, and naming and saving the query.

Within a simple query, you can sort and group data for specific kinds of results, you can build calculated fields not available in the underlying table or query, and you can directly print the results if you like. Essentially, the choices you make when you are constructing a query form the "question" you are asking of the database.

Of course, queries are meaningless without data to start with, and entering data can be very time consuming. Importing and exporting data, as well as linking to other applications, is an everyday occurrence for the effective database administrator. We will cover these topics in Chapter 7.

Practice Exercises

Exercise 1

> You need to create a query to retrieve certain information about employees. You're not quite sure what information is required or how you'll display it, so you decide to use Design view and run your query several times to make sure of the results.
>
> Create a query in Design view using the Employees table and fields.
>
> Sort your query in descending order on the Employee Name field.
>
> Run the query.
>
> Save the query as QryEmployees.

Answer To Exercise 1

To create a query in Design view, make sure the Queries tab is selected, click on the New button, and choose Design view on the next screen.

Click on the Sort row under Employee Name, and choose the sort order you prefer (descending in this case).

To run the query from Design view, click on the Run button on the Query Design toolbar.

Choose File|Save As/Export from the menu bar and then enter the name.

Exercise 2

You've created a query in Design view and then you ran it. Now, you want to get Design view back and make the query more specific. You also want to add a calculated field as well as print the results of your query.

Change from Normal mode back to Design view.

Add criteria to select only employees with two of the names entered in your table.

Create a new field named Raise, calculating its value as hourly pay multiplied by 1.05.

Save the query.

Run the query.

Print the results of the query.

Answer To Exercise 2

To go back to Design view, click on the Design View button on the Query Design toolbar.

To add criteria to select by Employee Name, enter a name in the Criteria row and another name in the Or row under Employee Name.

Go to a blank column and enter "Raise:[Employee Pay Per Hour]*1.05" in the row where the rest of the field names are.

Click on the Save button on the Query Design toolbar.

Click on the Run button on the Query Design toolbar.

Click on the Print button on the Query Design toolbar to print the results.

Exercise 3

You decide to make your query sort employees by employment date, so you can review the most recently hired first.

Open the new query in Design View.

Change the sort order of the Employment Date field to descending.

Save the query.

Answer To Exercise 3

Click on the Design View button on the Query Design toolbar.

Click on the Sort row of the Employment Date field.

Select the Descending sort order on the drop-down list.

Click on the Save button on the Query Design toolbar.

Need To Know More?

 Elmasri, Ramez and Shamkant B. Navanthe. *Fundamentals of Database Systems*, Addison-Wesley Publishing Company, Menlo Park, CA, 1994. ISBN 0-8053-1748-7. Chapter 16 contains an explanation of how queries work at the lowest levels.

 Viescas, John L. *Running Microsoft Access 97*, Microsoft Press, Redmond, WA, 1997. ISBN 1-57231-323-4. Chapter 8 provides information about select queries and retrieving data.

 www.e4free.com
The Query design page has detailed information about designing many types of queries.

Importing, Exporting, And Linking Data

7

Terms you'll need to understand:

√ SQL

√ ODBC

√ Importing

√ Exporting

√ Proprietary format

√ Comma-delimited

√ Linking

√ Data source

Skills you'll need to master:

√ Determining when to import and when to link

√ Copying and pasting objects and records

√ Importing and exporting from Access 97 databases

√ Importing and exporting from other applications

√ Importing and exporting text

√ Fixing import errors

√ Linking external data sources

Queries automate many of the data manipulation tasks you'll encounter, but they can't automate data entry. In truth, nothing can relieve you of manual data entry, unless the data is already in another database, spreadsheet, or text format (or an intern is handy).

But perhaps importing is not the solution. Importing data (or whole databases) creates a new object (a table, for instance) that you can manipulate within your Access 97 database. The external file is left unchanged, but, if you want to cause changes to it, creating a link will do the trick (although with some limits on property modifications).

If you need to cause changes to the external data file but want to do your work within the context of your Access 97 database, establishing a link between the two may be the answer. You may want to link, rather than import, whenever the external data file is too large (larger than 1GB), changed frequently by other users, or shared by other users on a network.

Access 97 imports to and exports from all the common formats in which you ordinarily find data, such as other Access versions, Excel, dBase, and text. Additional formats include FoxPro, Paradox, and HTML tables and lists. In fact, you can import from any SQL database that supports the Open Database Connectivity (ODBC) standard.

Keep in mind that when you encounter a proprietary format, the program that created it generally has an export function capable of converting from that format into one of the common formats—so all is not lost.

Finally, we cannot create complete examples for the tasks in this chapter, because it may not be possible for you to find or create every file format or database type. Therefore, we will explore the dialog boxes and commands involved rather than (for the most part) do the actual imports, exports, and links. Make sure you read and heed the instructions preceding each task, because we include important tips on successful importing, exporting, and linking.

 For the exam, any external data files or databases should already be present on your system, and you should receive instructions about their location. If you need to examine them to determine any preparation required, the correct applications to open or read them should also be present.

Importing And Exporting Access 97 Objects

Microsoft Access has undergone many changes over the years, and significant changes result in new version numbers. As consumers, we would prefer that new versions can always read or import databases from previous versions.

Access 97 imports from versions 1.x, 2.0, 7.0 (Access 95), and 8.0 (Access 97). Note that you must either create or open an Access 97 database to accomplish an import. When importing from an Access database, you can import all the major Access objects: tables, forms, queries, reports, macros, and modules.

By the way, if the external Access database is secured, you must have at least Open/Run and Read Design permission to perform an import. If you have these permissions, you can import the database and all the major objects, and you will be the owner of the new objects (meaning you will have full permission rights over them).

Copying And Pasting Objects And Records

Another way to (in effect) import from an Access database is to open the source database, choose the Edit|Copy command, open the target database, and choose the Edit|Paste command. This works well for one or two objects, but importing many objects is easier to do with the formal import process.

If you want to build a table in a Microsoft Word document based on records in an Access database, the procedure is very simple. Open the Access database and the table that contains the desired records, select the desired records, click on Edit|Copy to copy them to the clipboard, then open the Word document and click on Edit|Paste. The records are copied into the document and formatted as a table.

Task 1   *Importing from an Access database.*

1. Open the test database. Choose File|Get External Data|Import from the menu bar. The Import dialog box opens (see Figure 7.1).

2. The top of the dialog box resembles the typical file and folder listing in any Office application. In the bottom left-hand corner, a drop-down list lets you select the file type to import from. Click on the down-arrow to examine the file types available.

3. Next, choose the file type you want to import from, find and select the file (or files) you want to import, and click on the Import button.

4. Note that there is an Advanced button for opening the Advanced Find dialog box. Advanced Find lets you specify more criteria to aid your search for the proper files to import.

5. After you click on the Import button, the Import Objects dialog box opens. Specify the objects (tables, forms, and so on) you want to import.

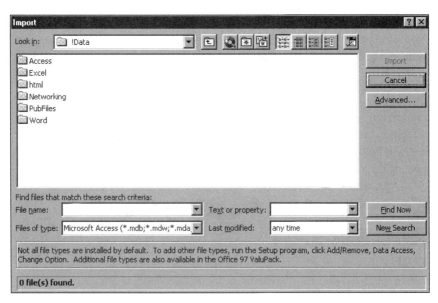

Figure 7.1 The Import dialog box.

6. Clicking on the Options button displays an additional section of the dialog box where you can specify the format for imported tables and queries. Here, you also have the option of specifying the import of Relationships, Menus and Toolbars, and Import/Export Specs.

7. When the import is successful, the new objects will have the name of the object that you selected. If the name is the same as an existing object, Access 97 inserts a number on the end of the name to differentiate it.

 You can install additional file types for import by rerunning the Office Setup procedure and choosing Add/Remove|Data Access|Change Option.

Exporting to an Access database is just about the reverse of the import procedure. You can choose the object you want to export, and basically save it as an object of the new Access version. You can even go as far as replacing an existing object of the same name if you choose. And when exporting macros, you have the option of saving the macro as a Visual Basic module in the current database.

Access 97 can export to Access database types, and quite a variety of other common formats as well. As when you are importing, you can load additional file types for export by rerunning the Office Setup procedure.

Task 2   Exporting to an existing Access database.

1. In the test database, select one of the tables.

2. Choose File|Save As/Export from the menu bar. The Save As dialog box opens.

3. Select the To An External File Or Database option, and click on OK.

4. The Save In dialog box, which displays the name of the object being exported as part of the title of the dialog box, opens. The purpose of the Save In dialog box is to let you select the database in which to save the object that you are exporting.

5. After you find the database folder and file, click on the Export button. The Export dialog box opens.

6. In the Export dialog box, enter the name of the new object. You have the option of exporting both the definition and the data, or the definition only.

Importing And Exporting With Excel

Spreadsheets are another common source of data. People frequently need to import data from them, primarily because many database applications start out as spreadsheets. Typically, someone has used a spreadsheet to build a rough application for solving a particular problem, but the application has been too successful. The amount of data in the application—and other people's desire to use it—has outstripped the spreadsheet program's ability to function efficiently.

In creating the new database application, your first order of business is to import all the data from the various sheets of the spreadsheet. You can import directly from Lotus 1-2-3 and Excel (version 2 and later) spreadsheets. If the data is in an incompatible spreadsheet format, try exporting from the program into a compatible format.

When importing a spreadsheet, Access 97 converts each row into a record and the data in each cell into a field, thus making a table. Access 97 uses the data in the first few rows to decide the data type for each field. You can also make Access 97 use the data in the entire first row as field names, as shown in Figure 7.2.

Make sure you're familiar with using the first row of a spreadsheet as the names for the fields in your newly imported table.

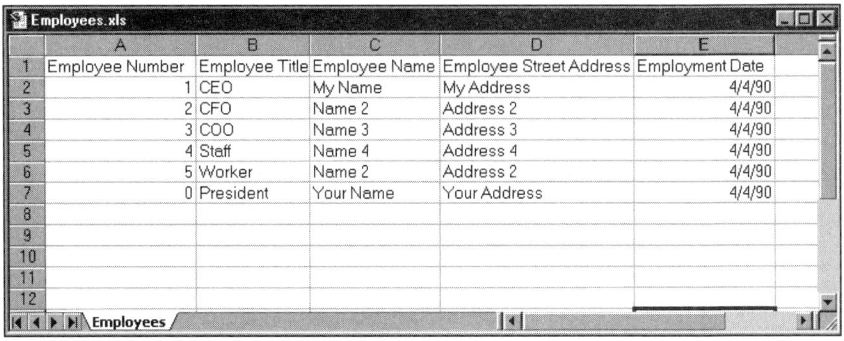
Employees.xls

	A	B	C	D	E
1	Employee Number	Employee Title	Employee Name	Employee Street Address	Employment Date
2	1	CEO	My Name	My Address	4/4/90
3	2	CFO	Name 2	Address 2	4/4/90
4	3	COO	Name 3	Address 3	4/4/90
5	4	Staff	Name 4	Address 4	4/4/90
6	5	Worker	Name 2	Address 2	4/4/90
7	0	President	Your Name	Your Address	4/4/90
8					
9					
10					
11					
12					

Employees

Figure 7.2 A sample Excel spreadsheet, with field names in the first row.

Prior to beginning the import process (assuming the data is in a compatible format), open the spreadsheet and determine whether the data needs to be massaged for the best import results. *Massaging* means spending a few minutes to place the correct data in the first few rows, resulting in exactly the table definition you're after. For instance, you can set the names for each field by creating a new first row that contains the correct name in each column. You can set the data type for each field by creating a couple new rows after the first one that have the correct type of data in them (called *dummy rows*). When you finish importing, open the new table, and remove any records that contain dummy data (the Field Name row won't become part of the data or affect the data types, so don't worry about that).

Task 3 Importing from an Excel spreadsheet.

1. Open the test database. Choose File|Get External Data|Import from the menu bar. The Import dialog box opens.
2. Click on the Files Of Type down-arrow to examine the available file types. Select Microsoft Excel.
3. Next, select the Excel file to import and then click on the Import button.
4. If your spreadsheet contains named ranges (or is an Excel 5 or later spreadsheet with multiple worksheets), the Import Spreadsheet Wizard dialog box opens.
5. In this dialog box, select the individual named range or worksheet for import and then click on Next.

6. The next screen of the wizard displays a sample of the spreadsheet. If your first row contains field names, indicate this by using the checkbox provided. Then, click on Next.

7. On the next screen, tell the wizard which fields to index and whether to skip certain fields. The name of the field and the data type are displayed on this screen as well. If you need to change the data type, you'll have to add dummy data rows by exiting the import process and massaging the spreadsheet data from within Excel.

8. In the next window, you can make one of the fields a primary key, unless several fields make up the primary key. If the primary key consists of multiple fields, you'll have to open the resulting table and establish the primary key manually.

9. In the final screen, enter the name of the new table. You can also choose to have the Table Analyzer Wizard analyze and optimize your new table automatically.

10. If another file is already using the name of the new table, Access 97 asks if you want to replace the old file. After you have decided whether to replace the file, click on the Finish button, and take a look at your new table.

HOLD That Skill!

If you have Excel on your machine, create a simple Excel worksheet with four or five rows of data in it. Make the rows contain textual, numerical, and date/time data. Create a first row that contains field names instead of data, and run through the process of importing this data as a new table in Access 97. It doesn't take very long to perform an experiment like this, and it'll improve your exam times if you've used the screens once or twice.

Exporting data to an Excel spreadsheet (or to a dBase, Paradox, or FoxPro file format) follows the same process as exporting to an Access 97 database, except that you choose a different file format and location for the exported object. Also, Access 97 cuts off long file names when exporting to dBase, Paradox, or FoxPro, and, if duplicate file names occur, Access 97 won't complete the export process.

Importing With dBase, Paradox, And FoxPro

Paradox, dBase, and FoxPro are common database formats in which you'll frequently find old data or applications. The import procedure for each is fairly similar to the one we just used, with the caveat that you'll need to install the Microsoft Data Access Pack before working with Paradox files (you can find it on the Microsoft Office Professional Edition 97 CD-ROM in the folder named \ValuPack\DataAcc). Also, Access 97 does not support the Paradox Graphic, Binary, and Formatted Memo data types. Other than these issues, the process is exactly the same as the procedure outlined in Task 3 (except, of course, you have to choose the appropriate file type).

Importing And Exporting Text

Text files are another common source of data for new Access 97 databases, although we're certainly not talking about using the contents of a letter or report as data. The kind of text files we're referring to are delimited or fixed-width text files (see Figures 7.3 and 7.4). These are files made up of records whose fields are separated by a delimiting character (such as a comma) or regular spacing (fixed-width). Typically, these files are the output of some other database or spreadsheet program, or mail-merge lists from a word-processing program. They can even be simple lists (of names, addresses, and phone numbers, for instance) created in a text editor, such as Notepad.

For Access 97, delimited data must use one of three standard separator characters: comma, tab, or space. The separator character indicates the beginning and ending of each field, and a carriage return indicates the end of a record. For instance, if a comma is used as the separator, it must be used consistently throughout the file, and, if the data in a field has any commas inside it, that

```
Employees.txt                                              _ □ ×
    · · · I · · · I · · · 1 · · · I · · · 2 · · · I · · · 3 · · · I · · · 4 · · · I · · · 5 · · · I · · · 6 · · · I ·
  1,"CEO","My Name","My Address",,4/4/90 0:00:00,,,"Free Child Care"
  2,"CFO","Name 2","Address 2",,4/4/90 0:00:00,,,"Onsite massages"
  3,"COO","Name 3","Address 3",,4/4/90 0:00:00,,,"Time off"
  4,"Staff","Name 4","Address 4",,4/4/90 0:00:00,,,"Vacations"
  5,"Worker","Name 2","Address 2",,4/4/90 0:00:00,,,"Coupons"
  0,"President","Your Name","Your Address",,4/4/90 0:00:00,,,"Coupons"
```

Figure 7.3 An example of comma-delimited text in Word.

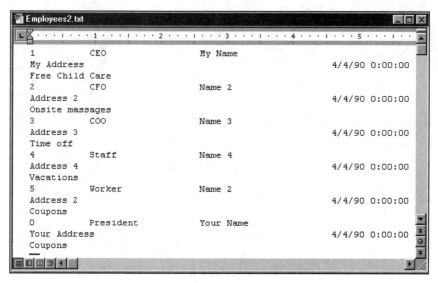

Figure 7.4   An example of fixed-width text in Word.

data must be enclosed in quotation marks. Each field is marked at the beginning and end by a comma, and, if there is no data for a particular field on a given record, there are two commas in a row (indicating a null value should be placed in that field).

Fixed-width text files contain field data that begins at the exact same location on each line. Access 97 ignores the character content (commas, spaces, and so on) and simply reads whatever it finds (starting at each location) into the new table. If you're planning to import a fixed-width file, you can view it using a mono-spaced font in Microsoft Word, with the Show/Hide Paragraph feature turned on (so you can see the carriage returns and other normally invisible characters). The file spacing becomes very apparent, and you can easily massage the data into the right format in Word.

In either case, you should create a first row that has field names instead of actual data (but it should be formatted as delimited or fixed-width, just like the other rows of data). Access 97 uses this first row of data to name the fields, just like it would if you were importing a spreadsheet.

HOLD That Skill!

If you have Word (or some other word-processing program) on your machine, create two simple text files—one delimited with commas and the other fixed-width. Enter four or five lines of data in them and make the rows contain textual, numerical, and date/time data. Create a first line that contains field names instead of data, and practice the process of importing this data as a new table in Access 97. If you want to finish exam exercises quickly, it's essential that you become familiar with the screens and how to manipulate textual data.

Task 4   Importing from a text file.

1. Open the test database. Choose File|Get External Data|Import from the menu bar. The Import dialog box opens.

2. Click on the Files Of Type down-arrow to examine the file types available.

3. Next, select Text Files and then find the folder and file you want to import. When you click on the Import button, the Import Text Wizard opens.

4. On the first screen of the wizard, a sample of the first few lines of text appears. The wizard's determination about the nature of the text file is indicated at the top of the screen (either Delimited or Fixed Width).

5. If the wizard has made the wrong choice, try exiting and massaging the data further. Then, resume the process.

6. When the wizard makes the correct guess, click on the Next button. Depending upon which text format you are using, Access 97 displays one of two windows next.

7. For delimited text, the wizard allows you to change both the separator character (this changes what Access 97 looks for, not the text file itself) and the text qualifier (for instance, the use of single or double quotation marks to identify the boundaries of a field). You can also choose whether the first line contains field names.

8. For fixed-width text, the screen displays the text with controls that let you change the location of the beginning of fields.

9. After making the necessary changes, click on Next.

10. The next screen gives you the option of creating a new table or appending the data to an existing table.

11. If you are creating a new table, the next screen is identical to the one you encountered during the spreadsheet-import process (it asks you to designate a primary key and choose which fields to import).

Note: *If you are appending data to an existing table, the columns must match exactly.*

12. When you've finished making your decisions, click on Next.

13. The final screen prompts you for the name of the new table (or the target table if you are appending data).

14. To end the process, click on Finish. If Access 97 encounters errors that cause the process to fail, the wizard remains open, allowing you to go back and change the settings if you choose.

Finding And Fixing Errors

Importing data files carries certain risks, and Access 97 is designed to mitigate the problems that can occur. If the first few rows of data for a given field appear to be numbers (the numerical portion of a street address, for example), Access 97 assigns a numerical data type. When other records are read and data that is obviously not the same data type appears, Access 97 stores these records in a special Import Errors table. At the end of the import process, Access 97 notifies you of the name and location of this special file.

If data is missing from the primary key field, you can open the resulting table and either supply the data or delete the record, then make the field a primary key in Design view. If the wrong data type has been chosen, you can change the data type in Design view. The special Import Errors table contains information that will help you locate the cause and location of erroneous data.

Linking External Data Sources

In some cases, you may want to use data in another application or file without importing to Access 97. *Linking* is the term that describes this process, and it differs from importing in that the source of the data is altered. For instance, if you link to a Paradox table, you can make changes to the data contained in that table from Access 97.

You can link to and work with data in Access 97 databases as though it were part of your current Access 97 database. This means that linking is a good method to use when you are sharing a particular database application. You can also link data from spreadsheets and text files—and from FoxPro, dBase, Paradox, and SQL databases—with a few limitations (text files can only be read, not changed; spreadsheet rows cannot be deleted). The primary drawbacks to these arrangements are that performance will suffer somewhat and there will be security implications.

Linking to other Access 97 tables is accomplished using a method very similar to what we've used for importing Access 97 tables:

1. Open the database in which you want to work from locally.

2. Choose File|Get External Data|Link Tables.

3. Select the location and file you want to link to.

4. Select the table you wish to link to.

5. Click on OK.

A new table with the same name as the table you chose, appears in your current database. It is marked with the Linked Table icon to distinguish it from local tables.

Fortunately, we live in an age when significant amounts of data are already in electronic format somewhere. Using Access 97 frequently means pulling that data in (importing) or shoving that data out (exporting). Access 97 can import and export directly from other versions of Access, Excel, dBase, and text documents. Often, other databases with proprietary formats can export to a format that Access 97 can import from, and vice versa. A key skill of competent database administrators is exporting and importing data.

Reports are the method by which the data, from a table or generated via a query, reaches the rest of the world. Reports can be used in applications to display data on screen, but their primary purpose is to format your data in a pleasing way, printed as hard copies. We'll cover this topic in Chapter 8.

Practice Exercises

Exercise 1

> You're ready to begin populating your database with plenty of real data, but the data is in lists, spreadsheets, legacy (previously developed in other formats) databases, and text files. You need to use the import and export functions in Access 97 to do the job.
>
> Import the data from the Employees.xls spreadsheet into your test database.
>
> Use the first row as field names.
>
> Make the first field a primary key.
>
> Save the table as ImportSpread.
>
> Import the data from a comma-delimited list (Employees.txt) into your test database.
>
> Use the first row as field names.
>
> Make the first field a primary key.
>
> Save the table as ImportList.

Answer To Exercise 1

Choose File|Get External Data|Import from the menu bar. Choose the file type, and find the file on your disk.

To use the first row as field names, click on First Row Contains Column Headings when it comes up on the second screen.

Choose Let Access Add Primary Key on the fifth screen.

To save the table with the name ImportSpread, enter that name in the appropriate screen, and click on Finish.

To import data from Employees.txt, choose File|Get External Data|Import from the menu bar. Choose the file type, and find the file on your computer.

Click on First Row Contains Column Headings when it comes up on the second screen.

Choose Let Access Add Primary Key on the fifth screen.

To save the table with the name ImportList, enter that name in the appropriate screen, and click on Finish.

Exercise 2

> You want to link a table rather than import it, because then you can make changes to the data in the table from Access 97.
>
> Link a table to an Excel spreadsheet.

Answer To Exercise 2

Choose File|Get External Data|Link Tables from the menu bar. Choose the spreadsheet file you wish to link to, and click on OK.

Exercise 3

> You need to export data from your Employees report to a text file for display as a preformatted list within an HTML file (rather than export it as HTML).
>
> Export the contents of the Employees report to a text file.

Answer To Exercise 3

From the Database window with the Reports tab selected, click on the Employees report to select it. Choose File|Save As/Export from the menu bar. A small Save As dialog box appears. The To An External File Or Database choice should be selected by default (click on the radio button to select it, if not). Click on OK. The Save Report dialog box opens. Choose a convenient directory to save the text file in.

Choose to Save As Type: Text Files (*.txt;*.csv;*.tab;*.asc) and then click on Export. The text file will be saved in the directory you chose.

Need To Know More?

Berson, Alex and Stephen J. Smith. *Data Warehousing, Data Mining, and OLAP*, McGraw-Hill, 1997. ISBN 0-07-006272-2. Chapter 17 contains an explanation of how to import data for data warehouses.

Viescas, John L. *Running Microsoft Access 97*, Microsoft Press, Redmond, WA, 1997. ISBN 1-57231-323-4. Chapter 10 provides comprehensive information about importing, exporting, and linking data.

www.e4free.com
The Import/Export design page has detailed information about importing and exporting data to and from Microsoft Access 97 as well as data about the formats supported.

Simple Reports

Terms you'll need to understand:

- √ Header
- √ Footer
- √ Detail
- √ Aligning and sizing
- √ Expression Builder
- √ Groups
- √ Calculated control
- √ Sorting and grouping
- √ Aggregate functions

Skills you'll need to master:

- √ Designing reports in Design view
- √ Building expressions in calculated controls
- √ Modifying report layouts
- √ Using a query as a source for a report
- √ Aligning and resizing controls
- √ Saving a form as report
- √ Manipulating data in reports
- √ Previewing and printing a report

Understanding The Parts Of A Report

Viewing data on screen with forms and queries is great, as long as the screen is convenient. In the real world, however, there are still many occasions when nothing but a printed report will do, and it's not uncommon to create reports specifically for on-screen use as well.

The secret to writing well-designed and informative reports quickly with Access 97 is to understand the basics of report sections: what goes where and why, and how the sections affect the data this is ultimately displayed. If you know what data the report must display, you can quickly identify the supporting tables and queries; if you know how placement in a particular section affects the data display, it's easy to format your report correctly.

Few reports are only one page or only lists of records. If they were, simply printing the table in Datasheet view would suffice. Most reports summarize data by groups and include header information that may be on the front page, on top of each page, or at the beginning of each group.

Reports are therefore broken into sections called *headers* and *footers*. Sections affect both your ability to summarize data and the action of page breaks. They are:

➤ **Report headers/footers** Controls (text boxes, labels, and so forth) that appear once at the beginning/end of the report

➤ **Page headers/footers** Controls that appear at the top/bottom of each page

➤ **Group headers/footers** Controls that appear when a group starts/ends

Report headers should include things that you want to see only once: at the front of your report or perhaps only on the front page. They can contain the title of your report, the date it was created, who wrote it, and what department that person works in.

Report footers appear once: at the end of the report. They can contain your conclusions, summary data for the report as a whole, or perhaps simply the words *End of Report*.

Page headers appear at the top of every page. If, for example, you have columns of data, you can label each column in the page header. Page footers are useful for page numbers and the date.

Group headers appear once each time a new group of records begins, no matter where that might be. Group headers should contain a control that specifies the current group's value. For instance, in a report that groups employees by department, each department's records begin with the department name.

The Detail section (in the middle of the report) contains data and controls that represent individual records within a group.

Group footers typically contain summary calculations. Another useful function for group footers is the page break control, which causes the report to start the next group at the top of the following page.

Creating A Report

Creating a report is similar to creating other objects in Microsoft Access 97. Simply click on New in the Database window when the Reports tab is selected. Access 97 offers several methods for creating reports as well as different kinds of reports. This chapter covers using the Report Wizard as well as Design view. We'll create similar reports using both methods.

Task 1   Creating a new report using the Report Wizard.

1. In the Database window, select Reports, and click on New.

2. The New Report dialog box, shown in Figure 8.1, opens. Select Report Wizard and then click on OK.

3. On the first wizard screen, select the table or query that you want to build your report from (in this case, Employees), then add the fields you want to use. Click on Next.

4. On the next screen, select the fields you want to use as groups. Click on Next.

 Field groups follow much the same pattern as sorted fields. The first group becomes the major category, and subsequent groups become subcategories, sub-subcategories, and so on.

5. On the next screen, choose the sort order for your Detail section records by selecting the field name and then clicking on the Sort Order button next to it. Click on Next.

6. On the next screen, choose the Layout you'd like from the options shown (try each one to get a preview on screen). Choose Portrait or Landscape orientation and then click on Next.

7. On the next screen, choose the style you want (again you can preview these on screen). Click on Next.

8. The last wizard screen lets you enter a name for your report and either preview it or go directly to Design view for modifying the report. Enter "Employees1", and click on Finish. Close the report.

 If you'd like to calculate a summary value on all the records in the group, click on Summary Options, and choose a function (Sum, Avg, Min, Max). The summary value appears in the header or footer of that group. Also, you can elect to show just the summary for that group and whether to calculate a percentage of the total (all groups).

 If you're creating a report with several tables, choose the additional fields on the first screen of the Wizard by clicking the drop down selection box under the Tables/Queries heading and then choosing the table form to which you'd like to add fields.

Task 2   Creating a new report in Design view.

1. In the Database window, select Reports, and click on New. The Report Dialog box opens.

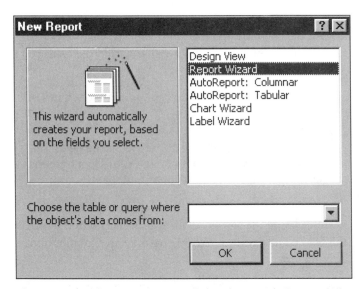

Figure 8.1   The New Report dialog box with Report Wizard selected.

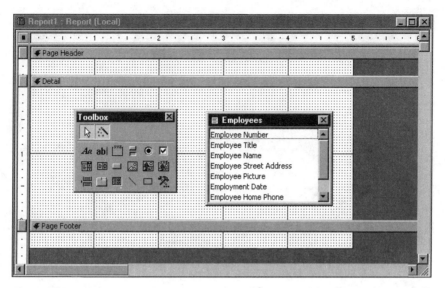

Figure 8.2   Report Design view with Field List and Toolbox showing.

2. Select Design view and then click on OK. You should see something similar to Figure 8.2.

3. In Design view, right-click on the gray area outside the report itself (but still within the Design View window). Choose Properties from the shortcut menu. The properties sheet opens.

4. Click on the down-arrow next to the Record Source text box, and select Employees1. By making this selection, you are binding the Employees table to your report.

5. Click on the Field List button. When the field list appears, click on and drag all the fields onto the report in the Detail section.

6. Your report should have a page header and footer. Click on View|Page Header (or View|Page Footer) to make it go away. Click on Report Header (or Report Footer) to display the report header and footer sections.

7. Click on View|Sorting And Grouping. When the Sorting And Grouping dialog box opens (as shown in Figure 8.3), select Employee Name for the first group, and select Yes for Header.

8. Close the dialog box, save the report as "Employees2", and close it.

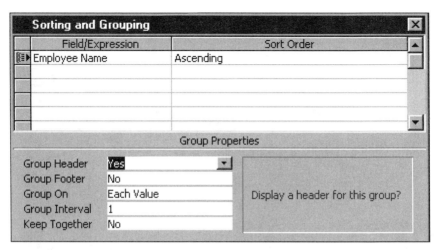

Figure 8.3 The Sorting And Grouping dialog box.

Modifying A Report

In Access 97 reports, you can add and remove sections; change, add, or delete groups on particular fields (as well as the group's properties); and size, format, align, and add or delete controls. In short, you can modify a report to your heart's content. Modifying a report is much like modifying a form. The controls react in a very similar manner, and the cursors and handles used are exactly the same.

Task 3   Modifying a report in Design view.

1. In the Database window, select Reports, choose Employees2, and click on the Design button. The Employees2 report opens in Design view.

2. First, change the size of the report by placing the cursor over the edge of the report until it turns into a cross. Then, click on and drag the report to the width you desire. You can use the same method to increase or decrease the height.

3. Next, select a field by clicking on it. Move the cursor over the field until the cursor turns into a hand. Then, click on and drag the field to a new location.

Task 4   Aligning and sizing controls.

1. Next, select several fields, and change their width and height by clicking on and dragging the handles (these modifications operate in a very

similar manner to aligning and sizing controls on forms). Notice that all
the selected controls react the same way when you resize one of them.

2. Choose Format|Size|To Narrowest to resize all the selected controls to
the same size as the narrowest control.

3. Now, move each field by hand to place them in a vertical row. To align
all of them with the leftmost control, select them all and then choose
Format|Align|Left.

4. Practice resizing, aligning, and setting horizontal and vertical spacing
until you feel comfortable with these functions. When you're finished,
close the report.

Arranging controls on a report in a pleasing and readable way
implies regular spacing, sizing, and alignment of similar objects.
Even slightly misaligned controls give an unprofessional, ragged
look. Access 97 has Grid and Snap features that allow you to simultaneously select, space, and size multiple controls—as well as
automatically align them.

Building Expressions In Reports

When building your reports, you can add controls bound to fields in the underlying table, or you can add controls that use expressions to display a value.
Expressions are a means of using existing values, built-in functions, and operators to create new values. You can complete an expression or perform a
calculation using operators, numbers, existing values from fields in records,
text, dates, or just about any combination you desire. Access 97 contains a tool
called the Expression Builder that assists you in composing your expressions.
It can be activated with the Build button on the properties sheet or the Report
Design toolbar. Once built, expressions are entered in the Control Source property of the designated control.

Task 5   *Adding an expression to a report control.*

1. Open the Employees1 report. Your report should have an Employee
Name header section on it. Click on the unbound Text Box button.
Next, using the cursor, draw a rectangle in the Employee Name section
header area. An unbound text box with a Label control to its left
appears.

2. Click on the Label control and then press the Delete key. The Label
control disappears.

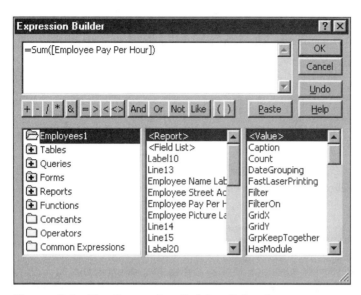

Figure 8.4   The Expression Builder dialog box.

3. Next, right-click on the remaining control. Select Properties from the shortcut menu. The properties sheet opens.

4. Click on the Control Source box and then click on the Build button. The Expression Builder opens (see Figure 8.4).

 To access the Expression Builder, click on the Control Source property (on the property sheet for the control). Be sure that you are familiar with the Expression Builder before you take the exam.

5. Click on the equal sign (=) and then double-click on Function|Built-In Functions. Scroll down on the bottom right-hand window of the Expression Builder to find the Sum function. Double-click on Sum. The top window should read (without the quotation marks) "=Sum(<<expr>>)". Click on "<<expr>>" to select it.

6. Click on Employees1 in the bottom-left window. All the controls on Employees1 appear in the bottom middle window; their attributes appear in the bottom-right window.

7. Double-click on Employee Pay Per Hour. "Employee Pay Per Hour" now appears in your expression where "<<expr>>" was.

8. Click on OK. The Expression Builder closes, leaving the expression you just created in the Control Source text box in the properties sheet.

9. Click on the Save button and then exit the report.

HOLD That Skill!

Navigating the Expression Builder is a key skill. If you practice using it frequently, you can polish your expression-building skills, enabling you to easily remember what's available and where to find it, and speeding up your construction of common Access 97 objects.

The top window is where your expressions appear. They should begin with an equal sign. The equal sign makes the value of the control equal to the result of the expression (assuming the expression is in the Control Source property of that control).

The middle row contains operators: plus, minus, times, divided by, and so on.

The bottom three windows, from left to right, are objects within your Access 97 database (some of them are automatically built into every database), items within those objects, and values those items can take.

Often, you can easily create the report you want based on data from a query. To do so, use the New Database Object function from the Formatting (Form/Report) toolbar.

Task 6   Creating a report from a query.

1. Open the Employees1 query.

2. With the data displayed, click on the New Database Object down-arrow, and select AutoReport.

3. Save the report as Employees3.

Creating A Calculated Field

In a report, *calculated fields* provide data that is not available within the underlying fields upon which the report is based. For instance, a table with fields for your cost and your sales price doesn't have a Gross Profit field. However, a report can calculate gross profit (based on the two fields) and display it when the report is viewed or printed. To create a calculated field, put an unbound control on your report and modify its Source property. This process is very similar to using calculated fields in forms or queries.

The important difference between spreadsheets and databases is that a report in a database program cannot calculate upon summaries of other calculations. If, for example, you calculate gross profit and net profit, and then summarize these two values at the bottom of a group, you cannot then make an additional calculation on the summarized calculations.

Task 7   Creating calculated controls in a report.

1. Open the Employees1 report in Design view. Click on the unbound Text Box button and then draw a rectangle in the Details section next to the other fields already there.

2. Delete the Label control.

3. Next, right-click on the remaining control. Select Properties from the shortcut menu. The properties sheet opens.

4. Using the Expression Builder in the Control Source text box, enter the expression "= [Employee Pay Per Hour] *0.15]".

5. In the Page Header and Detail sections, delete the label and control for Employee Number.

6. Move the other controls to the left and then create a new label for Social Security Tax.

7. Click twice on the label control to edit it and then enter "SST" as its caption.

HOLD That Skill!

A crucial point to remember when using calculated controls is that you can't calculate on a calculation in a report. This means that if you add two Detail fields together in a calculated control called DetCalCont—that is, "=[FieldA]+[FieldB]"—you can't create in the group section another calculated control that sums the Detail calculated control—that is, "=Sum([DetCalCont])".

Here's a way to achieve your objective: Take the sum of the first Detail control and add it to the sum of the second Detail control—that is, "=Sum([FieldA])+Sum([FieldB])". The arithmetic results in the same answer, and you avoid calculating on a calculation.

Saving A Form As A Report

You often use similar methods when you develop both forms and reports; simply saving a form as a report cuts your report-development time significantly. Access 97 lets you save a form as a report with minimal effort: Just open the form and choose New Database Object|AutoReport from the Formatting (Form/Report) toolbar.

Task 8   Saving a form as a report.

1. Open the Employees form.

2. Click on the New Database Object down-arrow and then select AutoReport.

3. Save the form as a report named Employees4.

Previewing And Printing A Report

Print preview and print functions are standard Windows functions, the same as in any other Windows application. Choose File|Print Preview or File|Print to use them.

Task 9   Previewing and printing a report.

1. To preview the Employees1 report you created with the Report Wizard, choose Preview (in the Database window, on the Reports tab with Employees1 selected).

2. If you like what you see, click on the Print button.

3. The report immediately begins printing, without offering you the chance to change print settings.

4. If you'd like to change print settings, click on File|Print. An ordinary Print dialog box opens.

In Access 97, you can create and modify reports—as well as place controls on reports—using many of the same techniques as you did for forms. The biggest difference between using forms and reports is that you can add sections to reports. Sections affect the output of the final report dramatically.

Advanced database applications frequently involve special table enhancements designed to minimize error and maximize data entry efficiency. Lookup tables, text validation, and required fields can simplify data entry and help ensure accurate data, both of which establish your database application's credibility. We will cover these topics in Chapter 9.

Practice Exercises

Exercise 1

> You want to print out a list of employees via an Access 97 report.
> You want to create a simple report using the wizard, because it
> offers great speed and convenience.
>
> Create a report using the Report Wizard.
>
> Name it rptEmployees.
>
> Save the report but leave it open.

Answer To Exercise 1

To create a report using the Report Wizard, make sure the Reports tab is selected and then click on New. Choose Report Wizard on the next screen, choose the table or query on which to base the report, and begin going through the wizard screens.

Enter "rptEmployees" in the last screen.

Click on the Finish button to save the report.

Exercise 2

> You want to add a calculated control to your report, then preview and print it.
>
> Open the report in Design view.
>
> Add a calculated control that shows the Social Security tax per hourly rate.
>
> Save and close the report.
>
> Preview the report.
>
> Print the report.
>
> Close the report.

Answer To Exercise 2

Click on the report in the Database window and then click on the Design button.

To add a calculated control to the report for Social Security tax, click on the Text Box button on the Toolbox, draw a text box on the report, and then remove the label. Right-click on the text box to bring up the shortcut menu, then choose Properties to bring up the properties sheet. Click on the Control Source area and then click on the Build Button to start the Expression Builder. Enter "=[Employee Pay Per Hour}*0.15".

Click on the Save button on the Formatting (Form/Report) toolbar, then exit the report.

Click on the Preview button in the Database window (make sure the report is selected first).

To print the report, click on the Preview button in the Database window.

Close the report by clicking on the exit button.

Exercise 3

> You want to remove the page header/footer portion of your report.
>
> Open the report in Design view.
>
> Remove the page header/footer portion.
>
> Save and close the report.

Answer To Exercise 3

Click on the report in the Database window and then click on the Design button.

Choose View|Page Header/Footer to remove the page header/footer.

Click on the Save button on the Formatting (Form/Report) toolbar and then exit the report by clicking on the Exit button.

Need To Know More?

 Litwin, Paul, Ken Getz, and Mike Gilbert. *Access 97 Developer's Handbook*, Sybex Inc., San Francisco, CA, 1997. ISBN 0-7821-1941-7. Chapter 9 covers various report-design topics for Access 97.

 Viescas, John L. *Running Microsoft Access 97*, Microsoft Press, Redmond, WA, 1997. ISBN 1-57231-323-4. Chapters 16 and 17 provide information about report-design basics.

Advanced Table Manipulation

9

Terms you'll need to understand:

√ Validation rule

√ Validation message

√ Combo box

√ Lookup table

√ Input mask

√ Zero-length string

√ Null value

√ Mandatory field

√ OLE object

Skills you'll need to master:

√ Setting validation for tables and fields

√ Making fields required and setting formats

√ Setting default values

√ Adding Combo boxes

√ Creating lookup tables

√ Adding pictures to tables

Setting up personal databases can be very easy—they may require only the crudest kind of table, form, query, and report features to get the job done. But if you need to create an application that the employees of your company or your clients use, you'll have to take a different tack. You can't expect them to understand the structures you take for granted, nor do you want them in the application messing around with its underlying components.

You need to shield users from the inner workings, just like your car's engine compartment shields you from the noisy, dirty, mechanical functions of the engine. To prevent users from entering inaccurate data, you should present simple lists of allowable values. To make each screen easy to identify, you should create distinctive colors (or even pictures).

Changing Table Properties

The properties of a table are essentially defined by the properties of its fields. Of course, you can rearrange the field order or change the way data is displayed in the datasheet, but setting field properties has the most impact.

There are, however, some properties that you can change for the table as a whole (we've already covered filtering and ordering in Chapter 3). They are:

➤ **Validation rule** Uses expressions to validate one or more fields

➤ **Validation text** Alerts the user when a validation rule is violated

➤ **Filter** Filters the data displayed

➤ **Order by** Sorts the data displayed

Task 1   *Setting a table validation rule.*

1. Click on the Tables tab in the Database window and then click on Employees|Design (see Figure 9.1).

2. Click on View|Properties. The Table Properties box opens.

3. In the Validation Rule text box, enter "[Employee Pay Per Hour]<100".

4. Close both the text box and the table.

Table validation rules let you use expressions that reference more than one field, as opposed to field validation rules, which can validate based on one field only (itself). For instance, suppose you want to make sure your selling price always exceeds your cost by at least 15 percent, no matter what discounts a salesperson tries to offer. You can set a table validation rule that compares the two fields and won't accept any selling price that is less than 15 percent higher than your cost.

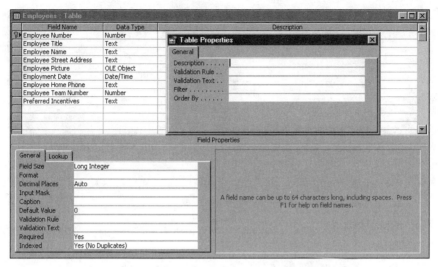

Figure 9.1   The Employees table in Design view with the Table
Properties dialog box open.

Changing Field Properties

Access 97 includes some very powerful tools for controlling just what the user can enter in a particular field. For instance, you can control the length of a text field, make a value list or lookup table for entries, and create an input mask that requires certain characters in certain places. Field entries can also be mandatory.

Table Design view displays all field properties so that you can modify them easily. Field properties, shown in Figure 9.2, include:

➤ **Field Size** Specifies the number of text characters allowed or the number type

➤ **Format** Controls the display of the data type entered: Number, Date/ Time, Text, Yes/No

➤ **Decimal Places** Specifies the number of decimal places to display for Number data types

➤ **Input Mask** Allows you to set a mask for data entry

➤ **Caption** Displays the field name of your choice

➤ **Default Value** Specifies a value that is automatically inserted when you create a new record

➤ **Validation Rule** Verifies that you are entering correct data into the field

➤ **Validation Text** Specifies an error message when you enter invalid data

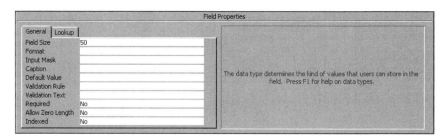

Figure 9.2 Field properties in Table Design view.

➤ **Required** Requires you to enter something in this field before you can exit a new record

➤ **Allow Zero Length** Enters a zero-length string instead of Null when blank

➤ **Indexed** Creates an index on this field

 Access 97 sets the properties of new controls in forms and reports according to the settings you choose in Table Design view (although you can change them later). Also, the predefined formats are standardized according to the country settings that are currently active in Windows itself (you can set these using the Control Panel's Regional Settings).

Task 2 Setting a field's data type.

1. Click on the Tables tab in the Database window. Click on Employees|Design.

2. Click on the Employment Date field. Tab to the Data Type text box and then click on the down-arrow. Choose Date/Time from the drop-down list. Notice that, on the General tab of Field Properties, the list of field properties available shrinks somewhat. Field properties always conform to the data type you've chosen.

3. Click on the Format property text area, click on the down-arrow that appears and then select Short Date.

 You can change a field's data type as you desire, but some changes may not work well. For instance, if you change a field from a Text data type to a Number data type, Access 97 may display a warning that "Some data may be lost." Keep in mind that each data type is handled differently within Access 97: Numbers can be added and subtracted, Memo fields cannot be sorted, and so on.

Like tables, fields can be set to validate data entered. You can ensure that only data of the proper type is entered (as we just did, by specifying Date/Time for the Employment Date field). In addition, you can check the data to make sure it matches a value or falls within a range of values as well as specify the format that data must follow.

Task 3   *Setting field-level validation rules and messages.*

1. Click on the Employee Pay Per Hour field and then click on the Validation Rule property on the General tab. Click on the Build button that appears (to the right of the Validation Rule text box). The Expression Builder opens.

2. Enter ">0" and then click on OK. The Expression Builder closes. In the Validation Rule text box, you see the expression you've entered. Any entry that you make into this field from any datasheet, form, or query recordset must now be greater than zero, or Access 97 will not accept the data and will display a warning message.

3. Click on the Validation Text text box and then enter "Must be greater than zero". If in the future you type "0" in the Employee Pay Per Hour field, Access 97 will display what you typed into the text box as a warning message.

 Interestingly, you can have a default value of zero appear in this field when a new record opens—without interfering with the validation rule you've just inserted. However, if you don't change this value, Access 97 does not let you move off the record.

Another way to help keep data pure is to set default values. Default values automatically appear in a new record when you set them at the field level. They are quite useful for making sure that the field at least contains something of the correct type (rather than a Null value). If you find that most of your records tend to have the same value for a field, you can speed up data entry by setting that value as the field's default value.

Task 4   *Setting default values.*

1. Click on the Employee Pay Per Hour field.

2. Click on the Default Value property on the General tab.

3. Enter "0". Whenever a new record is started, this field always has a zero in it, instead of being blank.

HOLD That Skill!

Notice that you could have started the Expression Builder in the Default Value text box. The Expression Builder comes in handy when the default value you want isn't static. For example, suppose you have a Delivery Date field that should always be 10 days into the future from whatever date an order is recorded in your database. You could use the Expression Builder to specify today's date—using the Now() function—plus 10. Then, whenever a new order record starts, that field would automatically calculate a date 10 days into the future and put it into the Delivery Date field.

Required fields are sometimes called *mandatory fields*. Either way, the meaning is clear: Access 97 does not allow you to move off the record until you enter something. Be careful when you set required fields; they are useful for ensuring that all necessary data is present before a transaction is completed, but it's common for data to be incomplete in real life. Too many required fields can make life miserable for users who are trying to get their jobs done.

 Before taking the test, be sure you are familiar with required fields and the procedure to set them. Also, ensure that you know about setting validation rules and validation text.

Task 5   Setting required fields.

1. Click on the Employee Name field.

2. Click on the Required Field property, and set it to Yes. Access 97 now prevents users from moving off the record until they enter a name (or some text value).

HOLD That Skill!

The Required Field property is designed to work effectively with other data validation field properties. For instance, setting the Employee Name field as Required ensures that you have to enter something; however, it does not prevent a user from entering an address instead of a name.

If you are adding the Required attribute to a field in records that already contain data (and some of them contain blanks for that field), Access 97 notifies you that your existing data doesn't conform to the rule (Required) you have just set. You'll have to enter appropriate data in that field for each record before you can return to Design view and make that field Required.

Inside the memory of your computer, Access 97 stores data as the basic values you enter; the number 25 is stored as an integer with a value of 25. By the way, you can manipulate the number that is displayed on screen. If you want to display 25 as "$25.00", you can set the Format property to Currency. If you want to display 25 as "25%", you can set the Format property to Percent. The underlying value doesn't change at all nor the way it's entered; just the display is altered.

Task 6   Setting the Format property.

1. Click on the Employee Pay Per Hour field.

2. Click on the Format property.

3. Set the Format to Currency.

4. Click on the Decimal Places property (notice that Decimal Places is a property of Number fields but not Text fields). Set the Decimal Places property to zero.

HOLD That Skill!

You can create custom formats (called *format images*) for Text and Memo fields. To do so, use *placeholders*—special characters that define the display of data at the character level. The Digit placeholders (0) or (#), the Percentage placeholder (%), the Force Uppercase placeholder (>) and the Decimal placeholder (.) are examples. You can find a complete list of all placeholder characters and examples of their correct usage in Access 97 Help.

For instance, if you want all characters in a particular field to be displayed uppercase, enter the greater-than sign (>) in the Format Property text box. Whenever the data is displayed, all characters will be uppercase, regardless of how you entered the data. Again, keep in mind that only the display is affected, not the underlying data.

You can think of an *input mask* as a character-level validation rule. It specifies what each character of the field may be. Think of it like the silverware holder in your kitchen drawer. Forks go in one slot, knives in another, big spoons over here, and little spoons over there.

Instead of a shaped plastic container, Access 97 uses special characters in the Input Mask property to define correct entries. Unlike the Format property, which affects only the display of data, input masks control what data you can enter.

Task 7   Setting input masks.

1. Click on the Employee Home Phone field. The default data type is Text. Change the number of characters allowed to 20.

2. Click on the Input Mask property and then click on the Build button. You are prompted to save the table. Next, the Input Mask Wizard, shown in Figure 9.3, starts.

3. Select Phone Number. If you'd like to change the stored input mask, click on Edit List, and make your changes. If not, click on Next. On the next screen, you can change the applied input mask.

4. Click on Next. The final screen allows you to choose whether the formatting characters (such as the dash between parts of a phone number) are stored with the value. When you click on Finish, the input mask is applied to the field.

 For the Input Mask Wizard to appear, you must have installed Advanced Wizards during setup. If you didn't load Advanced Wizards, rerun the Office 97 or Access 97 setup. Also, note that input masks only work with Text and Date/Time data types, even though the Input Mask property appears available for the Number and other data types.

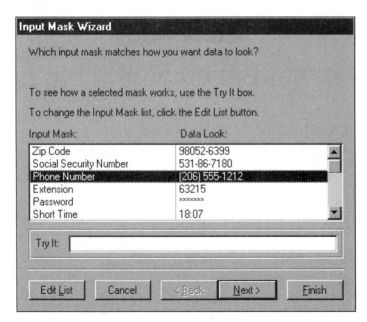

Figure 9.3   The Input Mask Wizard.

Creating Combo Boxes And Lookup Tables

Combo boxes are like the familiar drop-down lists or selection boxes. They consist of a text box with a value in it, a drop-down arrow, and more values that appear when you click on the arrow. They can support a single-column value list or multiple columns of values from a table or query (a lookup table). Lookup lists—whether the values they contain come from a list or a query/table—are convenient, because they speed up the data-entry process and improve accuracy. When you are using multiple columns, you can connect (bind) only one value to your table.

Combo boxes that use a value list are convenient for data entry, because the values are preset. You can allow the user to enter any value or choose a listed value; you can limit the user to values listed in the List Box only, if you like. If the list is fairly long, the user can find the value he or she wants by typing in the first few characters.

When you build a combo box in Table Design view, you specify either Value List or Table/Query as the source of the allowable values. It's common to use combo boxes supported by a value list when you know the choices will always be static (a lookup table may be appropriate if many choices are involved).

Task 8   *Addding a Value List combo box to a table.*

1. Click on Employee Pay Per Hour and then click on the Lookup tab (on the lower portion of the Design View window), shown in Figure 9.4. Display Control defaults to Text Box.

2. Click on the down-arrow next to the words *Text Box*; you are presented with three choices: Text Box, List Box, and Combo Box.

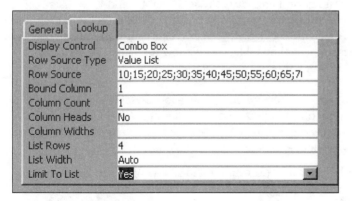

Figure 9.4   The field properties for a Value List combo box.

3. Select Combo Box. Nine additional options, starting with Row Source Type, appear below Combo Box.

4. Click on the Row Source Type text box to get the down-arrow, then open the drop-down list. Your choices are Table/Query, Value List, and Field List.

5. Select Value List. Enter values from 10 to 75 in the Row Source text box, separated by a semicolon (10;15;20;25;30; and so on). In this case, we've chosen Value List rather than Table/Query, so our Bound Column property is automatically set to "1". By the same token, we have only one column, so the Column Count property is also "1".

6. There is no table for Access 97 to get column headings from, so the Column Heads property defaults to No.

7. The Column Widths property allows you to specify column widths. Leave it blank.

8. The List Rows property specifies the maximum number of rows to display. Set it to "4".

9. The List Width property sets the width of the column of rows. Leave it set on Auto.

10. Set the Limit To List property to Yes. No off-list entries are allowed.

When entering Row Source values, you can right-click on the text box and get a shortcut menu. If you choose Zoom, you get a medium-sized window in which you can enter the values. The advantage is that it's easier to enter and view the values from this window than inside the tiny text box.

You use lookup tables generally where more than just a few values are involved. The important distinction here between lookup tables and value lists is that lookup tables make it easy for you to add additional values to the list without reentering Table Design view. In fact, you can create a form that allows users to update the values in the lookup table. If you know the values are dynamic (will be updated periodically), this is a good solution.

You need to know how to create a lookup table and set the number of columns it displays. Make sure you understand where the data comes from (another table that you have to understand how to find) and how to set the columns.

To demonstrate building a lookup table, build a table similar to Employees but with only two fields: Employee Name and Employee Address. Fill in three or four records with random data, name it MiniEmployees, save it, and you're ready to go.

Task 9   *Building a lookup table.*

1. Click on the Employee Name field and then click on the Lookup tab, shown in Figure 9.5. In the Display Control text box, select Combo Box.

2. In the Row Source Type text box, select Table/Query, and, in the Row Source text box, select MiniEmployees.

3. The Bound Column property should default to "1". (If you entered "2" into this property, the address field of MiniEmployees would be the value that you entered in MiniEmployees under Employee Name, and we wouldn't want that.)

4. For Column Count, we want "2" (so both fields of MiniEmployees will be displayed). For Column Heads, select Yes (so the field names of MiniEmployees will show). Leave Column Widths blank.

5. Set List Rows to "4" (so only four rows will display), leave List Width set on Auto (the width will match the current table's field width in the datasheet), and set Limit To List to Yes.

If you wanted to set the Column Widths for each field, you would enter a value in inches separated by a semicolon for each field (0.5;1;1.5; and so on). Keep in mind that your choice of width is affected by the column width you chose for the datasheet as well as by the List Width value.

Adding Graphics To Tables

Fields can contain graphics if the data type is designated as OLE Object (OLE stands for Object Linking and Embedding). You can either link to an object (an image, a Word document, a WAV sound file, a PowerPoint document, and so on), or embed a copy of the object in your Access 97 database.

General	Lookup
Display Control	Combo Box
Row Source Type	Table/Query
Row Source	MiniEmployees
Bound Column	1
Column Count	2
Column Heads	Yes
Column Widths	
List Rows	4
List Width	Auto
Limit To List	Yes

Figure 9.5   The field properties for a lookup table.

You can create new graphics or use existing images, and you have a variety of image formats to choose from. As the saying goes, "A picture is worth 1,000 words," and database records are no different.

Task 10   Inserting graphics.

1. Open Employees in Design view, and click on the Employee Picture field. For data type, select OLE Object. The only properties to set are Caption and Required (no Lookup properties are available).

2. Leave Caption blank, and set Required to No.

3. Save and close the table, and that's all there is to it.

To insert (embed) an image into a field for a particular record, you must have an OLE server (such as Microsoft's Paintbrush program) installed. Just right-click on the field in Datasheet view, select Insert Object, and then browse until you find the image file you wish to insert.

Business processes play an important role in database development. The way you collect and enter data into the database has to be effective, because the credibility of the resulting application depends on accurate data. No matter how good the design, users will declare "it doesn't work" if the data quality is poor.

Access 97's table design allows you to modify many field-level properties (such as default values, input masks, required fields, value limits, and text validation). It also lets you create lookup tables and combo boxes with value lists. If you use these capabilities liberally, you can help ensure accurate data.

Adding more tables and field properties to a database would seem, on the surface, to add more complexity to your database—and increase its size. However, that is exactly the case when you build a relational database. Although the database's true complexity increases somewhat, the benefits far outweigh the disadvantages. Truly relational databases dramatically reduce overall storage requirements, increase data accuracy, and allow you to perform functions that flat-file databases cannot offer. We will cover relational databases in Chapter 10.

Practice Exercises

Exercise 1

Data-entry clerks are now using your database frequently to enter new employee records and modify existing ones. You've received feedback that indicates incorrect data is beginning to pollute the database, and some of the clerks have asked if you could make the process more effective. You decide to set table and field validation rules as well as to add an employee picture field.

Make Employment Date a required field in the Employees table.

Set the validation text for Employment Date to read "Please enter the correct date of employment".

Save the table, but leave it open.

Answer To Exercise 1

Open the Employees table in Design view, select the Employment Date field, and then set the Required property to Yes.

Enter "Please enter the correct date of employment" into the Validation Text text box.

Click on the Save button on the Table Design toolbar to save the table.

Exercise 2

You want to make a value list for the Employee Title field in your Employees table, to make sure the title is entered correctly every time.

Make a value list for the Title field in the Employees table.

Set the values to Mr., Mrs., Ms, Dr., and President.

Save and close the table.

Answer To Exercise 2

To create a value list for the Title field, select the field and then click on the Lookup tab at the bottom of the screen. Click on the Display Control text area and then click on the down-arrow. Click on List Box|Row Source Type|Value List.

Enter the values Mr., Mrs., Ms, Dr., and President in the Row Source area, separated by semicolons.

To save and close the table, click on the Save button on the Table Design toolbar and then exit the table.

Exercise 3

You want to make the table a little more graphically appealing, so data entry clerks and managers have an easier time understanding the layout and entering data correctly.

Open the table.

Change the cells to have a sunken appearance and an Aqua background color.

Save and close the table.

Answer To Exercise 3

Open the table in the Datasheet view.

Right-click on the title bar to display the shortcut menu. Choose Cells from the menu. In the Cell Effects dialog box, choose Sunken as the Cell Effect. For Background Color, choose Aqua from the drop-down box.

Save the table by clicking on Save on the Table Datasheet toolbar, and close it by clicking on the Exit button.

Need To Know More?

 Elmasri, Ramez and Shamkant B. Navanthe. *Fundamentals of Database Systems.* Addison-Wesley Publishing Company, Menlo Park, CA, 1994. ISBN 0-8053-1748-7. Chapter 6 contains an explanation of tables constructed using the relational model.

 Viescas, John L. *Running Microsoft Access 97.* Microsoft Press, Redmond, WA, 1997. ISBN 1-57231-323-4. Chapter 5 provides a section of information about table and field validation.

 www.e4free.com

The Table design page has detailed information about making modifications to tables as well as setting up input masks, default values, and lookup tables.

Relational
Databases

Terms you'll need to understand:

√ Flat-file database

√ Primary key

√ Foreign key

√ One-to-many

√ Many-to-one

√ Many-to-many

√ Normalizing

√ Referential integrity

√ Cascading deletes

Skills you'll need to master:

√ Understanding relational databases

√ Identifying relationships

√ Analyzing data

√ Normalizing data and tables

√ Building simple relationships

√ Building complex relationships

√ Using the Relationships window

√ Understanding referential integrity

You've probably seen stacks of sales receipts at your local mom-and-pop store. If you think about these receipts—each one containing a complete record of the customer's name, address, phone number, items purchased, total price, tax, and so on—you'll have a good mental image of a flat-file database.

Flat-file databases used to be common. However, designers have abandoned them in favor of relational databases, because flat-file databases have severe limitations and inefficiencies. Simply put, a *flat-file* database keeps all its information in one huge table, repeating the data for every record. The mark of a relational database, on the other hand, is that each item of unique data is stored only once.

Understanding Relational Databases

The phrase *relational database* derives from the relationships between tables upon which such databases depend. A relational database breaks the database's information up into many tables, each related to the others by some unique value (the primary key).

When you initially create a relational database, you—of course—have to add data to create the multiple tables. However, you dramatically reduce the amount of total stored data as you use it. And because important data is stored only once, you significantly reduce the number of data-entry errors. These features make relational databases much easier to manipulate and maintain than flat-file databases.

Databases usually revolve around one major item of interest (customers, employees, work orders, and so on), and the item generally has its own table, with subtables of data that is related to the main topic. The phrase *parent-child relationship* is sometimes used to describe this situation. A *parent table* (Customers, for instance) contains one record for each customer, and a *child table* of orders for each customer (Orders) contains data about each order a customer has. The parent-child relationship is a *one-to-many* relationship. For every one customer, there may be many orders. Of course, the relationship of the Orders table to the Customers table is considered *many-to-one*.

Finally, think about the relationship of a Products table to an Orders table. One order may include many products, and there may be many orders for a single product. This type of relationship is called *many-to-many*.

Tying all these tables together are the Primary Key and Foreign Key fields. *Primary keys* are data that create a unique identity for each record, much like a Social Security Number (theoretically) uniquely identifies every American citizen. You can't use names, because many people share the exact same name. Primary keys don't have to be numbers, but they must be unique, different from all others in the table—forever.

Access 97 encourages you to create a Primary Key field for each table when you initially save it, but it's not always necessary. Make them whenever you think you might eventually create a relationship (link) between the table you are creating and the other tables in the database.

You must create a Foreign Key field when you want to link records in Table A to records in Table B via Table B's Primary Key field. In other words, a Foreign Key in one Table is another Table's Primary Key. These two common fields can be linked to establish the relationship between the two tables. Foreign Key fields can be indexed for performance (to speed up searching and sorting), and need to be of similar data type and size to the Primary Key in the other table.

Analyzing Your Data

The ideal relational database structure may not always be obvious, and if you are building as you go, it's easy to pile too much into a single table. You can use the Table Analyzer in Access 97 to help you find inefficiencies and even suggest ways to improve your table structure. Sometimes, splitting a table into several related tables is beneficial. For ease of use, the Table Analyzer creates a query that displays these related tables as one large table.

Task 1   Using the Table Analyzer.

1. Open your database, and make sure the Tables tab is selected. Click on the Analyzer button's down-arrow, as shown in Figure 10.1, and select Analyze Table. The Table Analyzer Wizard starts.

2. The first two screens are self-explanatory; they describe the negative effects that repeating data can cause and what the wizard will do to correct such a situation. The third screen asks you to choose the table to analyze.

3. Choose Employees, and click on Next. The next screen wants to know if you'd like the wizard to decide what fields go in what tables. Let the wizard decide, and click on Next.

4. For this table, the wizard recommends not splitting into separate tables (because you've done a good job of designing it). Click on Cancel.

If the table did have design flaws, the wizard would recommend splitting the table into several related tables, and it would propose the tables and fields to

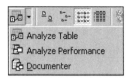

Figure 10.1 The Analyze button drop-down list.

create. You would have an opportunity to revise the wizard's suggestions according to your desires.

The Performance Analyzer differs from the Table Analyzer in that it makes suggestions for improving the search characteristics of your database as a whole. Frequently, these suggestions involve creating relationships between tables or changing data types.

Task 2 Using the Performance Analyzer.

1. Click on the Analyzer button's down-arrow, and select Analyze Performance.

2. The Performance Analyzer dialog box opens (see Figure 10.2). Click on the All tab and then click on the Select All button. All objects in your database are selected with a checkmark. Click on OK.

3. Notice in Figure 10.3 that each proposal the Performance Analyzer makes is marked by a symbol on the left: Recommendation, Suggestion, Idea, and Fixed (Fixed items have already been changed). If the Performance Analyzer has any Recommendations or Suggestions, you can have Access 97 make them by clicking on the Optimize button. You must manually put Ideas into action.

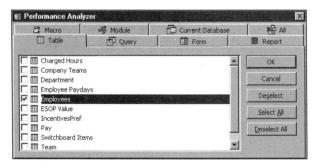

Figure 10.2 The Performance Analyzer dialog box.

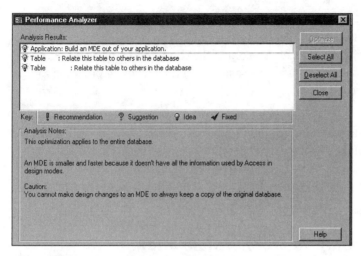

Figure 10.3   A completed analysis.

Sometimes, Access 97 suggests that you change data types, perhaps from Text to Long Integer. These suggestions can improve your database's performance by limiting the kinds of data you can enter (thereby reducing data-entry errors as well as speeding up searches). Creating relationships between tables also speeds up searches. Of course, Access 97 may have no suggestions at all, indicating a good table design.

Normalizing Data

The process of designing a relational database includes making sure fields contain only one item of data, eliminating redundant data, and making sure a table contains only data directly related to the primary key. These design considerations are called *data normalization*. Each step is called a *form*, and forms range from first normal form (1NF) through fifth normal form (5NF). There is also one higher level, called domain key normal form (DK/NF). Forms 4NF, 5NF, and DK/NF are of theoretical interest only; we will not discuss them here.

A very common error in table design is to put too much data into a single field, such as street address, city, and state. This is a problem, because it's very difficult to sort on State when the beginning character of the state is unknown (it could occur anywhere in the field, depending upon the length of the street address and city data).

Another common example of fields that often contain too much information is the Name field. You should have at least two fields for Name: First Name and Last Name—and possibly a Middle Initial field.

Another common deficiency is putting too many fields into a record. For instance, if you had a Customers table, you could easily add fields for transactions to the table. Then, you'd have a record of the customer ID information (name, address, phone number, and so on) along with transaction information for every transaction.

The drawback to this setup is that you'd have to reenter the customer ID information every time. Doing so could lead to data-entry errors as well as storage problems (a single customer could have thousands of transactions, so his or her name, address, and so on would be repeated thousands of times). The fix for this is to create a child table (Transactions) that is linked to the parent table (Customers).

Task 3   Analyzing for normalization.

1. Open the Employees table. Do any of the fields contain data that you could logically split into two or more fields? The answer is no. (If you had found some fields you could split, the appropriate action would be to create additional fields for each item of data.)

2. Next, ask yourself if any of the data is duplicated from record to record. The answer is yes. Although each record contains only one employee, the Employee Pay Per Hour data is duplicated for every employee who makes the same pay per hour.

Separating fields into individual items of data (each with their own field) and eliminating duplicate data (by creating separate linked tables) is called *conforming* to the first normal form (1NF).

Task 4   Normalizing to 1NF.

1. Create a table called Pay with four fields: Employee Number, Employee Pay Per Hour, Employee Deductions, and As Of Date.

2. Make Employee Number a primary key. Make Employee Pay Per Hour a number with a value-list lookup table that contains seven or eight different pay levels (such as $10, $15, $20, $25, $30, $35, and so on). Finally, assign Employee Deductions a data type of Number set to Integer; assign As Of Date a Date field.

3. In the Pay table, make up and enter employee numbers, pay per hour, deductions, and as of dates for all employees currently in your Employees table.

4. Open the Employees table. Delete the Employee Pay Per Hour field.

Second normal form (2NF) is really only a stepping stone to third normal form (3NF). Normalizing to 2NF means making sure each item of data has a *functional dependence* upon the primary key. You achieve full functional dependence when there is only one value for each field related to the primary key. 2NF eliminates redundant (non-functionally dependent) data by placing the data in a separate linked table.

For instance, the employees in the Employees table need to get paid, and each time a payday occurs, a record must be kept of the date and the pay amount. This means that each employee has many records. Employees, therefore, has a one-to-many relationship with the table that holds the pay records (Pay).

Task 5   Normalizing to 2NF.

1. Create a table named Employee Paydays with four fields: Payday Number (a primary key), Employee Number (the foreign key from Employees), Pay Amount (a Number in Currency format), and Pay Date (a Date field).

Before we create the link (relationship) between Employees and Employee Paydays, we need to normalize to 3NF. Normalizing to 3NF means eliminating *transitive* dependencies. Transitive dependencies occur when data depends upon data that itself depends upon the primary key in another table.

For instance, suppose each employee can be assigned to one or more company teams. In addition, suppose the teams work for various departments within the company, and you need to track hours charged for each employee (through the assigned team) to a department. In this case, charged hours would depend upon the team that the employee is assigned to, and through the team to the employee via the Employee Number primary key.

Normalizing to 3NF would mean creating a junction table called Team as well as separate Company Teams and Department tables. The Team table would connect Employees to the Company Teams and Department tables via relationships you create in the Relationships window (we will cover the Relationships window shortly).

Task 6   Normalizing to 3NF.

1. Open the Employees table. Click on the Employee Team Number field. Make the field a Number field set to Long Integer.

2. Create a table called Company Teams with two fields: Team Number and Team Name. Make Team Number a primary key set to the AutoNumber data type, and make Team Name a Text field.

3. Create a table called Team (the junction table) with two fields: Employee Number and Team Number. Select both fields simultaneously (click on the first field and then shift+click on the second), and click on the Primary Key button. Doing so creates a multiple-field, or *composite*, primary key made up of Employee Number and Team Number.

4. Create a table called Department with two fields: Department Number and Department Name. Make Department Number a primary key and Department Name a Text field. Make up and enter three or four departments (such as Accounting, Finance, Sales, Shipping, and so on).

5. Create a table called Charged Hours with four fields: Charged Hours Number, Employee Team Number, Department Number, and Hours Charged. Make Charged Hours Number and Employee Team Number a composite primary key, make Department Number a Number field set to Long Integer, and make Hours Charged a Number field.

When Primary Key fields are used in a related table, they are called *foreign keys*. If a primary key is made up of a combination of the primary keys from two or more other tables (as the Team table is), the primary key is called a *composite primary key*. Composite primary keys are typically used as junctions (connectors) in junction tables between other related tables to satisfy the requirements of 3NF.

Now you have normalized the database to 3NF by creating appropriate tables. Separating the data in this fashion means that you can build records for employees, their pay rates, their paydays, and the teams and departments they work for without duplicating data unnecessarily. The final step in the normalization process is to create the actual links.

Building Simple Relationships

Using the Relationship window, we will now establish the link(s) between the tables. With these links or connections established, Access 97 now allows us to build multiple-table queries, forms, and reports. You already have a table named Employees that contains a primary key: the Employee Number field. In order to establish a one-to-one relationship, you need at least one other table that contains data related to employees. The pay table fits this requirement. You can use the Relationships window to set a relationship between Employees and Pay. Start by clicking on the Relationships button, shown in Figure 10.4, on the Database toolbar.

Figure 10.4   The Relationships button on the Database toolbar.

You must be familiar with how to access and use the Relationships window to do well on the test. Be sure you know how to use the window and how to set and edit relationships within it.

Task 7   *Building a one-to-one relationship.*

1. Click on the Relationships button to open the Relationships window.

2. Select Employees, click on the Add button, and then do the same for Pay.

3. Click on Close to close the Table/Query selection box.

4. Create a one-to-one link between Employees and Pay by clicking on and dragging the Employee Number field from Employees to the same field in Pay (shown in Figure 10.5). Make sure to put a check in the Enforce Referential Integrity checkbox (we'll discuss why later). In the Relationships window, notice the join line that appears between the tables. You can tell the relationship is one-to-one because the number "1" is present at both ends of the link line.

Complex Relationships

Quite a bit more common than the one-to-one relationship is the one-to-many relationship. One-to-many relationships occur where a parent table (in this case, Employees) has the potential for many records in a child table (in this

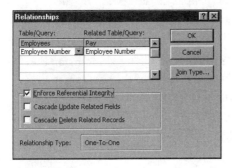

Figure 10.5   The Relationships dialog box.

case, Employee Paydays). Parent table records are not required to have more than one child table record (a person who quits after working only two weeks may have only one payday), but it is probable that they will.

You'll see these relationships appear with tables such as Customers and Orders, Orders and Order Details, Products and Shipments, Patients and Appointments, Buildings and Rooms, and School Districts and Teachers (that is, anything that has a subset of related entities).

Task 8   Building a one-to-many relationship.

1. Click on the Relationships button to open the Relationships window. The Employees and Pay tables should already be present.

2. Click on the Show Tables button, and add the Employee Paydays table. Click on Close to close the Table/Query selection box.

3. Create a one-to-many link between Employees and Employee Paydays by clicking on and dragging the Employee Number field from Employees to Employee Paydays. Make sure to put a checkmark in the Enforce Referential Integrity checkbox. Notice the join line that appears between the tables. You can tell the relationship is one-to-many because the number "1" is present at the Employees end, and the infinity symbol is present at the Employee Paydays end.

Task 9   Building a many-to-many relationship.

1. Click on the Show Tables button, and add the Team, Company Teams, and Charged Hours tables. Click on Close to close the Table/Query selection box.

2. Create a one-to-many link between Employees and Team on the Employee Number field. Create a one-to-many link between Company Teams and Team on the Team Number field.

3. Create a one-to-many link between Team and Charged Hours on the Team Number/Employee Team Number fields. Make sure to put a checkmark in the Enforce Referential Integrity checkbox. Notice the join lines that appear between the tables. A "1" appears on the Employees and Company Teams ends, and the infinity symbol appears on the Team and Charged Hours ends.

The many-to-many relationship is apparent when you look at the Team table in the Relationships window, as shown in Figure 10.6. Both the Employees and Company Teams tables have a one-to-many relationship to Team, resulting in a many-to-many relationship between Employees and Company Teams.

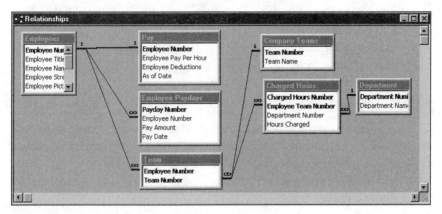

Figure 10.6   The Relationships window.

HOLD That Skill!

You can set your join type to one of three conditions in the Join window. The first join type displays only records from both tables that have a common value for the joining field. The second and third join types display either all records from one table and only those from the other table that have a common value, or vice versa.

For instance, if an employee is in training and has not yet been assigned to a team, that person has no team number. If you create a form that lists all employees that incidentally also shows team assignments, you can make the unassigned employees show up by choosing the join type that shows ALL employees but only those teams to which employees are assigned.

Referential Integrity

Referential integrity creates a special relationship between parent and child tables that helps you maintain your database. Specifically, when you enforce referential integrity, you can limit child records to only those that have a parent record. This also enables you to cascade updates and deletes, meaning that when you update or delete a parent record, all associated child records are also updated or deleted. You've already set referential integrity on all your joins in the Relationships window; setting cascading updates or deletes is simply a matter of checking the appropriate checkboxes during this process (refer back to Figure 10.5). By the way, if you do not check Enforce Referential Integrity when you establish joins in the Relationships window, the "1" and the infinity symbol do not appear on the join lines.

Relational databases consist of several tables, glued together (related) by primary key (unique) values. Tables can have a one-to-one, one-to-many, many-to-one, or many-to-many relationship. The theory of these relationships (called normal theory) begins with low levels of relatedness between data in various tables (Normal Forms 1, 2, and 3) and progresses to absolutely perfect relationships never seen in actual practice (Normal Forms 4, 5, and DKNF).

Using the Relationships window in Access 97 allows you to view, define, and remove these relationships. If you want to design high-performance database applications, it is critical that you understand the nature of these relationships, what fields they are made of, and how they can permit related concepts, such as referential integrity.

Advanced forms and queries use the relationships between tables as building blocks. Access 97 includes the ability to make forms and queries pull data from multiple tables; create crosstab queries that depict the relationship of two variables to a third; and even program queries directly in SQL, the national standard query language. We will cover these topics in Chapters 11 and 12.

Practice Exercises

Exercise 1

It should be obvious by now that, in order to get good performance from your database, you need to add more tables (by splitting existing tables or creating more fields for additional tables) and create links between them. Data entry, data selection, and reporting all benefit from using a relational database model.

Create a table named Employee Workspace, and include the following fields: Employee Number, Building, Location, Floor, and Computer Type.

Make Employee Number the appropriate type to serve as a foreign key for Employee Number in the Employees table. Make the other fields a data type of Text.

Open the Relationships window, and connect Employee Workspace to Employees with a one-to-one relationship.

Save the Relationships window, and close it.

Answer To Exercise 1

Click on the New button in the Database window (with the Tables tab selected, of course). Select Design View and then add the four fields. Set the data type of Employee Number to Number, Long Integer.

To set a one-to-one relationship using the Relationships window, click on the Relationships button on the Relationship toolbar, add your new table, and click on and drag the Employee Number field from Employees to Employee Workspace.

Click on the Save button from the Relationship toolbar and then exit the window.

Exercise 2

To properly normalize your database, you want to add a table for
employee computer hardware and relate it to each employee.

Create a table named Computer Hardware, and add the following
fields: Employee Number, Name, Model, and Serial Number.

Set the data type of the Employee Number field to the appropriate
type, and set the rest to Text.

Use the Relationships window to relate the Employees table to the
Computer Hardware table with a one-to-many relationship.

Save and close the Relationships window.

Answer To Exercise 2

Click on the New button in the Database window (with the Tables tab selected, of course). Select Design View and then add the four fields. Set the data
type of Employee Number to Number, Long Integer.

To set a one-to-many relationship using the Relationships window, click on
the Relationships button on the Database toolbar, add your new table, and
click on and drag the Employee Number field from Employees to Computer
Hardware.

Click on the Save button on the Relationship toolbar and then exit the
window.

Exercise 3

To ensure that orphan records are not left in your database when employees are laid off, you decide to set referential integrity.

Enforce referential integrity between the Employee Workspace table and the Computer Hardware table.

Save and close the Relationships window.

Answer To Exercise 3

Open the Relationships window, and display the Employee Workspaces and Computer Hardware tables. Right-click on the link between the tables.

Choose Edit Relationship on the shortcut menu. Choose Cascade Update Related Fields and Cascade Delete Related Fields.

Click on the Save button on the Relationship toolbar.

Need To Know More?

 Elmasri, Ramez and Shamkant B. Navanthe. *Fundamentals of Database Systems*, Addison-Wesley Publishing Company, Menlo Park, CA, 1994. ISBN 0-8053-1748-7. Chapters 12 and 13 contain an in-depth explanation of how to properly design and normalize tables.

 Viescas, John L. *Running Microsoft Access 97*, Microsoft Press, Redmond, WA, 1997. ISBN 1-57231-323-4. Chapters 5 and 6 provide information about creating relational tables and using the Table Analyzer.

 www.e4free.com
The Relational Database design page has in-depth information about how to create, normalize, and optimize relational databases.

Advanced Forms

Terms you'll need to understand:

√ Grouped controls

√ Shortcut menu

√ Concatenation

√ Argument

√ Label

√ DLookup function

√ IIf function

√ Switchboard

√ Record locking

√ Bitmap

√ Subform

Skills you'll need to master:

√ Working with advanced form controls

√ Working with the Expression Builder

√ Using the DLookup and IIf functions

√ Building calculated fields for forms

√ Adding graphics to a form

√ Creating and connecting a subform

√ Using switchboards

√ Creating charts and graphs

Forms (or screens, in the old mainframe database parlance) should be the mainstay of your user interface. Tables and queries should be hidden from the user, and even reports should be primarily used for printing, not as a user interface or display method. If you want to accomplish these goals, forms have to do more than just link to a table and allow data entry.

Access 97 lets you create forms with properties specifically designed for efficient user interaction. Forms can display controls that make your database operate much like a well-designed standalone program: command buttons, dialog boxes, checkboxes, calculated fields, and subforms that display the records in a child table related to the current records shown for the parent table. In addition, you can set startup options that control user interaction from the first time the database is opened.

Using Advanced Form Controls

In Design view, if the form is bound to a table, you can find the table's fields by opening the View|Field List menu choice. All other form controls are built from buttons on the Toolbox (see Figure 11.1). A list of available controls and their functions can be found in Chapter 5.

Creating controls on your form is basically a process of clicking on the form control button you want and then "drawing" the new control on your form. All controls can be configured manually, but many of them are best constructed with Control Wizards on.

Figure 11.1 The Advanced Controls Toolbox.

Among the advanced controls, there are several general categories:

➤ Drawn controls, such as lines and rectangles, for visual appeal

➤ Controls that allow you to select data options (list boxes, combo boxes, checkboxes, and toggle buttons)

➤ Grouped controls (option groups, option buttons, and radio buttons)

➤ Controls that allow you to initiate commands (command buttons)

Task 1   *Creating drawn controls on the Employees form.*

1. Open the Employees form in Design view. Maximize the form and then resize it to six inches wide. Relocate the heading label to the new center.

2. Relocate the Employee Picture field to the right side of the form, and resize it thinner and taller. Delete the Employee Picture label (there's no need for this label, because the field's content is obvious from the picture itself).

3. Relocate the Employee Name field and its label underneath the Employee Picture field. Click twice on the label. You should now be able to edit the label's text. Delete the word *Employee* and then resize the label to fit the remaining word (*Name:*).

4. Move the Employee Number, Employment Date, and Employee Street Address fields towards the top-left corner of the form. Draw a rectangle around them using the Rectangle button on the Toolbox. Just click on the Rectangle button and then start drawing on your form by clicking on and dragging the cursor. (Note that if you want to return to a normal arrow cursor without drawing the rectangle, you can click on the arrow button on the Toolbox.)

5. Right-click on the rectangle, and display the properties sheet. At Special Effects, select Sunken.

6. Click on the Line button on the Toolbox. Underneath the heading, draw a line that is slightly shorter than the heading itself. Right-click on the line, and display the Properties sheet. At Border Width, select 2 pt and then close the properties sheet. Your form should look like Figure 11.2. Save your form.

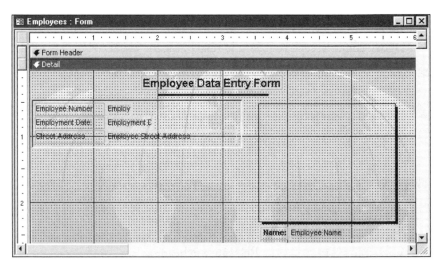

Figure 11.2 The Employees form in Design view with drawn controls.

Using The Properties Shortcut Menu

To open a control's Properties shortcut menu, shown in Figure 11.3, right-click on the control. The Properties shortcut menu contains frequently used/changed properties, such as Align, Size, Fill/Back Color, Front/Fore Color, and Special Effect. It also gives you a quick way to begin building an expression or VBA code for an event, convert a control from one type to another, change the tab order, edit text or objects, and access the entire properties sheet.

Use the Properties shortcut menu whenever you want to quickly set common properties; use the properties sheet for detailed property modification.

 Several questions on the test require you to be familiar with the properties sheet and the Properties shortcut menu. You may be asked to change the color of a control in one question, a line width in another, and the Control Source property in a third.

Using The Expression Builder

An *expression* is essentially a formula for arriving at a value. For instance, you can use an expression to add the contents of two fields or sum up all the field values in a group. Rather than force you to enter the formula manually (and with just the right syntax, no less), Access 97's Expression Builder does it for you with point-and-click ease.

Figure 11.3   The Properties shortcut menu.

You start the Expression Builder wherever you need to enter an expression; just click next to an event in a control's property sheet, for instance. The Expression Builder opens (depending upon what control's properties are displayed, you might get a dialog box that requests you to choose from the Expression Builder, Macro Builder, or Code Builder).

As you can see in Figure 11.4, the top part of the Expression Builder window shows your expression as you create it. The center section holds arithmetical and other operators (+, -, /, *, and so on). The three window sections on the

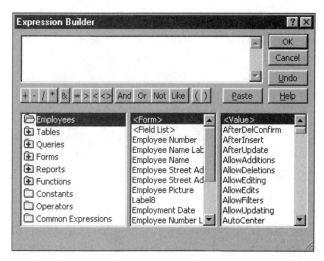

Figure 11.4   The Expression Builder.

bottom let you pick and choose database objects to use, fields and text boxes on your form or report, and built-in values and functions.

The cursor in the top box responds to typing, so you can simply enter the expression manually. You can also enter operators from the center section by clicking on them, or you can enter field or control names by double-clicking on them from the bottom sections. If you double-click on built-in functions, such as Sum(), the function becomes part of your expression and includes a placeholder for you to insert the actual field name.

The bottom-left window of the Expression Builder contains database objects, such as the current table; other objects within the current database; and functions, constants, operators, and common expressions that any Access 97 database can use.

These objects are similar to directories in that their own objects are in a hierarchy under them. For instance, if you double-click on Functions, then click on Built-In Functions, function categories appear in the bottom-middle window and specific functions within a category appear in the bottom-right window.

The purpose of these three windows is to make it easy to find, select, and use any available function, constant, expression, or database object in the expression you are constructing.

Designing Calculated Fields On A Form

Unlike bound controls (which use a table or query as their data source), calculated controls use expressions as their data source. Bound and unbound controls, whether visible on the form or not, can provide values for calculations. You can perform arithmetic on numbers; connect string values (text); and evaluate, add, and subtract dates. Text boxes are the most common type of calculated control, but you can use any control that has a Control Source property.

Typically, you use a calculated control in a situation where values must be calculated record by record but the value doesn't necessarily need to become part of the database.

For instance, suppose you want the Employees form to display employment length in years. That value is a function of the current date minus the Employment Date, divided by 365 (for a close approximation). Access 97 converts all dates to a numerical value internally, so you can accurately add and subtract dates from each other.

Task 2   *Creating a Years Employed control on the Employees form.*

1. The Employees form should already be open in Design view. Below the box that contains Employee Number, Employment Date, and Street Address, create another box (rectangle) about the same size.

2. Make sure Control Wizards is off and then click on the Text Box button. Draw a text box inside the rectangle. Open its property sheet, click on the Control Source text box, and then click on the Build button. The Expression Builder opens.

3. Click on the equals operator (from the row in the center) to begin your expression. Next, double-click on Functions and then click on Built-In Functions. Click on Date/Time in the bottom-center window and then double-click on Date. Your expression should read "=Date ()" (please note that quotation marks are not included in any of the Expression Builder entries offered here).

4. After the second parenthesis, enter a minus sign. Then, click on Employees (in the bottom-left window), and double-click on Employment Date. Add a parenthesis just after the equal sign and a closing parenthesis at the end of the whole expression. Your expression should now read "=(Date()-[Employment Date])".

5. The preceding expression gives us the number of days since the Employment Date in whole days, plus a fraction that represents the number of seconds. We want the number of years displayed, so enter "/365" after the last parenthesis. Close the Expression Builder by clicking on OK.

6. To prevent the Employees form from displaying the number of years followed by a long, meaningless fraction, click on the Format property, and change it to Fixed. Then, click on the Decimal Places property, and change it to 1. Close the properties sheet.

7. Select the calculated control by clicking on it (if it's not still selected) and then justify it to the left. Click on the Label button, draw a label to the left of the calculated control, and enter "Years Employed". Locate, align, and size your new control with the others on the form. Save your form.

8. Close the form and then reopen it in Normal view. If you see no Employment Date or Years Employed, enter some employment dates in the Employees table. The final product should resemble Figure 11.5.

Employee Number	Employ	
Employment Date	Employment D	
Street Address	Employee Street Address	
Years Employed	=(Date()-[Employment Date])/365	

Figure 11.5 The Employees form in Design view with the Years Employed control.

Access 97 converts dates and times into numerical values internally. These numbers indicate dates from Jan. 1, 100, to Dec. 31, 9999, and times from midnight (0:00:00) to 11:59 P.M. and 59 seconds (23:59:59). This range should be large enough to accommodate the vast majority of applications.

In Task 2, the expression obtains the numerical value of the current date (using the Date function) and the value of the Employment Date field for the current record, then subtracts the Employment Date value from the current date value. The result is a number that indicates whole days to the left of the decimal point and time (as a decimal fraction) to the right of the decimal point. For instance, the value 3.5 indicates 3 days and 12 hours.

As you already know, you cannot add or otherwise operate on text as you can a number value. However, Access 97 performs "addition" on text in the sense that it splices (concatenates) two text values together to create a longer string.

For instance, suppose you want to include a title for each employee. Assuming there is a Title field in the Employees table with titles already entered, you can just place both the Title and Employee Name fields on the form. The drawback to this method is that it is difficult to get exactly the spacing you want between the title and the employee's name. An easier method is to concatenate the two fields in a calculated control.

Task 3 Creating a Title and Name control on the Employees form.

1. Close the Employees form. In the Database window, click on the Tables tab. Open the Employees table in Normal view by clicking on the Open button. Enter titles for your employees using the value list that you created in Practice Exercise 2 of Chapter 9. Close the table.

2. Open the Employees form in Design view, as shown in Figure 11.6. Remove the Name label and the control underneath the Employee

Picture. Click on the Text Box button, and draw a box underneath Employee Picture. Size it as wide as the Employee Picture control.

3. Open the property sheet for the new control. Open the Expression Builder by clicking on the ellipsis next to Control Source.

4. Click on the equal sign to begin your expression. Make sure the Employees table is selected in the bottom-left window and then click on <Field List> in the bottom-center window. Double-click on Employee Title in the bottom-right window. To join the two text values, click on the & operator, and double-click on Employee Name in the bottom-right window.

5. To insert an aesthetically pleasing separation between the title and the employee name, type quotation marks, a space, a dash, a space, quotation marks, and another & operator between the first & operator and the bracket that begins the Employee Name field.

6. Your expression should now read "=[Employee Title]&" – "&[Employee Name]". Click on OK to close the Expression Builder, close the property sheet (ensure that your sizing and alignment of the control is even and nicely done), and save the form. Close the form and then reopen it in Normal view to check your handiwork.

The DLookup And IIf Functions

Sometimes, you need to get a value from a table/query other than the table/query to which your form is bound. You can do exactly that with the DLookup (Domain Lookup) function. For instance, you may want to display an employee's annual salary on your form. Using reverse engineering, we determine that annual salary equals pay per hour times the number of paid hours per year (we'll

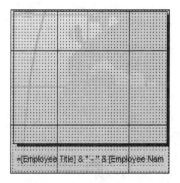

Figure 11.6   The Employees form in Design view with the Title and Name control.

use 2,087 hours per year for this example). In order to retrieve pay per hour and use it in a calculated control, we employ the DLookup function.

The syntax of the DLookup function is: DLookup(expr,domain,[criteria]). All functions begin with their name, followed by parentheses that enclose any arguments. *Arguments* is a rather negative term that refers to the numbers, fields, tables, values, and so on that the function takes into consideration as it does its job.

The job of the DLookup function is to find a particular value within another table or query, so the arguments of the function are, in order: field name (expr), table or query name (domain), and the value of a matching field in the appropriate record (criteria). The DLookup function takes the value of the matching field from the record that the form is currently on and uses it to look up a related value in the table or query we specify.

Task 4   Creating an Annual Salary control on the Employees form.

1. The Employees form should already be open in Design view. Enlarge the box around the Years Employed control, and, below it, create a label that reads "Annual Salary", as shown in Figure 11.7. Then, create another unbound text box to the right. Open the unbound text box's property sheet, click on the Control Source text box, and then click on the Build button. The Expression Builder opens.

2. Click on the equal sign to begin your expression. Double-click on Functions in the bottom-left window. Click on Built-In Functions in the same window and then scroll down the bottom-right window until you find DLookup. Double-click on DLookup to insert it into your expression.

3. Click on <<expr>> in the expression to select it. Enter "[Employee Pay Per Hour]" (including the quotation marks). Click on <<domain>> to select it. Enter "Pay" (including the quotation marks). Notice, there are no brackets around the name of the table. These two arguments define the field and table, respectively, from which we want to retrieve (look up) a value.

4. Your expression should now read: =DLookup("[Employee Pay Per Hour]","Pay", <<criteria>>) (including the quotation marks). Click on <<criteria>> to select it. Enter "[Employee Number] =

"&[Forms]![Employees]![Employee Number] (including the quotation marks). Notice that the quotation marks surround only the beginning portion that specifies the field name to match up. The value of the current record on your form is specified by the special notation [Form]![Employees]![Employee Number]. This argument tells the DLookup function to find the record in Pay where the Employee Number matches the current Employee Number on the Employees form. That way, we know the retrieved pay per hour value is for the employee we are currently viewing on our form.

5. After the last parenthesis in the expression, enter "*2087". The full expression should now read: =DLookup("[Employee Pay Per Hour]"","Pay","[Employee Number] = "&[Forms]![Employees]![Employee Number]) *2087.

6. Click on OK to close the Expression Builder. Click on the Format property, and change the number format to Currency. Click on the Decimal Places property, and change it to 2. Close the property sheet, and justify the contents of the control to the left. Save the form and then check it in Normal view. The annual salary of each employee should appear in the control as you view the Employees table record by record.

Another frequent application for calculated controls is performing calculations when users enter data into an unbound control. For example, you can multiply pay per hour by a user-specified number of work hours to gauge how much an employee makes for any period.

If we want to display several pre-calculated values (such as total salary for a week, month, or quarter), we can create a grouped control. This control lets the user select which period to compute and automatically displays the result.

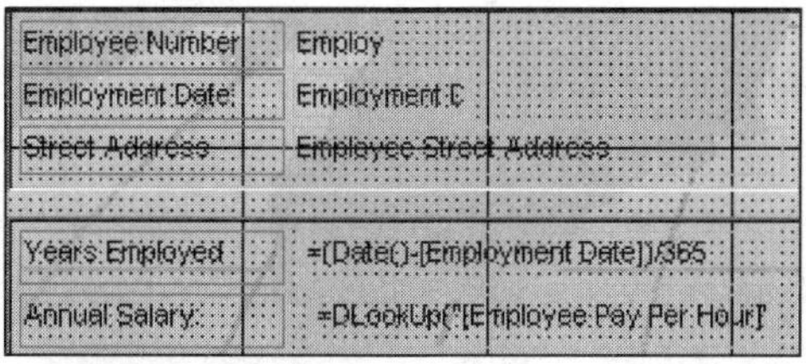

Figure 11.7 The Employees form in Design view with the Annual Salary control.

Task 5 Creating a salary calculator on the Employees form.

1. Open the Employees form in Design view. Enlarge the box around the Years Employed and Annual Salary controls. Below the Annual Salary control, create a label that reads "Pay Per Period Calculator". Then, next to it, add another that reads "Total Pay =". Next, draw an unbound text box following the Total Pay = label control.

2. Open the property sheet of the unbound control, and rename it TotalPay. Doing so makes it easier to refer to later.

3. Create another label (just below the one that reads "Pay Per Period Calculator"), and make it read "Enter Hours or". Create an unbound text box next to the label, and rename it HoursWorked.

4. Create a command button below the HoursWorked control. Open its property sheet, click on the OnClick event, click on the ellipsis (...), and start the Code Builder.

5. Using the Code Builder, we can create an event procedure that retrieves the current employee's pay per hour, multiplies it by the user-entered number of hours in the HoursWorked control, and then places the result in the TotalPay control. The cursor is automatically placed at the appropriate spot, so enter the following code:

```
TotalPay = DLookup("[Employee Pay Per Hour]", "Pay",
"[Employee Number] = " & [Forms]![Employees]![Employee Number])
* [Forms]![Employees]![HoursWorked]
```

Notice that we used the same expression as in the Annual Salary control to find the appropriate pay per hour and multiplied it by the value in the HoursWorked control. We could have specified the HoursWorked control simply by using its name, instead of the formal path to it— [Forms]![Employees]![HoursWorked].

6. In order to reset the value of TotalPay to zero after we change records or use another control, we need to insert a short procedure in one of the events inside the TotalPay control. *Events* are things that happen to objects during the operation of your application, and they are listed in the control's property sheet. For instance, the LostFocus event happens to a control when focus goes from it to another control or field. In this case, we'll create an event procedure in the LostFocus event that reads "TotalPay = 0" (without the quotation marks). Doing so sets the value of

the TotalPay control to zero when we move to the next record or shift the focus to another control.

7. Save the form, and check it in Normal view.

Task 6   *Creating an option group on the Employees form.*

1. Open the Employees form in Design view. Next to the HoursWorked unbound text box , create a label that reads "Choose One". To the right of that, create an option group frame. Open its property sheet, rename it HoursFrame, and then draw two option buttons (radio buttons) inside it. Note that the OptionValue of the option buttons you just created is automatically set to 1 and 2, respectively.

 As you draw the buttons inside the frame, the entire frame should become highlighted. If the frame doesn't highlight, your option buttons will not be a part of the group and will not work correctly.

2. Click on the buttons inside the frame, taking care to select the buttons and not their corresponding labels by mistake. Open their property sheets, and rename the first one you created OptionDay and the second OptionWeek. Arrange them in a short row so that OptionDay is to the left and OptionWeek is to the right.

3. Create another command button below the option group. Open its property sheet, start the Code Builder, and create an event procedure in the OnClick event. Enter the following code:

```
If HoursFrame = 1 Then
TotalPay = DLookup("[Employee Pay Per Hour]", "Pay",
"[Employee Number] = "
& [Forms]![Employees]![Employee Number]) * 8
Else
TotalPay = DLookup("[Employee Pay Per Hour]", "Pay",
"[Employee Number] = "
& [Forms]![Employees]![Employee Number]) * 40
End If
```

When you click on the command button, this code determines which option you have selected by checking the value of the option group (either 1 or 2, for OptionDay or OptionWeek). It then retrieves the Employee Pay Per Hour value, multiplies it by either 8 or 40 (the number of work hours in a day or week), and places the result in the

TotalPay control. Notice the use of the If...Then...Else structure in the code to choose which action to perform.

4. In order to reset the value of TotalPay to zero after we change records or use another control, create another event procedure in the LostFocus event that reads "TotalPay = 0" (without the quotation marks). Doing so sets TotalPay to zero when we move to the next record or shift the focus to another control.

5. Save the form, close it, and then check it in Normal view.

Task 7 Creating a combo box on the Employees form.

1. Open the Employees table in Design view. Add a 50-character Text field named Preferred Incentives. Save and close the table.

2. Next, create a new table named IncentivesPref, with a 50-character Text field also named Incentives. Enter your four or five favorite benefits in the new table: vacations, time off, on-site massages, free childcare, coupons from fine stores or restaurants, and so on.

3. Open the Employees form in Design view. Below the Annual Salary control, place a label that reads "Incentives Preference". Underneath that, draw a combo box with the combo box tool (make sure the Wizards button is pressed).

4. The first screen of the wizard opens. Choose "I want the combo box to look up the values in a table or query" and then click on Next. The second screen, with a view of tables as the default, opens. Choose the new IncentivesPref table and then click on the Next button.

5. The next screen asks you to choose the fields from which it will take data for the combo box. Only one field is available (Incentives), so make sure it's selected and then click on the top arrow button (the one that points to the right). Click on the Next button.

6. The next screen asks you to size the column of data to your liking. Use the default size and then click on Next.

7. On the next screen, you are offered two choices. You can either store the value for later use, or you can choose to enter the value in one of the fields present on your form. We want to enter the value into the Preferred Incentives field, so choose that option, and select the Preferred Incentives field. Click on Next.

8. On the last screen of the wizard, you can pick a descriptive name for the control. Name the control Incentives and then click on the Finish button.

9. Resize the field as necessary to complement the other fields, save the form, and then open it for data entry. Fill the records for that field with your employees' preferred incentives.

The IIf function (immediate if) is called a *program-flow function*. It is essentially a testing device that returns one of two values that depend upon a third value. You program all three values in, so you control its action by your entries.

For instance, if your company has a rule that anyone making more than $35,000 annually is Exempt (exempt from overtime pay requirements), you can create a control that tests for that value and returns the word *Exempt* or *Non-Exempt*, depending upon the value it finds. The IIf function evaluates the first argument to see whether it is true or false. Then, it displays the contents of the second argument (if the first argument is true) or the contents of the third argument (if the first argument is false).

Please note that a business rule such as this is poorly conceived. It would cause unnecessary maintenance, because it's likely that the value would change fairly frequently, and each change would require you to reprogram the form. However, the rule is well suited to demonstrating the IIf function.

Task 8   *Creating an IIf function control on the Employees form.*

1. Open the Employees form in Design view. Underneath the Title And Name field, create an unbound text box. In the Control Source property, create an expression that reads "=IIf([AnnualSalary]<35000, "Non-Exempt", "Exempt")" (without the external quotation marks).

2. Open the property sheet of the control where Annual Salary is calculated, and rename the control AnnualSalary. Save and close the form, and check it in Normal view.

3. This function examines the newly renamed AnnualSalary control for its value. If the annual salary value is less than 35000, the control displays the word *Non-Exempt*. If it is greater than 35000, the control displays the word *Exempt*. Note that you must not use a comma to separate the thousands in "35000". If you had used a comma there, the function would have misinterpreted it as a spurious argument, and you would be debugging your function now.

The IIf function evaluates both arguments every time, even if the first is true. Therefore, you should be careful to ensure that both arguments have the intended result, even if incorrect data has been entered. For instance, if the evaluated data causes division by zero, an error occurs, even if the other case is correct.

Creating Switchboards

Custom database applications ordinarily contain several forms for data entry or display, and several reports. These objects actually define the entire user interface, because the tables, queries, macros, and modules perform their work behind the scenes.

Typically, when a user first starts the application, a form called a *switchboard* appears. The switchboard usually contains some text that welcomes the user to the application, as well as some command buttons to open whatever forms or reports are available. The switchboard form itself is not connected to any tables and is not used for data entry.

Task 9   Building a simple switchboard form.

1. In the Database window, click on the Forms tab and then click on New. Choose Design View and then click on OK.

2. Enlarge the detail area of the form to 7.5 inches wide by 4 inches high. Set the background picture properties to the stone.bmp picture with Picture Tiling set to Yes.

3. Create a large, centered label at the top of the form. Enter "Personnel Database" into the label, and set the font to Bold, point size 24.

4. Click on the Control Wizards button on the Toolbox to turn Control Wizards on and then draw a command button on the form. On the first screen of the wizard, choose Form Operations (under Categories) and then choose Open Forms (under Actions). Notice that the actions available change according to the category you select. Click on Next.

5. On the second screen, the Employees form is the only one available. Choose it, and click on Next.

6. On the third screen, you can designate how the form opens—either with a particular record displayed or with all records displayed. Choose to display all records and then click on Next.

7. On the fourth screen, you can choose the caption for the button—either a picture or text you enter. Choose Text, and enter "Review Employees".

8. On the final screen, you can rename the button if you like, but there's no need (because we probably won't be referring to this button by name). Click on Finish. The wizard closes. Your button should be where you left it, with the caption "Review Employees" on it.

If your application needs only one top-level switchboard form, it might be easier to simply create an unbound form and put a few command buttons on it. On the other hand—depending upon how many functions your database has— you might have a top-level switchboard form that opens whenever the application starts as well as lower-level switchboard forms (which can be reached from the top-level form) for each category of functions. If that is the case, it is simpler to use Access 97's Switchboard Manager Wizard (see Figure 11.8).

Task 10   *Building switchboard forms with the Switchboard Manager.*

1. In the Database window, click on Tools|Add-Ins|Switchboard Manager. The Switchboard Manager Wizard checks your database for previous versions of the switchboard (by looking for a form named Switchboard) and asks if you'd like to create one. Click on Yes.

2. The first Switchboard Manager Wizard screen opens, with the Main Switchboard form selected in the upper window. You can add additional switchboard forms (called *pages*) by clicking on the New button.

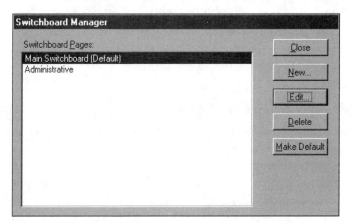

Figure 11.8   The Switchboard Manager Wizard.

3. Click on New. When the screen for the new switchboard opens, enter the name "Administrative" and then click on OK. Both the Main switchboard and the Administrative switchboard should now be on your screen.

4. Make sure the Main switchboard is selected and then click on Edit. Another very similar screen opens. It has the name of the current switchboard and, in the lower window, a blank listing of the commands you can put on the form (they show up as buttons).

5. Click on New. Another little window with three text boxes on it opens. The top box (labeled Text) shows the text that follows the button. The middle box (labeled Command) lets you select from several common actions to perform when the button is pressed. The bottom box (labeled Switchboard) lets you select which object (form) the action affects.

6. In the top box, enter "Review Employees". In the middle box, choose Open Form In Edit Mode. In the bottom box, choose the Employees form. Doing so creates a button on the Main Switchboard form that opens the Employees form so that you can review or edit records. Click on OK, then click Close to end editing of the Main switchboard.

7. Select the Administrative switchboard and then click on Edit. When the next screen opens, click on New, enter "Add Employees", and then choose Open Form In Add Mode (in the middle box) and Employees (in the bottom box). Click on OK and then click on New again.

8. The Administrative switchboard is one level below the Main switchboard, so it's wise to put a button on it that takes us directly back to the Main switchboard. To do this, enter "Back to the Main switchboard " in the top box, leave the middle box set to Go To Switchboard, and choose Main Switchboard for the bottom box. Click on OK|Close to end editing. Click on Close to close the Switchboard Manager Wizard.

Modifying Form Properties

Notice that in the Switchboard form, we've separated the data-entry function for adding employees from the function for reviewing employees. Because the database application should support the way the business works, there will likely be many instances where you set form properties so the application conforms to current business practices. In this instance, the Accounting department manager, for the sake of good internal controls, would not want the person who writes paychecks to be the same person who approves the time card. So, our Access forms should have these functions separated.

The preceding scenario implies that one set of users can review employees and another set of users can actually add employees. There is a way to set form properties so that data can be viewed only or only new records can be added. In addition, you can set form properties to restrict other users from editing the same record at the same time as the current user.

When you open your form in Design view, you can access its properties by clicking on the Properties button. Notice that (as shown in Figure 11.9) the following properties are available:

➤ **Allow Edits** Set to Yes by default. Setting it to No means records can't be edited, but additions and deletions are still allowed.

➤ **Allow Deletions** Set to Yes by default. Setting it to No means records can't be deleted, but additions and edits are still allowed.

➤ **Allow Additions** Set to Yes by default. Setting it to No means records can't be added, but deletions and edits are still allowed.

➤ **Data Entry** Set to No by default. Setting it to Yes restricts the user to only entering new records. Other records cannot be viewed or changed.

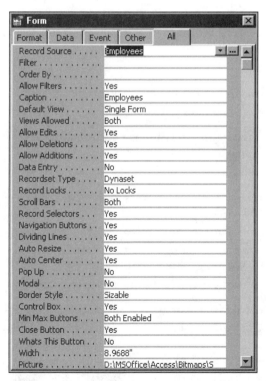

Figure 11.9   The properties sheet of the Employees form.

➤ **Recordset Type** Set to Dynaset by default. This means that you get an updateable set of records from the Record Source table. Snapshot is the only other choice, and it means the records supplied by the table are not updateable.

➤ **Record Locks** Set to No Locks by default. Allows you to lock records when a user opens the form. You can set it to varying degrees of locking—from no locks to locking the entire table that underlies the form.

These properties help you, as the database designer, control how users interact with the application during the business functions that the application supports.

Task 11   Restricting record changes for the Employees form.

1. Open the Employees form in Design view. The Object list on the Formatting (Form/Report) toolbar should be set to Form by default. Click on the Properties button. The form's property sheet opens.

2. Set Allow Edits, Allow Deletions, and Allow Additions to No. Close the property sheet.

3. Save the form, and examine how it functions in Normal view. You should be able to view the records as you like but make no changes whatsoever.

4. Return to Design view by clicking on the Design View button. Set Allow Edits, Allow Deletions, and Allow Additions to Yes.

5. Set Data Entry to Yes. Save the form, and examine how it functions in Normal view. You should be able to add new records but not see any other records (much less make changes).

Notice that we would need two copies of the Employees form—one for additions and one for viewing records—to support business rules properly, using these properties alone. There is a way to use only one copy of the Employees form: You can change form properties according to how the form is opened, but that involves programming VBA modules. You may review VBA module programming on my Web site at **www.e4free.com/access97examcram**.

Years ago, it was common for PC-based database applications to be standalone; that is, have only one user. These days, the reverse is true. Most database applications have multiple users. Designers are seldom the only user for the database, if they actually use it (as an end user) at all. Users are frequently networked, and they are the ideal candidates for data entry because they use or generate the fundamental data in their daily activities.

Many folks will be adding and editing records, so the designer must employ some form of record locking. Depending upon the circumstances, you may build in no locks, lock only the record being edited, or lock the entire underlying table.

Task 12   Locking records for the Employees form.

1. Open the Employees form in Design view. Open the form's property sheet, and set Record Locks to All Records. Doing so locks other users out of the entire underlying table until you close the form. This level of locking is appropriate when only one individual should be editing the table's records at a given time.

2. Reset the Record Locks property to Edited Records. Doing so locks the record you have open and other records nearby in the table. This level of locking is appropriate when few people are making changes but you need to allow access to the same table at the same time.

3. Reset the Record Locks property to the default—No Locks. Doing so ensures that all users can edit all records at the same time. If you attempt to save a record that someone else has already changed, you are given the option of overwriting the other person's changes, saving your changes to the clipboard, or discarding your changes. It is very convenient, but you can expect editing conflicts.

Adding Graphics And Other Objects To A Form

The Employees form already has a background image tiled over the entire background. Graphic images that mesh with themselves, or images of textures (metal, wood, stone, and so on), are appropriate for adding eye appeal to your forms (and reports).

Additional static images may be warranted to give your form exactly the professional appearance you need. You can insert them into the form in Design view, and they remain the same from record to record (unlike the contents of the Employee Picture field, whose images are inserted during record addition or editing in Normal view and change each time a new record is reached).

You insert static images into your form in an *image frame*. Image frames can display only bitmap and Windows metafile graphics, so, for this exercise, you'll need to create a bitmap image in Paint, Windows 95's included graphics utility program (in the Accessories group).

Task 13   Adding a static image to the Employees form.

1. Minimize Access 97 and then open the Accessories program called Paint by clicking on Start|Accessories|Paint. A new Paint file is displayed by default.

2. Choose Image|Attributes. A dialog box in which you can reset the image's width and height opens. Set the width to 100 and the height to 50 (these units are pixels, but you'll notice that you can also use centimeters or inches). Click on OK.

3. Click on the letter *A* on the toolbar and then click on the image space. A text box appears in the image, and a small dialog box opens. In this dialog box, you can choose the font, font size, and text attributes you'd like. Choose size 28, bold, and a font you like. Click on the image in the text box, and type in the word *Logo*. As shown in Figure 11.10, the word should appear on the image, in the current color (to reset the current color, click on one of the colored boxes at the bottom of the Paint program's window).

   This little image will be your company logo. Please feel free to change the colors, wording, and any other graphic aspects of this image, but keep the size on the small side. Also, if you happen to have an actual logo image (in bitmap format) on your hard drive or network, you can use that instead. After all, this is your company.

4. Save your file (as logo.bmp) in a directory that you will remember and then close the Paint program. Maximize Access 97.

5. Open the Employees form in Design view. Click on the Image button on the Toolbox, and draw a frame for your logo in the upper left-hand corner. An Insert Picture dialog box opens.

6. Find your bitmap logo file, select it, and click on OK. It appears in the frame you've drawn on the form. Resize the frame to accommodate the image. Save your form and then close it. The image appears at that location whenever the form is open.

Using Charts And Graphs With A Form

In the same way that a picture of an employee conveys much more information than just the person's name, a chart or graph conveys much more than columns and rows of numbers. Users frequently use forms to review data as

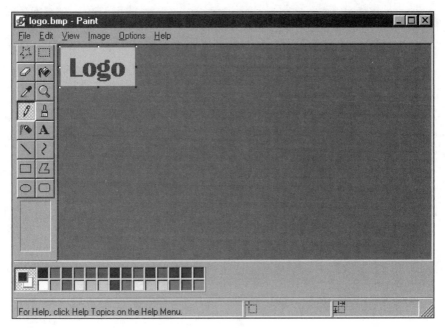

Figure 11.10   The Windows 95 Paint program with logo.bmp open.

well as perform data entry, so inserting charts and graphs can push productivity to new highs by compressing mountains of data into easily understood snapshots.

Access 97 contains charting wizards that make creating charts and graphs simple. The predefined styles are:

➤ **Column charts** Column, 3D Column, 3D Cylinder, 3D Cone, and 3D Pyramid

➤ **Bar charts** Bar, 3D Bar, 3D Cylinder, 3D Cone, and 3D Pyramid

➤ **Area charts** Area and 3D Area

➤ **Line charts** Line and 3D Line

➤ **XY (Scatter) charts** Data point charts

➤ **Pie charts** Pie and 3D Pie

➤ **Bubble charts** Bubble and 3D Bubble

➤ **Doughnut charts** Similar to Pie charts

The essence of making a chart is deciding which components to compare: sales per time period, number of employees per department, customer complaints

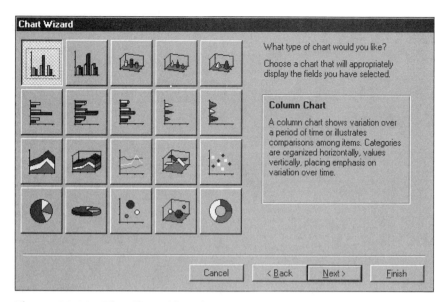

Figure 11.11   The Chart Wizard.

by complaint type, and so on. Once you know what you want to compare, it's relatively easy to begin defining your chart using the Chart Wizard, shown in Figure 11.11.

Task 14   Adding a chart to the Employees form.

1. To give us something relevant to chart on the Employees form, let's create a table for tracking the per-share value of your company's Employee Stock Ownership Plan (ESOP). Create a table with two fields: Date (Monthly) and Per Share Value. Set the Date (Monthly) field to a Data Type of Date using the Short Date format. Set the Per Share Value field to Currency with the number of Decimal Places set to 2. Save it with the name ESOP Value, open it, and then fill it in with some made-up dates and amounts (1/1/95, $4.00, 2/1/95, $4.25, and so on). After you create about 12 records, close the table.

2. Open the Employees form in Design view. Maximize the form, and create some room below the Pay Per Period Calculator.

3. Choose Insert|Chart from the menu and then draw a box for the new chart on the form in the space you just cleared. The Chart Wizard opens.

4. Select the ESOP Value table on the first screen and then click on Next. On the second screen, select the Date (Monthly) and Per Share Value

fields. Then, click on the arrow in the center to move them to the window on the right side for inclusion on your chart. Click on Next.

5. Click on Line Chart from the chart styles displayed on the third screen and then click on Next. On the fourth screen, you can drag and drop the fields so that the values display along the side (the Y axis) or across the bottom (the X axis). Put Per Share Value along the side and Date (Monthly) across the bottom. Click on Next. If we were charting data that changed for each new record displayed on the form, we could use the sixth screen to connect the form to the chart. Because we're charting data from a completely unrelated table, click on Next to bypass this feature.

6. On the seventh screen, the name ESOP Value should be entered by default. Click on Finish to complete the chart.

7. When your chart appears on the form in Design view, it has sample data in it to give you an idea of what kind of chart it is. The idea is to check for placement of the titles and legends, and to make sure the chart is centered properly. To see actual data, save the form and then open it in Normal view.

8. If the chart is not properly centered or you need to make changes, right-click on the chart in Design view. A shortcut menu opens. Choose Chart Object|Edit to open up the chart for editing.

Creating And Connecting A Subform

Database applications that contain tables linked to one another in a parent-child relationship are quite common. For instance, students regularly receive grades, orders frequently contain multiple products, divisions within a company usually have multiple employees, clients often make several payments for an order, and so on. All these situations call for tables that are bound together by a parent-child relationship.

Creating a subform and connecting it to a master form is a convenient way of facilitating that relationship through forms. For each record entered into the parent table, you can enter multiple records into the child table as well as review them all from the same form. The primary key value from the master table automatically appears in the corresponding field of the child table whenever a new child record is created, saving a data-entry step and ensuring that the records are always correctly linked.

For our growing sample application, we will build a subform that contains a payment history for each employee. The required data includes payday number, employee number, pay date, and pay amount.

Task 15   Creating and connecting a subform.

1. In the Database window, with the Forms tab selected, click on New. In the dialog box that opens, choose Design View (it should already be selected by default) and then select the Employee Paydays table from the drop-down list below. Click on OK. A fresh form in Design view opens.

2. Choose View from the menu, and select Field List. The Field List box appears. Click on and drag all four fields to the form.

3. Move and resize the fields as necessary to place them compactly in the top, left-hand corner of the available form space. Set the background color to a dark greenish to complement the color of the Employees form. Save the new form, and close it.

4. Open the Employees form in Design view. Widen the Employees form to approximately eight inches, so there is enough space to insert the Paydays subform next to the Employee Picture field. Using the Subform/Subreport tool in the Toolbox, draw a Subform control next to the Employee Picture field. A wizard opens.

5. On the first screen of the wizard, choose the Forms option and then select the Paydays table from the drop-down box. Click on Next.

6. The next screen allows you to determine how the tables are connected. Microsoft Access 97 generates a linking method, or you can choose to define your own linking fields. You want the records to be linked from the Employee Number field in the Employees table to the Employee Number field in the Paydays table, so choose the second option. The screen changes, and you can then select these fields from the option boxes. Note that you can choose more than one field to link from each table (although we don't need to do so for this exercise). Click on Next.

7. Finally, name the control Paydays and then click on the Finish button. Save the Employees form. Then, open it to check the size, placement, and visibility of the Paydays subform. Resize the fields in the subform as necessary to obtain a pleasing effect.

8. Enter several sample paydays for each employee. Notice that the Employee Number is automatically entered for each new record.

Perhaps you recall standalone applications programs from the '80s: single-function programs that contained everything you needed to perform a specific job, such as maintaining personnel records. Upon launching these programs, you were greeted with a welcome screen with several available menu choices. Each choice took you to another screen with data-entry, query, or reporting capability, and perhaps a few special functions.

Access 97 gives you the tools to build standalone applications like these, and forms are the objects used to simulate the workings of a standalone program. You can create advanced controls that select from various options, command buttons that open other forms or reports, calculated fields for unique values that are missing from the underlying data, even customized help systems. Startup options let you start forms when the database first opens; charts, graphs, and subforms round out the picture.

Practice Exercises

Exercise 1

> Managers are now using your database to retrieve and review
> employee information, and they want to manipulate records us-
> ing a form, rather than read printed reports. You need to create
> additional features on your Employees form to satisfy those re-
> quirements.
>
> Create a control on the Employees form that indicates when a
> person has passed his or her probationary period of 90 days.
>
> Make the control a text box that reads "Yes" when the person's
> employment date is 90 days or greater in the past.
>
> Save the form.

Answer To Exercise 1

To create a control that reads "Yes" when a person's employment date is 90 days
or more before the present, add an unbound text box. Open the Control Source
property, and open the Expression Builder. Using the Immediate If (IIf) function, enter the following code:

```
=IIf(Now()-[Employment Date]<90,"No","Yes")
```

To save the form, click on the Save button in the Form Design toolbar.

Exercise 2

> Managers have asked to see data about each employee's pay rate and deductions on your form.
>
> Add a subform to the Employees form that shows Employee Pay Per Hour and Employee Deductions from the Pay table.
>
> Save and close the form.

Answer To Exercise 2

To add a subform to the Employees form that shows Employee Pay Per Hour and Employee Deductions from the Pay table, click on the Subform/Subreport button on the Toolbox and then draw the subform where you want it to appear. On the wizard screens, choose the Pay table as well as the Employee Pay Per Hour and Employee Deductions fields, and select Employee Number as the linking field. Use the default name for the subform.

To save and close the form, click on the Save button on the Form Design toolbar and then exit the window.

Exercise 3

> You decide to set the Employees form to display continuous records, to facilitate data entry and review.
>
> Open the Employees form in Design view.
>
> Set the form to display continuous records.
>
> Save and close the form.

Answer To Exercise 3

Click on the Employees form in the Database window, and click the Design button.

Click on the Properties button on the Form Design toolbar. In the Default View property, choose Continuous Forms. Exit the property sheet by clicking on the Exit button.

Click on the Save button on the Form Design toolbar.

Need To Know More?

 Litwin, Paul, Ken Getz, and Mike Gilbert. *Access 97 Developer's Handbook*, Sybex Inc., San Francisco, CA, 1997. ISBN 0-7821-1941-7. Chapter 8 contains an in-depth look at advanced form design topics.

 Viescas, John L. *Running Microsoft Access 97*, Microsoft Press, Redmond, WA, 1997. ISBN 1-57231-323-4. Chapters 14 and 15 provide detailed information about designing forms and subforms as well as adding special objects.

 www.e4free.com

The Advanced Form design page has detailed information about designing forms with advanced features, subforms, and multiple pages.

Advanced Queries

Terms you'll need to understand:

- √ Record grouping
- √ Equi-join
- √ Outer-join
- √ Multitable query
- √ AutoLookup
- √ Crosstab
- √ SQL

Skills you'll need to master:

- √ Using the Query Wizard
- √ Querying for top, first, and last records
- √ Creating multitable queries
- √ Creating AutoLookup queries
- √ Creating crosstab queries
- √ Using action queries
- √ Using parameter queries
- √ Creating SQL queries

Advanced queries expose the true power of relational databases by allowing you to compose information from practically any angle. You can join multiple tables several ways; format data to see the effects of two variables on a third; even program queries using SQL, the standard "plain English" language for creating and querying databases. Access 97 makes it easy with the Query Wizard, and understanding the choices available in each type—as well as the results displayed—is the key to using advanced queries effectively.

Using The Query Wizard

A very quick way to construct new queries is to use the Query Wizard. You can save lots of time by running through the wizard screens first, and then modifying the results later. We've waited until now to discuss the Query Wizards because they're much easier to use when you understand query basics.

Query Wizards come in four types:

➤ **Simple** Builds an ordinary select query.

➤ **Crosstab** Builds a query that displays the effects of two variables on a third.

➤ **Find Duplicates** Builds a query for finding duplicate values.

➤ **Find Unmatched** Builds a query for finding values that have no match in another table. See Table 12.1.

We'll use a Query Wizard from now on whenever we create a new query, but we'll always return to Design view to see what we've built or whenever we need to make changes.

Querying For Top Values, First And Last Records

Access 97 queries can group records to obtain summary data, as we discussed in Chapter 6. You might have noticed the First and Last selections in the drop-down box in the Total row. If you choose First, the query returns only the value of the first record for that field, and vice versa for Last. Of course, if you choose not to sort the records during the query, you'll simply get whatever record happened to appear first or last in the selected recordset.

Apart from the selections in the Total row, you can have the query return only records with the highest or lowest values by choosing a Sort Order (Ascending or Descending) and by setting Top Values (a combination button and text field

Table 12.1 Query Wizard types.		
Query Wizard Type	**Query Name**	**Query Purpose**
Simple	Action	Modifies the database by updating, appending data in a table, deleting data in a table, or making a new table.
	Parameter	Allows the user to enter the criteria for record selection.
	AutoLookup	Automatically obtains field values for a new record based on the linking field value.
	Select	Retrieves data from a table and displays it in a data-sheet for review.
Crosstab		Builds a query that displays the effects of two variables on a third.
Find Duplicates		Builds a query for finding duplicate values.
Find Unmatched		Builds a query for finding values that have no match in another table.

on the Query Design toolbar) to a number or percentage. Only those records that fall within the specified top value limits are displayed. For example, if you set Top Values to 5 and choose Ascending as the Sort Order for a numeric field, the query returns the records with the lowest 5 numbers in that field.

Task 1 Finding the highest-paid employees.

1. Click on the Queries tab in the Database window. Click on New, select Simple Query Wizard, and then click on OK. The Simple Query Wizard, shown in Figure 12.1, opens.

2. From the Tables/Queries drop-down box, choose Table:Employees. From the Available Fields drop-down box, choose Employee Number, and add it to the query by clicking on the right-arrow in the center. Do the same for the Employee Name field and then click on Next.

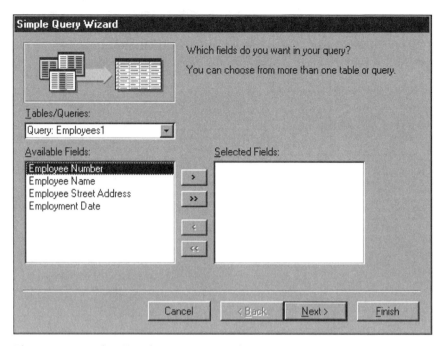

Figure 12.1 The Simple Query Wizard.

3. On the last screen of the wizard, enter "HighestPaidEmployee" and then choose Modify The Query Design. Don't enable the "Display Help on working with the query?" checkbox. Click on Finish.

4. Your new query (HighestPaidEmployee), shown in Figure 12.2, appears in Design view. Click on the Show Table button on the Query Design toolbar. The Show Table dialog box opens. Select the table named Pay and then click on the Add button. The Pay table is added to the query, and a one-to-one relationship should automatically be established.

5. Drag the Employee Pay Per Hour field onto the query design grid. Click on the Sort row, and select Descending. Click on the Top Values text box on the Query Design toolbar, and enter "1". Run the query by clicking on the Run button. The highest-paid employee is displayed.

The Top Values property on the query's property sheet works identically as the Top Values button on the Query Design toolbar. Keeping this in mind, you may wonder how the query knows which records to select when several fields are sorted. The answer is that the Top Values property works on the first field sorted upon, from left to right.

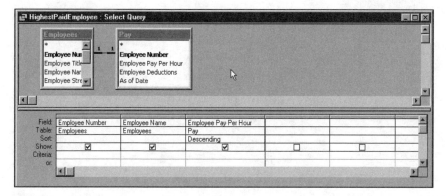

Figure 12.2   The HighestPaidEmployee query.

Creating Multitable Queries

Designing a query, especially a multitable query, is a little reverse-engineering job. You must decide what data you want and then determine the underlying data that will produce it as well as where that data resides.

Adding and deleting tables from queries is a key skill.

For instance, using the sample tables we've created so far, suppose you want to build a query that shows the names and teams of all employees who work for the Marketing Department. You need the Employees table, the Company Teams table, and the Department table, but how do you connect them? You must include the Team table as well as create *joins*.

Task 2   *Creating a query that joins three tables.*

1. Before doing this task, open the Team, Department, Charged Hours, and Company Teams tables, and make sure you have some data in them. In particular, make sure there are entries that show someone charging hours to the Marketing Department.

2. Click on the Queries tab in the Database window. Select Simple Query Wizard and then click on OK. The Simple Query Wizard opens.

3. Choose the Employees table from the drop-down box. Select and transfer the Employee Number, Employee Name, and Employee Team Number fields to the text area on the right-hand side of the screen. Next, select the Department table from the drop-down box. Then, select

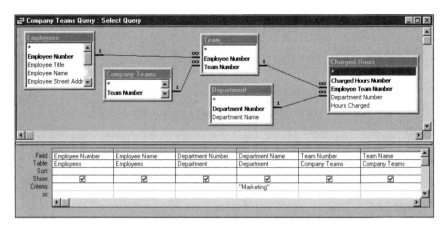

Figure 12.3 A multitable query with five tables.

and transfer the Department Number and Department Name fields to the text box. Finally, select the Company Teams table, and select and transfer the Team Number and Team Name fields to the text box. Click on the Next button.

4. The wizard automatically names the query for you (Company Teams Query is the name it chose). Change the name to Company TeamsQ1 and then click on Finish. The results of the query are displayed.

5. Click on the Design View button to open the query in Design view. Notice in Figure 12.3 that the wizard has included the additional tables required to complete the links, and has connected the tables for you. Make more room in the top half of the Design screen and rearrange the tables to get a better look at the linkages.

In the Design view in Figure 12.3, you see the tables that the Query Wizard has included in the query (in addition to the tables/fields that you specified when you constructed the query) as well as the join lines. You may recall from the work we did in Chapter 10 that joins can be of several types and that you can change the type of join by double-clicking on the join lines. The same holds true for queries. You can change join types, and their effect on the query's results is dramatic. The join types are:

➤ **Equi-join** Includes records where joined fields from both tables are equal.

➤ **Outer-join** Includes all records from one of the tables and only those records from the other table where the fields are equal. An outer join is said to be "right" or "left" depending on which table has all its records included.

Use the Query Wizard to make these types of joins.

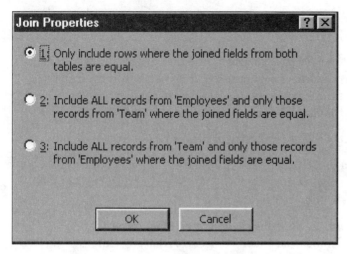

Figure 12.4   The Join Properties dialog box.

 If you double-click on the join lines in the Design View window, the Join Properties dialog box, shown in Figure 12.4, opens. It displays the three types of joins: equi-join and both types of outer-join. You can easily change the type of join by using this dialog box.

Creating An AutoLookup Query

AutoLookup is a multiple-table query used to look up and enter several items of data for you when you enter a single key piece of data. AutoLookup queries are frequently useful when you need to enter new data for an existing entry onto a form. For instance, suppose you're running a health spa and you have a table whose fields include ID Number, Name, and Weight. Each day your clients visit, you weigh them and record their weight. You can configure Access 97 to automatically look up a client's name from the Client table and fill it in for you when you enter that client's ID Number. AutoLookup queries perform this function on many records at the same time.

Task 3   Creating an AutoLookup query with the Query Wizard.

1. Before doing this task, open the Employee Paydays table, and enter some sample data.

2. Next, create a new query from scratch using the Design view. Add the Employees table and the Employee Paydays table. Access 97 automatically creates a one-to-many join line for you, from the Employee

Number field in Employees to the same field in Employee Paydays (see Figure 12.5).

3. From Employee Paydays, drag and drop the Payday Number field and the Employee Number field onto the design grid. Add the Employee Name field from Employees, and add the Pay Amount and Pay Date fields from Employee Paydays.

4. Save the query as PaydaysAuto and then close it.

5. Create from scratch a form that is bound to the PaydaysAuto query you've just made. Display the field list, and put all the fields onto the form. Save the form as PaydaysAuto.

6. Open the form in Normal view, and insert a new record. Enter an Employee Number, and you'll see Access 97 look up and insert the Employee Name and Pay Amount that correspond to that number.

Creating Crosstab Queries

Ordinary queries show data based on two variables: "How many golf stores are there in California?" (the variables are golf stores and California), "What is the average age of Southern California residents?" (age and Southern California), and so on. *Crosstab queries* show data based on three variables: "How many golf stores are there in California by ZIP code?" (golf stores, California, and ZIP code), "What is the average age of Southern California residents by income level?" (age, Southern California, and income level), and so on.

Looking at the results of a crosstab query, you would see, for example, golf stores across the top row (the X axis), ZIP codes down the left-most column (the Y axis), and the number of golf stores in each ZIP code as the data in each intersecting cell.

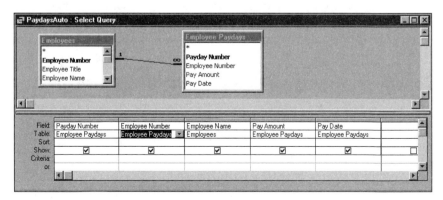

Figure 12.5 An AutoLookup query.

The Crosstab Query Wizard, shown in Figure 12.6, makes setting up a crosstab query simple. Just choose the underlying table or query, specify the variables on the X and Y axes, and it's done. These types of queries can be difficult to set up from scratch, so the Crosstab Query Wizard comes in handy whenever you need to compare data in this fashion.

Task 4   *Creating a crosstab query with the Query Wizard.*

1. Open the Company TeamsQ1 query in Design view, and add the Hours Charged field from the Charged Hours table to the design grid. Save the query as Company TeamsQ2.

2. In the Database window, with the Queries tab selected, click on the New button, select Crosstab Query Wizard, and then click on OK. On the first screen, select the radio button for displaying queries only and then choose the Company TeamsQ2 query as the source for your crosstab query.

3. On the next screen, choose Department Name as the row headings field and then click on the arrow to put it in the Selected Fields column.

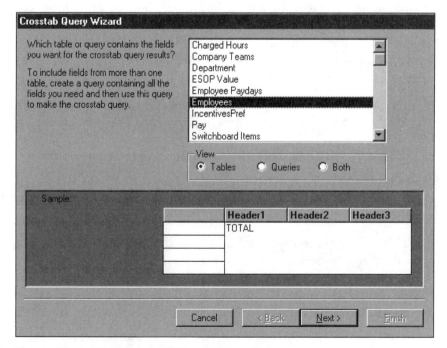

Figure 12.6   The Crosstab Query Wizard.

Notice that Department Name fills the sample results on the bottom of the screen. Click on Next.

4. On the next screen, the remaining fields are available to become column headings. Choose Team Name as the column headings field (notice that Team Name becomes the header for each column). Click on Next.

5. On the next screen, choose Hours Charged in the Fields box and Sum in the Functions box. The Yes, Include Row Sums checkbox should be checked by default (meaning an extra column of sums for each row is included in the results). Click on Next.

6. The final screen lets you rename the query as well as choose whether to open the query or go directly into Design view for further modifications. Keep the name that Access 97 gives the query (it chose Company TeamsQ2_Crosstab), and click on Finish. The results appear.

7. Add more data to all the involved tables, and run the query again until you get a nice cross section of data. It should then be clear to you just what a crosstab query is and how it works.

Using Action Queries

During the process of defining and building your database application, it's easy to overlook a critical part of successful application design—maintenance. Maintenance functions are discussed in more detail in Chapter 15, but for now, we need to examine the role of action queries in populating and updating the contents of your database.

Often, data originates in other applications (as we discussed in Chapter 7) or other databases. Sometimes, new reports or queries require that you merge data from several tables. Finally, it's not uncommon to make archive records from tables or queries and then remove those records from the main application.

Action queries help perform these functions by letting you make tables from queries, update records in batches, append records from one source or table to another, and delete selected records.

For instance, suppose you want to take a "snapshot" of all employees as of a particular date and store it in an archive database for future reference. Why would you need to perform such an action? Every time you make changes to employee records, you essentially destroy the old information, unless you store the "transactions" in an archive database.

Task 5   Creating a Make-Table query.

1. First, create a new database, and name it Archives. Close this database, open the test database again, and then click on the Queries tab of the Database window. Open the Employees1 query in Design view.

2. Choose Query|Make-Table Query from the menu. The Make Table dialog box, shown in Figure 12.7, appears. Enter the name "Employees3-15-98" for the new table and then click on the Another Database checkbox. Enter the file name "Archives.mdb" as the name of the database in which to insert the new table. Click on OK.

3. Click on the Run button. Then, save and close both the query and the test database (the query is saved as a Make-Table query).

4. Open the Archives database. You'll see in the Database window (see Figure 12.8) the table that your new query created. Close the Archives database.

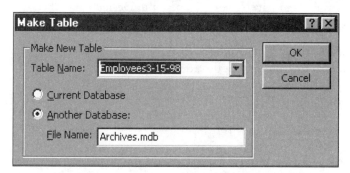

Figure 12.7   The Make Table dialog box.

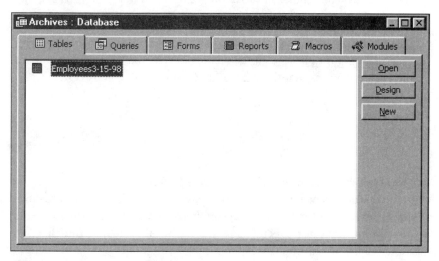

Figure 12.8   Your new query.

Update queries are extremely useful, because you can use the selective powers of queries to make simple or complex changes to any set of records you want. This means you can use one table to hold various blocks of records, and update all the records in a given block simultaneously without making any changes to other blocks.

Task 6   Creating an update query.

1. You have the pleasant task of giving everyone in the company his or her annual 25 percent raise (hey, it's just make-believe). Open the test database and then click on the Queries tab. Click on the New button to design a new query.

2. When the New Query dialog box opens, choose Simple Query Wizard, and follow the steps. Use the Pay table as the source for the query, and insert only the Employee Pay Per Hour field into the query. Name the query Annual Raise and have Access 97 open it in Design view when the wizard is finished.

3. Choose Query|Update Query from the menu. The design grid changes, and an Update To row appears. In this row, enter the value to which you would like to update that field for each record in the table. Enter the following in the Update To row:

```
[Pay]![Employee Pay Per Hour]*1.25
```

Entering this expression causes the query to find the current value in the Employee Pay Per Hour field (for each record), multiply it by 125 percent (which is equivalent to adding 25 percent to the original value), and insert the new value in the record when you run the query.

4. Save the query and then run it. Access 97 prompts you to confirm that you really want to update all the records (it tells you the record count and also mentions that there is no "undo" function). Choose OK.

5. Close the query and then open the Pay table. You should see the Employee Pay Per Hour values increased by 25 percent. If you didn't check the values first, reset them, and do it again to make sure you're getting the right values.

Append queries work by adding the records from one table to another. You frequently use them when you need to archive the same types of records over and over. A likely scenario is that you simply create your table once (as we did in Task 5) and then just append more records to it. That way, the table has multiple snapshots that you can pull up using a select query.

Task 7   *Creating an append query.*

1. Open the Employees1 query in Design view. It should currently be a Make-Table query. Click on Query|Append Query on the menu to begin the append query process. The Append dialog box opens.

2. The Append dialog box looks very similar to the Make Table dialog box, and it should have the name of the Employees3-15-98 table and Archives database already showing by default.

3. Click on the OK button and then click on the Run button. Access 97 warns you that you are about to append records to an existing table in another database. Click on OK.

4. Close the test database, open the Archives database, and then open the Employees3-15-98 table. The table should have the additional records you just appended.

Lastly, the delete query lets you delete specified records in batches, again according to whatever criteria you choose.

Task 8   *Creating a delete query.*

1. In the Archives Database window, click on the Queries tab. Click on the New button to start a new query. When the New Query dialog box opens, select Design View and then click on OK. A new query should appear with the Add Table dialog box open.

2. The only table available should be the Employees3-15-98 table, and it should already be selected, so click on the Add button to add it to the query.

3. Double-click on the title bar of the Employees3-15-98 table in the query to select all the fields and then drag them onto the query grid. All the fields should now be part of the query.

4. Notice the design grid has a row called Where. If you want to select specific records from a table for deletion, you add criteria just as you would for a normal select query. The only difference is that in this case, those records are deleted. For this example, we won't add any criteria.

5. Click on the Run button. Access 97 prompts you that you are about to delete records from the Employees3-15-98 table. Click on OK, save the query (name it DeleteEmployees), and then close it. Open the Employees3-15-98 table to confirm that the records have been deleted. Close the table and the Archives database.

Using Parameter Queries

Another very useful type of query is the parameter query. It works just like an ordinary select query, except that you get to insert the search value or criterion in a little dialog box each time the query runs, instead of redesigning the query. Although it might not seem like that much trouble to open a query in Design view and change the criterion, doing so is often not practical for users—and that's where the parameter query comes in handy.

Task 9   Creating a parameter query.

1. Open the test database and then open the Employees1 query in Design view. Choose Query|Select Query from the menu.

2. In the Employee Name field, enter "[Enter Employee Name]" in the Criteria row. The brackets and text tell Access 97 to treat the entry as a label for a dialog box that opens when the query runs. The idea is that the user sees the dialog box open, reads the label, and understands what value to enter. Access 97 uses that value to process the query with any other parameters that you have entered.

3. Run the query, and when the dialog box opens, enter an employee name that you know is in your database. The results should show the record or records for that name only.

You can enter parameters in more than one field, and you can specify the data type for each in the Query Parameters dialog box, shown in Figure 12.9, while you're in Design view (use the Parameters choice on the Query menu). Access 97 uses the Text data type by default, but you can set the data type to Number, for instance, if you know the parameter entered should always be a number.

Using SQL Queries

Microsoft Access 97 queries are based on the database command language Structured Query Language (SQL). All queries, even simple select queries designed with the design grid, are stored as SQL statements. You can design the most commonly used queries with the design grid, but some of them require knowledge of SQL.

SQL statements are based on the English language and attempt to follow a common logic. For instance, the SQL statement **SELECT** when followed by a list of fields directs the query to select (retrieve) specific rows and columns from database tables. Quite naturally, the next statement, **FROM**, when followed by a table name directs the query to use the table named to retrieve those rows and columns.

Figure 12.9   The Query Parameters dialog box for setting data types.

 Fortunately, you won't be required to write SQL from scratch, but you may need to know how to view the underlying SQL.

The easiest way to learn more about SQL is to design queries with the design grid and then view the SQL. Figure 12.10 shows the SQL view of the Employees1 query.

Task 10   Viewing the SQL in a query.

1. Open the Employees1 query in Design view. Choose View|SQL View from the menu.

2. Read the commands in SQL view. Notice the **WHERE** command (immediately following the **FROM** command). Choose View|Design View from the menu.

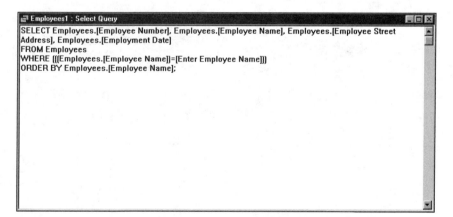

Figure 12.10   The Employees1 query in SQL view.

3. Enter "4" in the Criteria row of the Employee Number field.

4. Choose View|SQL View from the menu. Notice the **WHERE** command has changed to include the additional criterion you specified.

5. Close the Employees1 query without saving the changes.

Access 97's Query Wizard is the best starting point for you to perform many types of advanced queries. Often, queries are built from multiple tables with a variety of joins, and you have to be concerned with referential integrity. Action queries can perform much more than simply "pulling data," including appending and deleting records. More specialized types, such as crosstab and parameter queries, gather and present data focused precisely the way you want it. Finally, SQL queries give you complete control over query functions with a standard language that is widely used.

Practice Exercises

Exercise 1

> Another day, another data call. Your manager has asked for a listing of employees, as well as their names, street addresses, and phone numbers—for everyone in the local area code (555).
>
> Use the Simple Query Wizard to create such a query, using the Employees table as a data source.
>
> In Design view, enter the local area code and any other data necessary to retrieve employees whose phone numbers fall within it.
>
> Name the query LocalEmployees, save it, and then close it.

Answer To Exercise 1

To start the Simple Query Wizard, make sure the Queries tab is selected in the Database window and then click on the New button. Choose Simple Query Wizard from the dialog box that opens and then click on OK.

Choose Table:Employees from the drop-down box on the next screen. Then, add the Employee Name, Employee Street Address, and Employee Home Phone fields to the Selected Fields box. Click on Next. In the final screen, name the query, and save it, but make sure to select the Modify The Query Design radio button, because you're going to add some criteria.

In Design View, enter "555*" so that the query searches for phone numbers beginning with that number.

Click on the Save button. Close it by clicking on the Exit button.

Exercise 2

> Your manager now wants the same query to be automated, so that the database can be searched for lists of employees in any area code. You decide a parameter query is in order.
>
> Open the LocalEmployees query.
>
> Add the appropriate entry to make it into a parameter query that searches on the Employee Home Phone Number field.
>
> Save the query.

Answer To Exercise 2

Open the LocalEmployees query by selecting it and clicking on the Design button.

Erase the existing text in the Criteria row of the Employee Home Phone Number field, and enter "[Enter area code followed by *]".

Click on the Save button.

Exercise 3

The phone company has changed the area code for employees in the 555 area, from 555 to 565. You decide to create an update query to make the change, rather than changing each record by hand.

Create an update query.

Code it so that for every entry in the area code where the first three digits are 555, they are changed to 565.

Run the query.

Answer To Exercise 3

From the Database window with the Queries tab selected, click on the New button. Choose Design View when the New Query dialog box opens and then click on the OK button. From the Show Tables dialog box, choose Employees, and click on the Add button. Close the dialog box. Add the Employee Home Phone field to the query. Change the query to an update query by choosing Query|Update Query from the menu bar.

In the Criteria row, enter the following: Like "555*".

In the Update To row, enter the following: "565"+Right([Employee Home Phone],9).

Save and run the query by clicking on the Save button on the Query Design toolbar and then clicking the Run button on the Query Design toolbar.

Need To Know More?

 Litwin, Paul, Ken Getz, and Mike Gilbert. *Access 97 Developer's Handbook*, Sybex Inc., San Francisco, CA, 1997. ISBN 0-7821-1941-7. Chapter 5 contains lots of information about Access 97 SQL.

 Viescas, John L. *Running Microsoft Access 97*, Microsoft Press, Redmond, WA, 1997. ISBN 1-57231-323-4. Chapters 8, 9, and 11 provide detailed information about designing select, parameter, and SQL queries.

 www.e4free.com
The Query Design page has detailed information about designing many types of queries, and how to set up wildcards for retrieving selected data.

Advanced Reports

Terms you'll need to understand:

√ Styles

√ Templates

√ Autoformat

√ Avery number

√ Summary expression

√ Microsoft Graph editing screen

Skills you'll need to master:

√ Creating multitable reports (adding subreports)

√ Using report templates

√ Creating AutoFormat entries

√ Grouping data on a report

√ Sorting data on a report

√ Creating mail merge labels

√ Using summary controls

√ Using colors, images, and special effects

√ Creating charts

First impressions are everything. Because reports are usually printed, they tend to be the first (and sometimes only) view of your database that some people will ever get. Your reports must be easy to read and understand, contain exactly the data necessary, and convey that information as graphically as possible.

Access 97 installs with report styles that are designed by professionals, a good starting point for easy-to-understand documents. You, too, can design your own report templates. You can group data on a report into logical sections, add colors and graphics for eye-appeal, use multiple tables and subreports, and include custom pages with charts and graphs. Advanced reporting features ensure that low-quality printed output does not sabotage your hard work.

Creating Multitable Reports (Adding Subreports)

Multitable reports, like multitable forms and queries, combine the data from several tables or queries into one report. Multitable reports can contain data from tables with parent-child relationships as well as data from unrelated tables or queries.

When you use the Report Wizard, you can choose from several predefined report *styles* to give your report a professional look. It's easy to add punch to your report using styles in the Report Wizard, and then modify it in Design view until it looks just right.

 Make sure you've created a relationship (in the Relationships window) between the two tables before doing the next exercise. Access 97 does not let you combine the data from two tables in a report unless a relationship exists.

Task 1   Creating a multitable report with the Report Wizard.

1. Open the test database, click on the Reports tab, and then choose New. When the New Report dialog box opens, choose Report Wizard. The Report Wizard opens.

2. On the first screen, select the Employees table from the drop-down list. Then, select and transfer the Employee Number and Employee Name fields from the Available Fields box to the Selected Fields box.

3. Next, choose the Employee Paydays table, and transfer all of its fields except Employee Number. Click on Next. You should see a screen that resembles Figure 13.1.

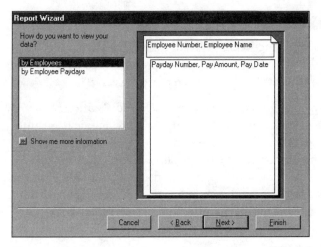

Figure 13.1 The third screen of the Report Wizard.

4. By default, your report shows your data by Employee, and this is what we want. Click on Next. On the next screen, you can choose additional grouping levels, but don't. Just click on Next.

5. On the next screen, click on the drop-down arrow on the first box and then select Payday Number as the field to sort on. Note that you can change the Sort Order by clicking on the Sort button on the screen, but don't change it.

6. On the next screen, choose your page orientation and your layout (you'll see examples on the screen). Also, make sure the checkbox that fits all the fields on the page is checked. Click on Next.

7. The second-to-last screen gives you several options for style, but just choose Corporate (unless you feel adventurous). Click on Next.

8. On the final screen, enter the name "EmployeePaydaysReport" and then click on Finish. Your report should open, and it should resemble Figure 13.2.

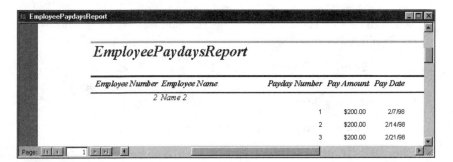

Figure 13.2 EmployeePaydaysReport.

Using Report Templates

In the previous task, we used the Report Wizard to add styles to our report. If you've used Microsoft Word or PowerPoint, you've probably used templates in addition to styles. Templates work a little differently in Access 97.

The default template named Normal is the only one included with Access 97. However, you can use any other report as a template by typing its name into the Report Template box on the Forms And Reports tab of the Options dialog box (under the Tools menu). Of course, this means you can create and use as many new templates as you like with a particular database, but only one at a time. Each time you want to use a different template, you have to go back into Options and change the name of the template in use. Unfortunately, the Options dialog box doesn't have a drop-down feature to let you easily switch to previously used templates.

 To use a template with another database, you must copy or export the report to that database. If you use your own template in one database and then open another database without copying or exporting the report to that database, the Options dialog box still shows the name of your template, but Access 97 uses the Normal template by default.

Once you've started your report using a template, you can make any changes you desire in Design view, just like you can with any other report. And if you want to make changes to the template, just change the underlying report in Access 97. All your new reports reflect the changes you've made when they are first created. Keep in mind, though, that a template doesn't create controls (even labels) on a report, so you'll still probably have a fair amount of work to do to each new report.

Task 2 Creating a report template.

1. Open the test database, click on the Reports tab, and then choose New. When the New Report dialog box opens, choose Design View. A new report in Design view opens.

2. Right-click on the Detail section, and choose Fill/Back Color on the shortcut menu. Choose a bright color, such as red, by clicking on it in the palette that appears. The Detail section turns bright red.

3. Save the report as Norm1. Close the report.

4. Choose Tools|Options from the menu bar. Click on the Forms/Reports tab. In this tab, type the name "Norm1" in the Report Template box, replacing the word *Normal*. Click on OK.

5. In the Reports tab of the Database window, click on New. When the New Report dialog box opens, choose Design View, and click on OK. The new report in Design view should have a bright red Detail section.

6. Exit the new report without saving it. Change Report Template back to Normal. Delete the Norm1 report.

Creating AutoFormat Entries

The formal term for the styles we used in the Report Wizard is *AutoFormat entries*. They are used to set the font, color, and border of controls (their properties don't apply to sections or backgrounds of the report itself). There are six AutoFormat styles already present when you install Access 97: Bold, Casual, Compact, Corporate, Formal, and Soft Gray.

To apply an AutoFormat entry to a control, just select the control and use the Format|AutoFormat dialog box, shown in Figure 13.3. You can also create your own autoformat by creating a control with properties set as you desire, then selecting the control and using the Format|AutoFormat dialog box. When you create your own AutoFormat entries, they show up in the list of entries available. You can delete the ones you make but not the ones that come with Access 97.

Task 3   Using AutoFormat entries in existing reports.

1. Open the test database, click on the Reports tab, and then open EmployeePaydaysReport in Design view.

2. Click on the label control that reads Payday Number to select it. Choose Format|AutoFormat from the menu bar. The AutoFormat dialog box opens.

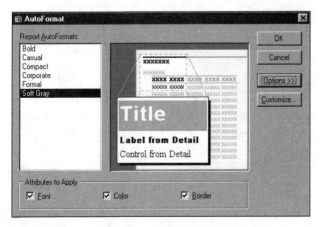

Figure 13.3   The AutoFormat dialog box.

3. The current style of this label is Corporate. Choose the Soft Gray style from the list. Notice that Access 97 shows you what it will look like in the preview section. Notice also that there are three kinds of styles in this Autoformat entry: Title, Label From Detail, and Control From Detail.

4. Before clicking on OK, click on the Options button. Another section of the dialog box opens. In this section, you can tell Access 97 which parts of the style to apply: Font, Color, and Border. Don't make any changes.

5. Click on the Customize button in the AutoFormat dialog box. Another dialog box (Customize AutoFormat) opens. In it, you can create, update, and delete AutoFormat entries. Again, don't make any changes. Close the Customize AutoFormat dialog box.

6. Click on OK to apply the new style to the label control you've selected. Redo the process by reopening the AutoFormat dialog box, selecting another style, and then clicking on OK.

You can create your own AutoFormat entries by creating a new blank report in Design view. Just add label and text box controls in the Report Header and Detail sections; specify font, color, and border properties for these controls; and then invoke the Customize AutoFormat dialog box as we did in Task 3. Choosing Create New AutoFormat Entry allows you to save the new format with its own name. It appears whenever you use the Report Wizard thereafter, unless you delete it from the list.

Grouping Data On A Report

In Chapter 8, we discussed some of the basics of grouping data on reports; now, it's time to delve into the subject in more detail. Reports are frequently about data in groups: employees by department, projects by employee, items by manufacturer, and so on. Of the various sections that make up a report, headers and footers for groups of data offer you the most control over how your data is displayed and summarized on your report.

You can group your data in a report using a single table or multiple tables; you can also group it into several levels. Each level can be summarized to show statistics for that level, and the summaries operate on all the records within each group *at its particular level*. For instance, if you create a report that groups employees by their state of residence and within state by their grade level, your report shows headers for state of residence as well as for grade level, and then your report details records for each employee.

Task 4   *Grouping records in a report.*

1. Open the test database, click on the Reports tab, and then open EmployeePaydaysReport in Design view.

2. Click on View|Sorting And Grouping from the menu bar. The Sorting And Grouping dialog box, shown in Figure 13.4, opens. Click on the Payday Number row to select it, and notice that the Group Header and Group Footer properties are turned off.

3. Set both of these properties to Yes. Headers and footers for Payday Number appear on your report.

4. Increase the height of the Payday Number header. Select the Payday Number control in the Detail section and then copy it to the clipboard. Click on the Payday Number header section to select that section and then paste the copied field into that section.

5. Resize the field to a larger square, move it to the left-hand side, make the font bold, and resize the font to about 16 points.

6. Save the report and then view it using the View button on the Report Design toolbar. Each payday should now be denoted by the Payday Number value within the Employee Number group.

Report sections, such as the report header and footer and the page header and footer, also help keep your data organized. Instead of listing column heading titles (using label controls) within each grouped section of the report, you can use the page header instead. That way, the column headings show up only once per page, even if the groups happen to repeat four or five times on a single page. Your reports will use less paper and be easier to read.

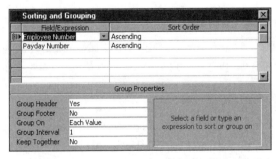

Figure 13.4   The Sorting And Grouping dialog box.

Sorting Data On A Report

Sorting and grouping are closely tied together. In fact, you sort data on a field and create group headers and footers using the same dialog box. You don't have to show each grouping level in its own section on the report, so you can sort records as finely as you like by adding more fields to the Sorting And Grouping dialog box. Just set the Group Header properties to No (this setting is the default) and then set the Sort Order to Ascending or Descending as you wish.

If you like, you can sort records at the table or query level before generating a report. Queries run prior to report generation automatically if a report is based on them, so you're pretty safe using this method. The downside is that several different reports may be based on the same query or table. If the reports use a different Sort Order, setting the table or query to a particular order does not work for them.

Creating Labels—Mail Merge

Another common type of report that doesn't really fit the typical description of a report is the mailing list (or mail merge). Mailing lists can print labels, print an address directly on an envelope, or print form letters. You can print the report directly from Access 97, or you can merge it with Microsoft Word. The advantage of using Word is that this program gives you extensive control over your document's format.

In either case, you start by creating a table that holds the values you wish to use for your mailing list. Then, you can format them as labels using the Label Wizard in Access 97, or you can use the Merge functions to inject the values into Word documents.

Task 5   Creating labels in Access 97.

1. Open the test database, click on the Reports tab, click on New, and then select Label Wizard and the Employees table. The Label Wizard opens (see Figure 13.5).

2. Notice the Avery Number listing, along with the dimensions and number of labels across. When you purchase labels for your printer, make sure you buy the right kind, or you'll have trouble matching sizes. If you have an odd size, you can customize a size using the Customize button at the bottom of the screen. Notice also that you can specify whether to use English or Metric units for label size, and you can specify Sheet Feed or Continuous paper stock. Click on Next.

3. On the next screen, you can set the font size and other text characteristics. Set the font to underlined italics by clicking on the checkboxes provided and then click on Next.

4. On the next screen, you can choose the fields to include and their placement on the label. Choose Employee Name and then click on the arrow button in the center to put it on the label. Press the Enter key to make a new line on the label, choose Employee Street Address from the list, and then put it on the label. Click on Next.

5. On the next screen, you can sort your labels as they print (by one or more of the fields). Choose Employee Name as the Sort field. Click on Next.

6. The final screen gives you the option of naming your label report (or using the default name supplied) and opening the labels in either Preview or Design view. Keep the default name, and click on Finish. The Labels report opens in Preview view. After reviewing it, close it. Your label report has already been saved with the default name in the Reports tab of the database.

Task 6   *Merging records with mail merge.*

1. Open the test database, click on the Tables tab, and then select the Employees table.

2. Click on the down-arrow on the Office Links button on the Database toolbar and then choose Merge It With MSWord from the menu. The Microsoft Word Mail Merge Wizard, shown in Figure 13.6, opens.

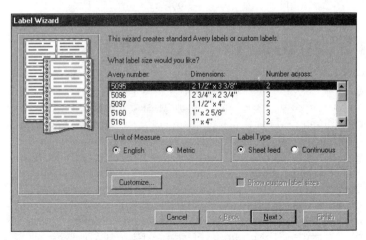

Figure 13.5   The first screen of the Label Wizard.

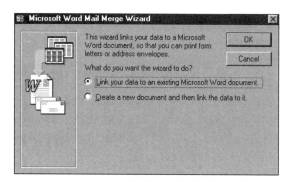

Figure 13.6 The Microsoft Word Mail Merge Wizard dialog box.

3. Choose Create A New Document And Then Link The Data To It (the second choice in the box) and then click on OK. Word starts with a new document open, ready for you to insert merge fields.

4. Click on the Insert Merge Field button from the Database toolbar in Word. This brings up a drop-down list of fields to choose from. Choose Employee Name. It appears on the new document. Press Enter to make a new line and then put Employee Address in.

5. Press Enter twice and then write a line of text as you normally would in Word (something like "This is a test of the mail merge functions in Word and Access").

6. Save the document as MailMergeTest. Click on the View Merged Data button on the Database toolbar to see your actual data in the Word document. Click on the first-, last-, and previous-record buttons on the Database toolbar to cycle through the records. Then, close the document and Word. You should be back in Access 97.

Using Summary Controls

In Chapter 8, we inserted calculated controls into a report. In this section, we'll discuss the particulars of summary controls and how to properly place and customize them in a report. Summaries are frequently used in reports to show the Sum, Average, Minimum, Maximum, Count, and other summarized data, and summary controls usually follow Detail sections in group, page, or report footers.

You can define the scope of the summary by using the Running Sum property of the control. The default for this property is No, meaning the summary reflects the results from the current Detail records. If you choose Over Group, the scope includes a summary of all records in the group; if you choose Over All, you see a summary of all records in the entire report.

Task 7   *Using summary functions with report controls.*

1. Open the test database, click on the Reports tab, and then open EmployeePaydaysReport in Design view.

2. Click on the unbound Text Box button on the Toolbox (if the Toolbox isn't visible, choose View|Toolbox to make it appear). Draw an unbound text box in the Payday Number Footer section. Click on the label attached to it (to select it) and then press Delete to get rid of it.

3. Right-click on the text box, and open its Properties dialog box. Click on the ellipsis in the Control Source area to open the Expression Builder. Use the Expression Builder to create an expression that reads:

```
=Count([Payday Number])
```

4. Close the Expression Builder.

5. Click on the Running Sum property area, and choose Over Group from the drop-down list. Close the Properties dialog box.

6. Preview the report. The number of paydays over the group should appear on the report. When a different employee group starts, the count should reset to 1.

Using Colors, Images, And Special Effects

After you study the material about placing images in forms, it should come as no surprise that you can insert pictures (images), add color, and otherwise use special effects to embellish and enhance your reports. Images can be bound to a table (as part of the records, say a photo of each employee) or unbound, like a company logo. You can use color with the report background or with objects drawn into the report. Other objects, such as charts, can be bound or unbound as well.

In addition, you can add page breaks to give the pages in your report a cleaner look. Doing so is especially important when groups of records tend to finish in varying places on the page.

Each section of the report has its own properties, and you can set the Back Color and Special Effects properties to display a multitude of colors as well as Flat, Raised, and Sunken effects. Adding graphics to reports is as simple as adding the proper bound field from the Field List, or inserting an image using the Insert Image button on the Toolbox. Finally, you can place background images on the report (and you can tile them in, if you like) using the Picture properties of the report.

Task 8   Tiling a background image onto a report.

1. Open the test database, click on the Reports tab, and then open EmployeePaydaysReport in Design view.

2. Report should be the object selected by default in the Object box on the Formatting (Form/Report) toolbar. Click on the Properties button on the toolbar to open the Properties dialog box for Report.

3. You can set six picture properties: Picture, Picture Type, Picture Size Mode, Picture Alignment, Picture Tiling, and Picture Pages.

4. First, set Picture Tiling to Yes. Doing so tiles the background image over the entire background.

5. Next, choose a picture from any clipart you have available by clicking on the Build button in the Picture property area. A dialog box (labeled Insert Picture) that lets you choose image files from any directory on your hard drive displays.

6. Leave Picture Type as Embedded. This means the picture will become a part of the report, rather than be linked to every time the report is opened.

7. Leave Picture Size Mode as Clip. Stretch and Zoom make the image fill up more of the report. We don't need to make these adjustments here, because we're using tile to cover it all, but you might use these features if you have an image that doesn't tile well.

8. Leave Picture Alignment set to Center.

9. Leave Picture Pages set to All Pages. You can set this so only certain pages contain the image, but that's not what we want to do here.

10. Save the report, and preview it. The image you've chosen should be tiled all over the background. Close the report.

Creating Charts

We discussed using charts in forms in Chapter 11. Like forms, reports can contain charts based on values in the underlying tables. Access 97 includes quite a variety of charts you can add: Column, Line, Bar, Pie, and so on. Figure 13.7

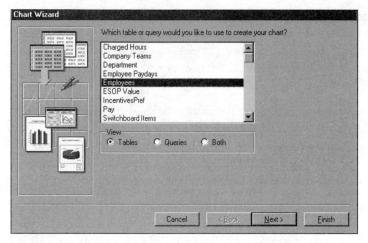

Figure 13.7   The first screen of the Chart Wizard.

shows the first screen of the Chart Wizard. We'll cover editing charts in addition to making them.

Charts that are placed in different sections of a report reflect the contents of those sections rather than the contents of the report as a whole.

Task 9   Placing a chart on a report.

1. Open the test database, click on the Reports tab, and then open EmployeePaydaysReport in Design view.

2. Use the cursor to increase the height of the report header section. Choose Insert|Chart from the menu bar. Draw the outline of your chart in the report header section using the cursor.

3. After you let go of the mouse button, the Chart Wizard appears. Select the Pay table as the source of the data for the chart. Click on Next.

4. On the next screen, choose the Employee Number and Employee Pay Per Hour fields to be included on the chart. These are going to be the X and Y axes of your chart. Click on Next.

5. On the next screen, choose the type of chart you'd like. In this case, choose the second from the top-left—3D Column chart. Notice the variety of charts available. Click on Next.

6. On the next screen, you can manipulate which of the two fields is which axis. You can also preview the chart to get an idea of what it will look like on the report. Leave the axes alone, but click on the Preview button to see your chart. It should have several bars, one for each employee, with the rate of pay going up the Y axis. Close the preview, and click on Next.

7. On the next screen, you can link the chart to fields within the report itself, so that the chart changes for each record. Doing so might have been a good idea if we had put the chart in the Detail records. However, it's in the header, so we'll leave the linking fields blank. Press the Delete button to delete the contents of each text box on this screen. Click on Next.

8. On the final screen, change the name of the chart to PayBarChart, leave the Legend setting as is (Yes), and click on Finish. Save the report, and preview it. Your chart should look the same as the preview, except that it is in your report now.

9. Go back to Design view (click on the Design View button on the toolbar) and then right-click on the Chart object. The Microsoft Graph editing screen, shown in Figure 13.8, opens.

10. Choose Chart|Chart Type from the menu bar. Change the Chart Type to another type. Close the editing screen, and examine the results of your change in the finished chart. Close the report without saving your latest change.

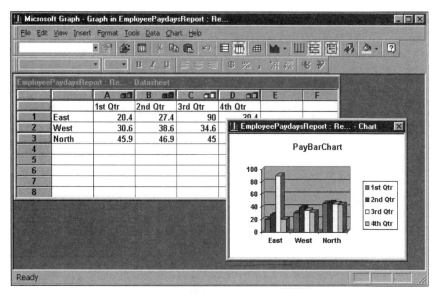

Figure 13.8   Editing a chart.

Multitable reports, like multitable forms and queries, make full use of the properties of relational databases. Report templates replace days of hard work, allowing you to spend perhaps a few hours experimenting with the various preformatted reports available. Intelligent use of the sections of a report, as well as summary controls, produces information rolled up exactly as you desire. Colors, special effects, charts, and graphs combine to get your message across visually.

Macros bring a new level of functionality to your database as a whole. The AutoRun macro can set the stage for your users every time the database is opened. Macros can synchronize forms, run at startup, or even run from other macros. Access 97 automates macro creation as well as gives you tools for debugging macros. We'll cover macros in Chapter 14.

Practice Exercises

Exercise 1

> Your manager asks you to create a report that lets him review employees according to what they work on. You decide to create a report that groups employees by team.
>
> Create a report using the Report Wizard.
>
> Make the report group employees by team, and include the employee name, street address, team number, and team name.
>
> Save the report as EmployeesOnTeam. Leave the report open.

Answer To Exercise 1

To begin the report, click on the New button in the Database window (with the Reports tab selected, of course). Select Report Wizard and then choose the Team table on the first screen of the wizard.

Add both fields from the Team table, add the Team Name field from the Company Teams table, and then add Employee Name and Employee Street Address from the Employees table. On the next screen, choose to view the data by Company Team.

Use the default choices until you get to the last screen, name the report EmployeesOnTeam, and then save it by clicking on Finish.

Exercise 2

> Your manager asks you to modify EmployeesOnTeam so that it counts the number of employees assigned to each team and places that number at the bottom of each team grouping.
>
> Put the EmployeesOnTeam report into Design view.
>
> Create a Company Teams footer.
>
> Add a text box, and make it display the number of employees in the group, using Employee Name to count by.
>
> Save the report.

Answer To Exercise 2

To put the report in Design view, click on the Design button on the Report Design toolbar.

To add a Company Teams footer, choose View|Sorting And Grouping from the menu. Click on the Company Teams field in the dialog box, click on the Group Footer property, and change it to Yes. Close the Sort And Grouping dialog box.

In the Company Teams footer, draw a text box by clicking on the Text Box button on the Toolbox and then drawing with your mouse. Right-click on the text box, and choose Properties from the shortcut menu.

Click on the Control Source area once and then click on the Build button to bring up the Expression Builder. In the Expression Builder, enter the following code:

```
=Count([Employee Name])
```

Click on OK to close the Expression Builder, close the properties sheet, and save the report.

Exercise 3

> Your new boss doesn't like the look of your reports and asks you to change the background image.
>
> Change the background image on the EmployeePaydaysReport to the flower.wmf image.
>
> Tile the image.
>
> Save the report.

Answer To Exercise 3

Open the EmployeePaydaysReport in Design view by clicking on the Design button in the Database window with the EmployeePaydaysReport selected. Click on the Properties button on the Report Design toolbar. Click in the Picture property, and find the flower.wmf image file (it should be in the Program Files/MicrosoftOffice/Clipart/Popular folder).

Click in the Picture Tiling property, and change it to Yes.

Close the properties sheet, and save the report.

Need To Know More?

 Litwin, Paul, Ken Getz, and Mike Gilbert. *Access 97 Developer's Handbook,* Sybex Inc., San Francisco, CA, 1997. ISBN 0-7821-1941-7. Chapter 9 contains topics about report design.

 Viescas, John L. *Running Microsoft Access 97,* Microsoft Press, Redmond, WA, 1997. ISBN 1-57231-323-4. Chapter 18 is dedicated to advanced report design.

 www.e4free.com

The Advanced Reports page has more information about how to use Access 97 to create great-looking reports and solve annoying problems.

Creating Macros

Terms you'll need to understand:

- √ AutoExec
- √ Argument
- √ Object
- √ Run command

- √ AutoKey
- √ Single-stepping
- √ Conditions

Skills you'll need to master:

- √ Creating macros
- √ Referencing object properties
- √ Adding actions and arguments
- √ Creating macro groups
- √ Running macros in macros
- √ Running macros at startup
- √ Using Access 97 keystroke syntax

- √ Troubleshooting macros
- √ Assigning macros to events or command buttons
- √ Commenting-out macro commands
- √ Referencing macros in macro groups

Long ago, programmers and users alike noticed that some tasks were very repetitious. In fact, repetitious tasks are what computers were designed to eliminate in the first place. Programmers can simply program a function to perform these tasks over and over till they're done, but what can users do? Creating macros is the answer.

Any good database program allows you to create macros. Access 97 automates quite a bit of the process, and puts your macro into a consistent logical format that is easy to create and modify. All the actions your macro can take and all the objects upon which those actions can be performed are at your fingertips; you only have to point and click.

Understanding Macros

Originally, macros were designed to let the user automate repetitive tasks by "recording" keystrokes or mouse clicks, then playing them back at the push of a button (usually one of the function keys, F1 through F12). Access 97 includes a dialog box (see Figure 14.1) that helps you build macros that perform a wide array of functions. You can set macros to send standard keystrokes and mouse clicks as well as to pause for input or to make decisions.

You can use macros for opening forms, checking the contents of fields, querying a table, applying filters, resizing windows, displaying messages, printing reports, synchronizing forms, quitting an application, and so on. You can run macros in several ways:

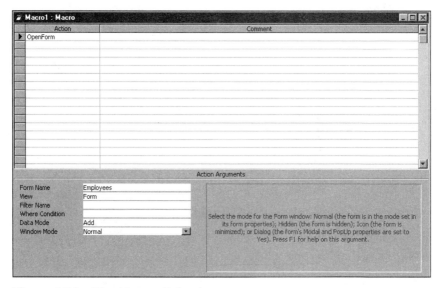

Figure 14.1 The Macro dialog box.

➤ By selecting them in the Database window and clicking on the Run button

➤ By clicking on a command button attached to a macro

➤ By pressing keys (the macro's author sets the combination)

➤ By responding to events, such as a form opening or a certain value being entered in a field

Essentially, macros contain a list of commands that run when the macro is activated. These commands take place one-by-one (including commands to open other macros) until all the commands have been completed. In addition, you can set the macro to test for certain values and proceed along different paths of actions based on the value found.

Creating And Running A Simple Macro

Macros use actions to accomplish their tasks; *arguments* tell them the particulars of the action you want them to perform. Some arguments are names of objects, and others are values. In Task 1, we use the OpenForm action to open a form. We have to include the name of our Employees form because the macro needs to know the name of the form to open as one of its arguments.

Task 1   *Creating a macro to open a form.*

1. Start Access 97, and open the test database. Click on the Macros tab.

2. Click on the New button to open the Macro dialog box.

3. Click on the top row of the Action text field. A list of available actions appears. Choose OpenForm.

4. In the bottom section of the dialog box (Action Arguments), click on the Form Name text field. A list of form names appears.

5. Choose Employees.

6. Below that, in the Data Mode field, click on the down-arrow, and choose Add.

7. Click on the Save button. Doing so begins saving the macro.

8. A small dialog box in which you can enter the name of the macro you're saving appears. Enter "AddEmployees" and then click on OK.

9. You now have a macro that opens the Employees form in Add mode when you run the macro from the Database window. You should be in the Macros tab of the Database window with the AddEmployees macro selected, so click on the Run button to run it. If it runs OK, close the Employees form.

Running Macros At Startup

Ideally, any application you create should hide most of the details from the users. During startup, when a database is opened, Access 97 looks for and runs a macro called AutoExec. AutoExec is unique from all others only by its name; as with any other macro, you can program it to perform any functions you like. Using AutoExec to open a "Welcome to this database!" form effectively hides the rest of your application from users, and, from there, you can limit their actions to only those you've programmed in.

The AutoExec macro runs automatically when the application starts, *unless the user holds down the Shift key during the startup sequence.* It is usually used with the Switchboard form, so that the switchboard is the first form that users see. This is particularly useful for applications where you want users to use only the interface you create, from the very start.

Task 2   Creating an AutoExec macro.

1. In the Macros tab of the Database window, click on the New button to open the Macro dialog box.

2. Click on the top row of the Action text field. A list of available actions appears. Choose Hourglass.

3. In the bottom section of the dialog box (Action Arguments), the Hourglass On field should read Yes.

4. Click on the next Action field (in the top portion of the screen). From the drop-down list of actions, choose Echo.

5. In the bottom of the dialog box, change the action for Echo On to No, and enter the following text in the Status Bar Text field: "Opening Employees database".

6. Click on the next Action field, activate the drop-down box, and choose OpenForm from the list of actions.

7. In the bottom of the dialog box, click on the Form Name field, and choose Switchboard from the list. Leave the other arguments as they are. Note the Macro dialog box for the AutoExec macro in Figure 14.2.

8. Click on the Save button and then save the macro with the name AutoExec.

9. You now have a macro that opens the Switchboard form automatically whenever the database is opened. Close the database and then reopen it. The Switchboard form should automatically open.

Creating AutoKey Macros

In many popular application programs, you can create macros that run when a particular keystroke combination is used. After users are familiar with the keystrokes and their associated actions, they can accomplish common tasks more quickly, hopefully becoming more productive. You can assign keystroke combinations to Access 97 macros; they are called AutoKey macros (see Figure 14.3 for an example of an AutoKey macro under construction).

Only one AutoKey macro group per database is allowed, and, if you assign keystroke combinations that are predefined by Access 97 (such as Ctrl+C or Ctrl+X), your AutoKeys take precedence. However, it is best to leave the predefined Access 97 combinations out of your AutoKey macro group, because you could confuse your users.

 Note that if you enter keystroke combinations in other macro groups, they do not run; only the macro group can perform this function.

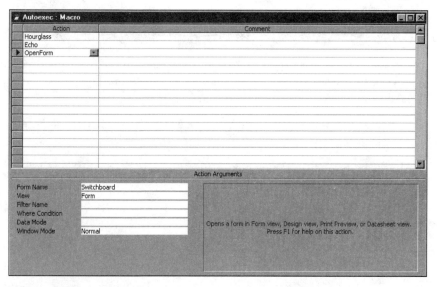

Figure 14.2 The Macro dialog box for the AutoExec macro.

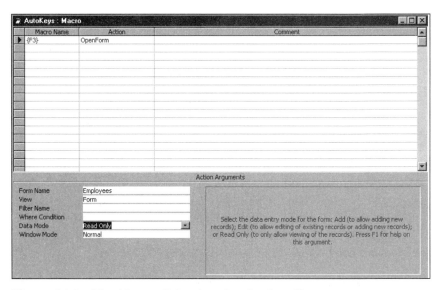

Figure 14.3 The Macro dialog box for the AutoKeys macro group.

AutoKey macros don't have normal names. They use a special syntax that sets them equal to a keystroke combination. For instance:

➤ {F3} means the macro is activated when users press the F3 key

➤ +{F3} or ^{F3} means the macro starts when users press Shift+F3 or Ctrl+F3

➤ ^G or ^7 means the macro starts when users press Ctrl+G or Ctrl+7

Task 3   Creating an AutoKeys macro group.

1. In the Macros tab of the Database window, click on the AddEmployees macro to select it and then click on the Design button. The AddEmployees macro should open in Design mode.

2. Click on the Macro Names button. The Macro Names column appears. Click on the top row of the Action text field. Type "{F3}".

3. In the bottom of the dialog box, change the Data Mode to Read Only.

4. Save the macro with the name AutoKeys. Close the macro.

5. Press the F3 button. The Employees form should open in read-only mode.

6. Close the Employees form.

Referencing Object Properties

Within a macro, you can reference and affect the properties of database objects and the controls inside them. For instance, you can set the value of a control in a form to a particular number. This capability is handy when you have various uses for the same form or report, and want to change values accordingly.

Task 4   Referencing a control with the SetValue action.

1. Click on the Forms tab in the Database window, and select the PaydaysAuto form. Open it in Design view.

2. Add an unbound field (in the location shown in Figure 14.4), open its Properties dialog box, set the Format property to Currency, and set the Decimal Places property to 2.

3. Name the new control Minimum Wage. Close the Properties dialog box.

4. Add a label next to the new unbound field. Enter "Minimum Wage=".

5. Save the form, and close it. Click on the Macros tab of the Database window. Click on the New button.

6. In the first Action cell of the Macro dialog box, choose the OpenForm action. Specify PaydaysAuto as the form to open. Leave the other fields as they are.

7. In the next Action cell, choose SetValue. Click on the Build button in the bottom of the dialog box (next to the Item field). The Expression Builder opens.

8. From the left-hand box, double-click on Forms|All Forms|PaydaysAuto. The controls of the PaydaysAuto form appear in the center box.

9. Double-click on the Minimum Wage control. The following expression appears in the text-entry box at the top of the Expression Builder:

```
[Forms]![PaydaysAuto]![MinimumWage]
```

10. Close the Expression Builder by clicking on the OK button. The expression appears in the Item field.

11. Enter "425" in the Expression field just below the Item field in the Macro dialog box. Save the macro with the name LookupPaydays.

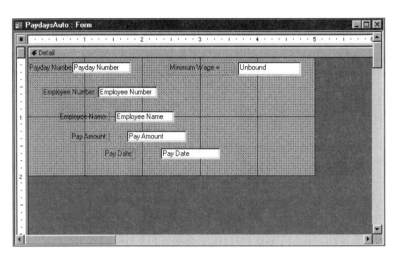

Figure 14.4 The PaydaysAuto form with a new field, Minimum Wage.

12. Close the macro. Run it from the Macros tab in the Database window using the Run button.

13. The PaydaysAuto form should open, and the Minimum Wage control should display "$425.00".

Creating Conditional Macros

Another nice feature of macros is that you can set conditions for activation. If you want to keep a macro from operating unless a certain condition is met, just build the condition into the macro, and the condition restricts its operation. Doing so is especially useful when you need to choose among several macro actions based on user input or current data.

Conditions are defined by expressions entered into the Conditions column on the same row as the macro name and action. The expression can take data from any valid object in the database and must evaluate to either True or False. If the condition is False, the macro is ignored (as well as any other macro actions tied to it with an ellipsis in the Conditions column); if the condition is True, all macro actions associated with the condition are performed.

Task 5 Creating a conditional macro.

1. Click on the Macros tab in the Database window, and select the LookupPaydays macro. Open it in Design view.

2. Click on the Conditions button to display the Conditions column. In the first free Conditions row (below the existing actions OpenForm and SetValue), click on the text area, and click on the Build button. The Expression Builder opens (see Figure 14.5).

3. Using the Expression Builder, enter the following condition:

```
[Forms]![PaydaysAuto]![Pay
Amount]<[Forms]![PaydaysAuto]![MinimumWage]
```

4. Click on OK. The Expression Builder closes, and the expression is entered into the Conditions field.

5. In the Action column, choose MsgBox.

6. In the bottom of the dialog box, enter this message: "This person earned less than minimum wage".

7. In the Type field, choose Information. In the Title field, enter "Part-Time Employee".

8. Save the macro, close it, and then run it from the Database window using the Run button.

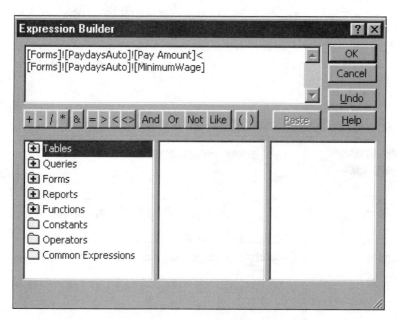

Figure 14.5 The Expression Builder with a condition.

Macros In Events Or Command Buttons

Starting a macro should be convenient. Creating macros to run at startup makes it quite convenient for you, the developer. But suppose you're building an application for users, and you want them to be able to initiate the macro at a given point. You can assign the macro to an event or to a command button on a form. Assigned to an event, the macro starts automatically whenever the event is activated. If a macro is assigned to a command button, the user can start it whenever the form is open. In the next section, we do both in the context of creating a macro group.

Creating A Macro Group

You can consolidate macros into groups for organizational purposes. After all, you may accumulate quite a few macros for any given function or set of functions, and sometimes it's easier to manage them if they are grouped according to function.

To construct a macro group, you put several macros into one macro dialog box, each denoted by its name in the Macro Name column (you can display this column by clicking View|Macro Names from the menu bar when you're in Design mode). To run a specific macro from a macro group, you enter the name of the macro group followed by a period and then the name of the macro. You can activate the macro from another macro using the RunMacro command or from an event.

Task 6   Running a macro within a macro group.

1. Click on the Macros tab. Click on the New button to open the Macro dialog box.

2. Click on the Macro Name button to display the Macro Name column. Enter the name "Macro1" in the first row of the Macro Name column.

3. In the Action column, choose the OpenForm task and then choose the Employees form on the bottom of the dialog box. Leave the other settings as they are.

4. Insert a Beep as the second action.

5. In the next row, enter the name "Macro2" as the second macro.

6. In the Action column, choose the OpenReport task and then choose the EmployeePaydaysReport on the bottom of the dialog box. Change the View entry to Print Preview (from Print). Insert a Beep as the second action.

7. Save the Macro as Mgroup and then close it.

8. Open the PaydaysAuto form, and place a command button on the form. Open its properties, and enter the name "Mgroup" next to the OnClick property. Put the form in Normal mode, and click on the Command button.

9. Although you might expect nothing to happen, because you didn't specify one of the macro names, you should see the first macro run but not the second. Close the form and reopen Mgroup in Design mode.

10. Put the cursor in the top row, and click on the Insert Row button. A blank row appears. Save the macro, and close it.

11. Open the PaydaysAuto form, and click on the command button. Nothing should happen. To run the macros, change the reference in the OnClick property to read "MGroup.Macro1" or "MGroup.Macro2". Either of these entries should make your first or second macro run, respectively.

Troubleshooting Macros

Naturally, creating macros isn't an exact science, and it's simply inevitable that you'll find errors in yours, especially as they grow more complex. In fact, creating macros is one technique programmers use to develop prototypes of applications they intend to formally program in Visual Basic or VBA later on. Therefore, Access 97 comes with some valuable troubleshooting and debugging tools that help you find and correct your errors.

One of those tools allows you to cause Access 97 to single-step through a macro. To activate single-stepping, you use the Single Step button on the Macro Design toolbar in the Design mode of a macro (but don't forget to go back and click on the button again to turn it off; all of your macros will single-step until you turn off the feature). You can actually see the actions your macro is taking as it runs, and you have complete control over what it's doing with the dialog box that pops up during each step.

Another tool lets you comment-out macro commands. To do so, type "False" in the Conditions column of the command you wish to disable. When the macro is next run, that particular command won't be implemented, allowing you to see if that command was causing the problem.

Task 7 Single-stepping through a macro.

1. Click on the Macros tab and then click on the LookupPaydays macro to select it.

2. Click on the Design button to open the macro in Design mode.

3. After the macro is open, click on the Single Step button to activate the single-stepping function. Notice that the button is now pushed in; it stays that way for all macro execution until you reset it.

4. Close the macro (there's no need to save it).

5. With the LookupPaydays macro selected, click on the Run button. The macro should execute the first step and then a dialog box should pop up (see Figure 14.6).

6. Click on the Step button. The macro should execute another step.

7. Continue clicking on the Step button until the macro executes the remaining steps.

8. Open the macro again in Design mode, and reset the single-step function by clicking on the Single Step button again. Close the macro.

Macros are the automated equivalent of keystrokes, mouse clicks, and keyboard data entry. Their main advantage is they are recorded and automatically repeated until some repetitive task is completed, saving you time (as well as your sanity). Building macros using Access 97 is fairly automated; all actions and objects (to be acted upon) are available in the New Macro window. You can combine several macros into a group as well as assign them to events, command buttons, and the toolbars. You can run macros at startup or from inside other macros, and they can open and synchronize forms. Access 97 also contains tools for debugging your macros.

As database administrator, you may be called upon to apply and manage security, repair, backup, replication, and synchronization of your database applications. You might need to analyze your database for performance and then tune it appropriately. Finally, you need to prepare documentation for future database administrators so that they can understand your application and its characteristics. We will cover these topics in Chapter 15.

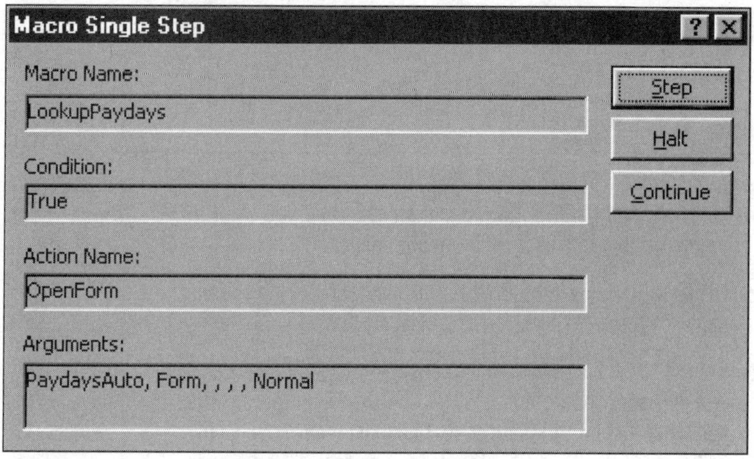

Figure 14.6   The Macro Single Step dialog box.

Practice Exercises

Exercise 1

> Your application is getting more use than ever, and you want to create a macro that makes it easier to administer.
>
> Create a blank, unbound form. On the form, create command buttons that open each form. Near the forms, put labels that describe them.
>
> Create a macro for each form that opens the form, and place that macro in the appropriate event of its command button so it is activated when the button is pressed. Make the macro open each form in Form view with the Normal Windows mode. Name each macro after the form that it opens.
>
> Save the form as Administrative.

Answer To Exercise 1

Use Design view to create a blank, unbound form. Use the Toolbox button for command buttons (with the wizard tool turned off) to create command buttons and the Label button to draw the labels.

Make a button and label for each form.

Go to the Macros tab of the Database window, and click on the New button. In the Action column, choose OpenForm. In the Action Arguments area, enter the name of each form (you can choose it from the drop-down list), and use the defaults from there.

After naming and saving the macro, go back to the Administrative form, and open the properties sheet for each command button. In the OnClick event, enter the name of the macro associated with that button.

Save the form with the name Administrative by clicking the Save button and entering a name for the form.

Exercise 2

Your application is getting more use than ever, and you want to create a macro that automates some repetitious functions.

On the Employees form, create a command button.

Build a macro that sets the value of all fields to zero or blank spaces.

Save the macro as Cleared. Place the macro in the command button in the appropriate event.

Save the form.

Answer To Exercise 2

Open the Employees form in Design view by clicking on the Design button in the Database window (with the Forms tab selected). Create a command button by clicking on the Command tool on the Toolbox and drawing the button on the form with the mouse. Minimize the form.

Start a new macro by clicking on the New button on the Database window (with the Macros tab selected). Choose the SetValue function for your first action. Then, find the appropriate item, and enter it in the Arguments area (the item is the name of the control or field you want to set to zero or blank spaces). In the Expression area, enter either zero or blank spaces.

Save the macro as Cleared, and close it. Maximize the form, and open the command button's property sheet. In the OnClick event, enter the name of the macro. Close the property sheet, and save the form.

Exercise 3

One of the data entry folks is complaining about having to click to get a frequently used report open for preview, and wants to know if there is a way to use a keystroke to get the same action accomplished. You come to the rescue with an AutoKey macro.

Create a macro that opens the EmployeePaydaysReport.

Make the macro execute when the F5 key is pressed.

Save the macro as AutoKeys.

Answer To Exercise 3

In the test database, click the New button from the Database window (with the Macros tab selected, of course).

Display the Macro Names column by choosing View|Macro Names from the menu bar. Enter "{F5}" in the Macro Names column. Click in the Action column, and choose OpenReport from the drop-down list. Click in the Report Name area of the Action Arguments and then choose EmployeePaydaysReport from the drop-down list. Choose Print Preview by clicking in the View area of the Action Arguments.

Click on the Save button, and enter the name AutoKeys (erase the previous AutoKeys macro if necessary). Click on Save to finish saving the macro.

Need To Know More?

 Klander, Lars and Dave Mercer. *Access 2000 Developer's Black Book*, The Coriolis Group, Scottsdale, AZ, 1999. ISBN 1-57610-349-8. Chapters 10 and on provide an overview of the inner workings of Access 2000.

 Litwin, Paul, Ken Getz, and Mike Gilbert. *Access 97 Developer's Handbook*, Sybex Inc., San Francisco, CA, 1997. ISBN 0-7821-1941-7. Chapter 2 contains an informative review of the events that Access 97 uses and how the event model works.

 Viescas, John L. *Running Microsoft Access 97*, Microsoft Press, Redmond, WA, 1997. ISBN 1-57231-323-4. Chapters 19 and 20 provide detailed information about creating and modifying macros.

 www.e4free.com

The Access Macros page has more information about how to use Access 97 to create macros.

Managing Database Objects

15

Terms you'll need to understand:

√ Database password

√ Back up

√ Rename

√ Encrypt

√ Encryption key

√ Decrypt

√ Compaction

√ Replication

√ Documentation

√ Conflict resolution

Skills you'll need to master:

√ Copying, renaming, and deleting database objects

√ Saving and securing database objects

√ Repairing and compacting database objects

√ Replicating and synchronizing databases

√ Splitting a database

√ Analyzing and improving database performance

√ Documenting database objects

Depending upon the purpose of the application you are creating, you may need to apply formal security measures, network your database, tune it for performance, and document it carefully for future administrators. Not all applications may need this level of effort, but having the tools available to perform these actions is the mark of a high-quality database program.

Access 97, of course, lets you do all these tasks in an automated and friendly way. In order to successfully administer your database, you should know what choices Access 97 offers and what results they produce.

Copying, Renaming, And Deleting Database Objects

When you have the Database window open, any item you click on is selected (highlighted). Once an object is highlighted, you can copy, rename, or delete that item using toolbar or menu functions.

I like to keep database object names similar so I can easily tell which ones go with which. For instance, the J1 query would support the J1 report. Older versions of Access let you use the same name for queries and reports, but Access 97 doesn't. The current convention is to include an abbreviation of the object name in the beginning of the name you choose for an object. For example, a form object named Customers would be named frmCustomers, using frm as the abbreviation for the word *form*.

Task 1 Copying, renaming, and deleting database objects.

1. Open the test database, click on the Forms tab, and then click on the Employees form to select it.

2. Click on the Copy button. The object is copied onto the clipboard, just like any other image or piece of data.

3. Click on the Paste button. A small dialog box (shown in Figure 15.1) opens. It asks what name you would like for your new object. Enter "EmployeesNew" and then click on OK. The EmployeesNew object should appear in the Database window.

4. The EmployeesNew form should already be selected. Click on it once to begin the renaming process. It should become editable. Enter the name "NewEmployees" and then click outside the area. The form should take on the new name.

Figure 15.1   The Paste As dialog box.

5. The NewEmployees form should already be selected, so click on Edit|Delete. An information box that asks if you're sure you'd like to delete the object opens. Click on OK to delete the NewEmployees form.

Saving And Securing Database Objects

With Access 97, all database objects and data are combined into one file. One advantage of this arrangement is it's easier to save and back up your applications; a disadvantage is that the file can get large. As with all important data, you should back up your database frequently.

Just for the record, *backing up* means copying your data to a secure place, whether that is a floppy, a network drive, or a tape cartridge especially designed for the purpose. A useful application is typically used quite often, so its data changes quite often. Backing up frequently is a necessity to maintain an up-to-date copy, so you need a backup method that is very easy to perform.

Backing Up Your Database Files

You can back up your database in many ways, but the basic process consists of simply copying your database file to a safe place. You can also use a method as simple as copying to and pasting from the clipboard. The database file contains all the data and the objects you've created, so it can get quite large. You can copy small databases (under 1.4MB in size) to an ordinary 3.5-inch floppy disk. However, the majority of your databases will most likely be large enough to require some other backup medium (such as a tape backup, Zip or Jaz drive, or optical storage medium). Of course, if you have a backup program, it might be able to split larger database files into smaller components that can fit on several floppy disks; however, this is a cumbersome backup method you'll probably dislike.

Task 2   Backing up a database file.

1. Close the test database. Minimize Access 97, and start Windows Explorer (click on Start|Programs|Windows Explorer).

2. Find the Test.mdb file. Put a disk in your A: drive, and copy the file to it (just click on and drag the file to the A: drive).

3. Close Windows Explorer. Maximize Access 97.

Setting A Database Password

Another aspect of keeping your data and database safe is to set a password. This is just a preliminary form of database security, but it does begin to protect your data from unauthorized access.

This kind of password is called a *database password*. When you set a database password, everyone who wishes to use the database must enter the password before they are granted access. However, once they are in, no other measures are available to prevent them from taking any actions they desire, unless you've set user-level security.

 A good first step to perform, prior to setting a password on a database, is to make a backup copy (as we've done) and store it in a safe place.

Task 3   Setting and removing a database password.

1. The test database should already be closed (this procedure starts with a closed database). Click on File|Open Database (note that if you choose to open the database from the File menu's list of recently opened databases, you do not have the opportunity to choose the Exclusive option). The Open dialog box appears.

2. Click on the Exclusive checkbox, click on the Test database to select it, and then click on the Open button. The Test database opens in Exclusive mode.

3. Click on Tools|Security|Set Database Password. The Set Database Password dialog box opens (see Figure 15.2).

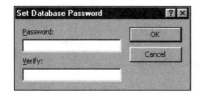

Figure 15.2   The Set Database Password dialog box.

4. Enter a password in the top field (Password) and then enter the same password again in the Verify field. Click on OK.

5. Close the Test database and then reopen it. A dialog box that requests you to enter the password for the database appears (see Figure 15.3). Enter the password, and open the Test database.

6. Close the Test database and then reopen it in Exclusive mode.

7. Click on Tools|Security|Unset Database Password. A dialog box that requests your current password opens. Enter it, and click on OK. The password is now unset.

Encrypting A Database

Encryption is the process of encoding a file and exchanging characters with other characters, in a sequence known only to the encryption program. Encrypted files can be read only with an *encryption key*, usually contained within the program that performed the encryption. Reversing the process is called *decryption*.

Encrypting a database provides an additional level of security, because it makes the database unreadable by word-processing or utility programs. Not everyone is aware of this, but much of the data in a database is stored on the hard drive in files that contain text, and many ordinary programs can read that text. Encryption scrambles the text so it can't be read directly from the database files.

Task 4   Encrypting and decrypting a database.

1. Close the test database (this procedure fails if the database is open, even if another person has it open). Choose Tools|Security|Encrypt/Decrypt Database. The Encrypt/Decrypt Database dialog box opens (see Figure 15.4).

2. Select the test database by clicking on it (the files displayed should include the Test database; if not, use the file-finder functions available in the dialog box). Click on OK. Another dialog box opens. It asks you what name to save the encrypted database as.

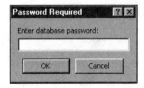

Figure 15.3   The Password Required dialog box.

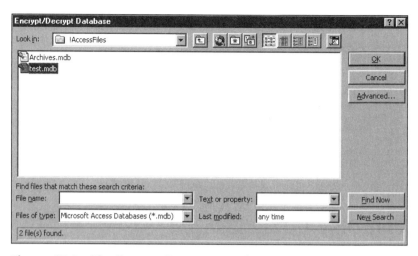

Figure 15.4 The Encrypt/Decrypt Database dialog box.

3. Enter "Entest.mdb" and then click on Save. With no further prompts, Access 97 saves the database in encrypted form using the name you provided.

4. Click on File|Open Database. You should see the new file name in the Open dialog box. Click on Cancel.

5. Choose Tools|Security|Encrypt/Decrypt Database. When the dialog box opens, select the Entest database, and click on OK.

6. When the Decrypt Database As dialog box opens, click on the Test database to save the decrypted database over the existing Test database. Click on Save. Access 97 asks you if you want to replace the existing database. Click on Yes. With no further prompts, Access 97 decrypts the Entest database and saves it over the existing Test database.

 The encryption/decryption process fails if there is not enough room on disk to save the encrypted database, or if user-level security has been established and you don't have the correct permissions.

Repairing And Compacting Database Objects

Power outages inevitably occur. If you are working with a database application when one happens, it might become damaged and unstable. Access 97 includes tools that can repair such damage. In some cases, however, the database may be beyond repair. Nevertheless, it's worth a try.

Another common maintenance task is to compact your database. Whenever you delete tables, the database may become fragmented and use disk space inefficiently. The compacting process defragments the database and frees disk space.

Task 5   *Repairing and compacting a database.*

1. Open the test database (you can repair a database that is open or closed).

2. Choose Tools|Database Utilities|Repair Database.

3. Access 97 automatically repairs the open database and responds with a message that it has successfully repaired the database. Click on OK.

4. Choose Tools|Database Utilities|Compact Database.

5. With no further prompts or messages, Access 97 automatically compacts the open database

Replicating And Synchronizing Databases

Replicating a database means making more than one copy of it (that is, one for your desktop and one for your portable computer or for someone else on your network). You can use replicas independently. The idea is to make sure records in both computers stay up-to-date. Bringing both sets of records to the same condition is called *synchronizing*. Therefore, to work effectively on the road and at home, you must replicate and synchronize your database.

Access 97 provides you with a variety of replication tools, some of which are available only if you are running the Developer edition. You can replicate and synchronize databases using the menu bar, using the Briefcase tool, programmatically with Data Access Objects (DAO), and with the Replication Manager. We cover using the menu to perform replication.

The Replication/Synchronization Process

The replication process starts with a database that has not been replicated. Once you replicate a database, Access 97 converts the original database into a Design Master. This means, it becomes the model upon which replicas are based. If it becomes damaged, you can use a special command to assign Design Master status to another, undamaged replica.

As you add records and data, the replicas become unsynchronized; at some point, you should synchronize them to make the data identical across all replicas once again. Access 97 employs a command (Resolve Conflicts) that permits you to view conflicting updates and decide which one should be accepted.

Note that when databases are synchronized, all databases accept records and data from each other as long as no conflicts are present. This means that neither database (not the Design Master nor the replicas) takes precedence over the other.

Database Replication Changes Database

In order to perform replication and subsequent synchronization properly, Access 97 makes some changes to your database. These include changes to the AutoNumber function (all new AutoNumbers become random); the size of the database file (it increases); and the addition of tables, fields, and properties (for replication tracking and control purposes). You should make a backup copy of your database and store it in a safe place prior to beginning the replication process, in case an unexpected result occurs.

Task 6   Replicating a database using menu choices.

1. With the test database open, choose Tools|Replication|Create Replica.

2. Access 97 asks you if you want to close the database. Click on Yes. An information box opens. It recommends that you create a backup copy of the Test database, and suggests a name and location for it.

3. Click on OK to make the backup copy that Access 97 recommends. Another dialog box opens. It asks where you wish to put the replicated database, and offers a name for it (starting with Replica Of).

4. Click on OK to accept the recommended location and name.

5. You should now have both the original database (saved as a copy with the extension .bak), a Design Master, and a replica of the original. Click on File|Open Database to verify that these files exist. If they do, close the Open Database dialog box. If not, the procedure has failed, so try it again.

 Using Access 97 menu choices to perform replication functions requires that Briefcase DLLs be installed on your system, even if you don't use the Briefcase Manager to perform the replication. You can install them from your installation disk using a custom install if they are not already installed on your system.

How Synchronization Works

Assuming you've replicated a database and have added different data to the copies, synchronization updates each copy with the data in the others. Of course, when data differs, only one version of the data can take precedence. Access 97 therefore needs some mechanism for establishing which is which. That mechanism is called *conflict resolution*.

Access 97 stores data about conflicting records in special tables. Among these special tables are MSysSidetables, MSysErrors, MSysSchemaProb, and MSysExchangeLog. You can see these tables if you make system objects visible.

After you perform the synchronization function, you should check to see if conflicts have occurred and, if so, correct them. Then, all your data is updated properly, and you can go back to work.

Task 7   Synchronizing replicas and correcting conflicts.

1. With the test database open and the Tables tab selected, choose Tools|Options to open the Options dialog box. Click on the View tab. You should see a screen like the one in Figure 15.5.

2. Click on the checkbox for System Objects, under Show. Click on OK. In the Database window of the test database, you'll see many additional tables, as in Figure 15.6.

3. Choose Tools|Replication|Synchronize Now. The Synchronize Database 'test' dialog box opens (see Figure 15.7). Note that you have the option of converting the replica into the Design Master.

4. Click on OK to accept the file Access 97 suggests, which should be the replica you just made. When synchronization is complete, Access 97 reports success and asks if you'd like to close and reopen the database in order to view whatever changes have occurred.

5. Click on OK. Viewing the tables in the Database window, you'll notice no MSysSidetables or MSysSchemaProb tables exist, whereas MSysErrors and MSysExchangeLog are present. This is because there were no changes to the data in either table, so no conflicts occurred.

Splitting A Database

Many of us work on a local area network (LAN). As database applications grow more sophisticated and usage climbs, effective performance declines unless you take steps to improve database architecture. One of those steps is splitting the database.

In this context, *splitting the database* means creating two new databases, one with the underlying tables and one with the rest of the database objects. The tables database goes on the LAN inside a server. Servers usually have more processing horsepower and larger and more secure hard drives, so there's plenty of room for new records and searches to be performed more rapidly. And the load on the network is reduced, because data is all that's being transmitted.

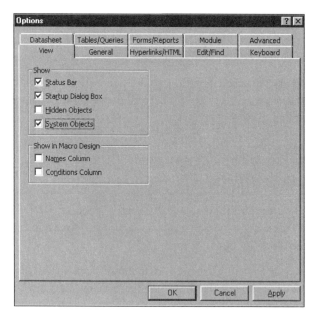

Figure 15.5 Making system objects visible.

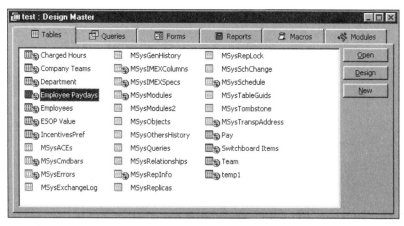

Figure 15.6 System objects in the Tables tab of the Database window.

Figure 15.7 The Synchronize Database 'test' dialog box.

You can distribute the rest of the objects to individual computers across the LAN. Each user uses the same data, but can create new queries, forms, and reports designed specifically for his or her own needs. The changes don't affect other users.

Task 8   Splitting a database.

1. With the test database open, choose Tools|Add-Ins|Database Splitter. The initial screen of the Database Splitter Wizard opens (see Figure 15.8). Access 97 asks you if you want to split the database now.

2. Click on Split Database. Another dialog box opens. It suggests a name and location for the back-end database (consisting only of tables).

3. Click on OK to accept the suggestions Access 97 makes. The next message you should see tells you the database has been successfully split. You can check this by choosing File|Open Database and verifying the existence of the file named test_be.mdb.

Analyzing Performance

As your database grows, you add new functions according to users' needs, and this usually means new fields. Too many fields in a table, or redundant data, can cause poor performance. Access 97 has tools that automatically analyze table structure and make recommendations for improvement. You can even have the adjustments made automatically for you.

Task 9   Improving database performance.

1. With the test database open, choose Tools|Analyze|Performance. The Performance Analyzer dialog box, shown in Figure 15.9, opens. It gives you the opportunity to select which objects in the database you wish to

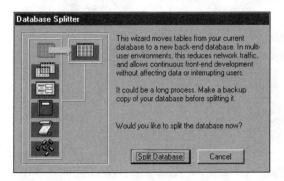

Figure 15.8   The initial screen of the Database Splitter Wizard.

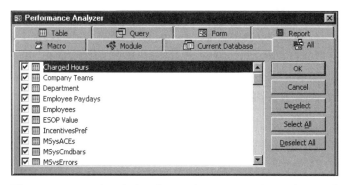

Figure 15.9 The dialog box where you select objects for performance analysis.

analyze and possibly improve. Click on the All tab and then the Select All button.

2. Click on OK to start the analysis process. Shortly, Access 97 produces a screen like the one in Figure 15.10, with recommendations for improvements.

    Note the first suggestion, regarding the fact that the database has not been saved in a fully compiled state. At the bottom of the Performance Analyzer dialog box is additional information about this suggestion.

3. Click through the suggestions, and note how the additional information at the bottom of the box changes. Each suggestion is categorized as

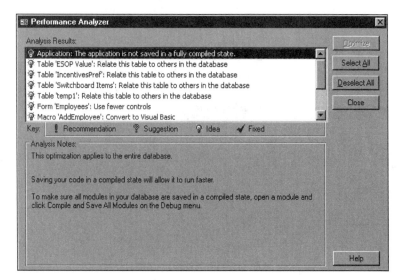

Figure 15.10 The dialog box with Performance Analyzer results.

Recommendation, Suggestion, Idea, or Fixed (meaning Access 97 has taken it upon itself to make the change it notes). If Access 97 can make the change within this wizard, the Optimize button becomes active.

Documenting Database Objects

Ever try to figure out how someone constructed a database, and what the purpose for each field and object was? If you have, you understand the importance of good documentation. Without it, it's very possible that the next database administrator will have to scrap the entire application and start over.

Fortunately, Access 97 includes tools that automatically document key features of your application: fields, properties, even relationships between tables. You can easily print out definitions for individual objects in Access 97 or for all objects in the current database.

Task 10   Printing object definitions.

1. With the test database open, choose Tools|Options to open the Options dialog box. Then, click on the View tab. Click on the System Objects checkbox to make system objects once again invisible and then click on OK.

2. Choose Tools|Analyze|Documenter. The Documenter dialog box appears.

3. In the Documenter dialog box, you can choose which object type you'd like to document by clicking on the appropriate tab. Choose All Object Types.

4. You can also select which options you choose for printing tables, and fields, and indexes (see Figure 15.11). Click on the Options button to display your options, but don't make any changes.

5. Click on OK to begin the process of documenting objects in the database. This may take several minutes.

6. The end result should be a rather long report that details every aspect of the database's structure. You can print it out if you like, but a better choice is to simply review it for the information you want.

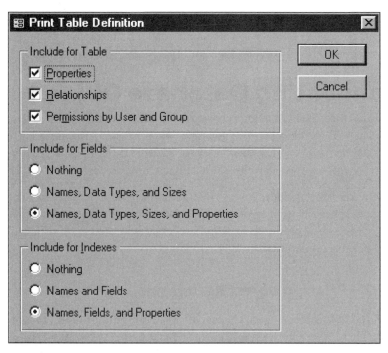

Figure 15.11 Setting options for printing documentation.

Practice Exercises

Exercise 1

> You've been working on your staging version of the database for awhile, and you need to clean up some of your experimental objects that no longer serve any useful purpose.
>
> Delete the Administrative form.
>
> Delete the command button for clearing values on the Employees form.
>
> Delete the Cleared macro.

Answer To Exercise 1

To delete the Administrative form, select it in the Database window (with the Forms tab selected), and press the Delete key.

To delete the command button from the Employees form, open the form in Design view, select the command button, and then press the Delete key.

To delete the Cleared macro, select it in the Database window (with the Macros tab selected), and press the Delete key.

Exercise 2

> Your database is in production now, and you want to begin preventing unauthorized users from misusing it.
>
> Set a database password (pwrd1) on the Test database.
>
> Remove the database password on the Test database.
>
> Change the database password on the Test database.

Answer To Exercise 2

To set a database password, close the database and then open it in Exclusive mode. Choose Tools|Security|Set Database Password. Enter your password, verify it, and then click on OK.

To remove the database password, close the database and then open it in Exclusive mode. Choose Tools|Security|Unset Database Password. Enter the password, and click on OK.

To change the database password, remove the existing password and then set the new password.

Exercise 3

It's time to clean up the database, and you have a few stray objects you need to get rid of.

Delete the DWP and EmployeesOnTeam reports.

Change the name of the LocalEmployees query to AreaEmployees.

Answer To Exercise 3

Delete the two reports by selecting them and pressing the Delete key.

Change the name of the LocalEmployees query to AreaEmployees by selecting the query and clicking twice (with a short pause between clicks) and then enter the new name.

Need To Know More?

 Klander, Lars and Dave Mercer. *Access 2000 Developer's Black Book*, The Coriolis Group, Scottsdale, AZ, 1999. ISBN 1-57610-349-8. Chapters 10 and on provide an overview of the inner workings of Access 2000.

 Litwin, Paul, Ken Getz, and Mike Gilbert. *Access 97 Developer's Handbook*, Sybex Inc., San Francisco, CA, 1997. ISBN 0-7821-1941-7. Chapters 13 and 14 contain tons of in-depth information about database management techniques as well as putting the final touches on your applications.

 Viescas, John L. *Running Microsoft Access 97*, Microsoft Press, Redmond, WA, 1997. ISBN 1-57231-323-4. Chapters 23 and 24 provide comprehensive information about managing databases, security, and replication.

 www.e4free.com
The Access Application Management page has examples of optimization techniques, security configurations, and general database management.

Web Functionality

Terms you'll need to understand:

√ Hyperlinks

√ Universal Resource Locator (URL)

√ Universal Naming Convention (UNC)

√ World Wide Web (WWW)

√ Ecommerce

√ Hypertext Markup Language (HTML)

√ Tags

√ Common Gateway Interface (CGI)

√ JavaScript

√ File Transfer Protocol (FTP)

√ Telecommunications Control Protocol/Internet Protocol (TCP/IP)

√ Active Server Pages (ASP)

√ Internet Database Connector (IDC)

√ Personal Web Server (PWS)

Skills you'll need to master:

√ Designing Web pages

√ Importing and exporting Web documents

√ Creating hyperlink fields

√ Creating hyperlinks for the Web and for Microsoft Office 97 products

√ Building order forms for Internet use

√ Printing reports for your Web site

It's safe to say that everyone working in computers (and possibly everyone on the planet) has encountered some information about the Web. The Web is changing communications and commerce on a grand scale probably not seen since the invention of writing, or TV, or the telephone. Regardless of all the hype about Hypertext Markup Language (HTML), the real secret to effective Web sites is database interactivity. You can program databases to customize (or individualize) a Web site for each user—automatically and on-the-fly. The real magic, the real potential of the Web, is only just beginning.

Access 97 incorporates Web functions into your database at a very fundamental level, and, if you run an Internet Information Server (IIS) with Active Server Pages (ASP), you can let users reach into the database for all kinds of information, even build a completely automated business. Understanding the functions allowed and how they relate to the Web is the secret of mastering Web database power.

Understanding The Web And Access 97

The Web isn't a *thing*, per se. It's simply a subset of the Internet, which uses Telecommunications Control Protocol/Internet Protocol (TCP/IP) as its common language. As with English, anyone who "speaks" TCP/IP can communicate with anyone else who understands it. The Web is the most popular of the software services that are standard on the Internet, but email is actually the most used. Other services include File Transfer Protocol (FTP), Internet Relay Chat (IRC), the Usenet (newsgroups), and Telnet (a remote operator protocol).

The Web is popular because of the graphical nature of Web pages. The original reason for the Web, however, was to post information for worldwide distribution. More recently, commercial and organizational sites have started using the Web to perform transactions, especially sales transactions. Commercial transactions over the Web are called *Ecommerce*, and projections indicate it will grow extremely rapidly over the next 10 years, eventually encompassing much of today's business-to-business and business-to-consumer commerce.

Access 97 and other database programs are so important to this trend because most organizations have their inventory, sales, and shipping data in the form of databases. If a business can connect this information to the company's Web site, it can come close to automating the entire business. Access 97 is also important because members of an organization can easily share this information via an internal Web site, or *intranet*.

To publish on the Web, you need Web space—whether it's on your company's Web server or rented from an Internet Service Provider (ISP)—browser software, and some kind of access connection. Your message (Web page) is constructed in HTML text files and might also use image files, media files, Java, VBScript, and even CGI scripts.

The first crude Web pages used HTML and image/media files exclusively. Now, however, most Office 97 programs (including Access 97) can convert their output to HTML. Therefore, you can store Universal Resource Locators (URLs)—www.e4free.com, for instance—in your database (allowing users to browse the Internet or your intranet directly from your database) as well as output the contents of your database as an HTML report. In fact, Access 97 lets you output a table, form, query, or report to the Web in static or dynamic HTML.

The term *Internet* refers to the open, public network of networks that use TCP/IP. The term *intranet* refers to an internal network that uses the same software services and protocols, but is accessible only to those inside a certain company. The term *extranet* refers to a portion of an organization's intranet that is open to a restricted set of users outside the firewall (a *firewall* is software that prevents unauthorized entry to a company's internal network, while allowing access to the Internet from inside the company).

The *Hyper* in Hypertext Markup Language stands for *hyperlinks*. Hyperlinks represent a new way of perusing and accessing information in a nonlinear fashion. You'll want to be familiar with how to create them in order to take advantage of their power in your databases.

Creating Hyperlink Fields In Access 97

A hyperlink in the traditional sense contains the Internet address of a Web site, such as www.microsoft.com. An Access 97 hyperlink is a specific data type and has several additional components. It actually stores three items of data separated by the number sign (#):

➤ **Display text** The text that actually displays (like a link on a Web page). If you include no display text, Access 97 displays the address itself.

➤ **Address** The URL or Universal Naming Convention (UNC) from which a hyperlink retrieves a file when the user clicks on the display text.

➤ **Subaddress** The specific destination within the file. For example, if you want the file to open halfway down the page, include a subaddress in the link.

Hyperlinks are stored as plain text in Access 97, like this:

```
DisplayText#Address#Subaddress
```

Office 97 applications can open ordinary links by starting the browser, or they can open links created by other Office 97 apps by starting the app and displaying the file.

To create a hyperlink field in Access 97, you can put a field in a table and simply set the data type to Hyperlink. Following that, create a text box on a form using the Hyperlink field, and you can enter your link. The easiest way is to use the Insert Hyperlink dialog box, shown in Figure 16.1.

Although you can use the Insert Hyperlink dialog box to enter the URL and subaddress of your link, you can't enter the display text. For that, you must use the Display Text entry area on the menu bar, as we discuss in the following task.

Task 1   Creating a Hyperlink field in a table and form.

1. Open the test database. Create a new table in Design view with the following fields and data types: Department Number (Number, Long Integer, Indexed with no duplicates, primary key), Department Web Page (Hyperlink), Author (Text, 50 characters), and Most Recent Update (Date).

Figure 16.1   The Insert Hyperlink dialog box.

2. Save the table with the name DWP and then close it.

3. Using the Form Wizard, create a form based on the DWP table. Use the default choices in the wizard, including all fields.

4. Name the form DWP, and let the wizard open it for data entry.

Task 2   Entering data in a Hyperlink field.

1. In the DWP form, enter a department number ("1" will do).

2. Right-click on the Department Web Page field. A shortcut menu opens. Choose Hyperlink|Edit Hyperlink.

3. In the Insert Hyperlink dialog box, enter the URL in the Link To File Or URL text area. Enter "www.e4free.com/examcram/ch16department/". Leave the subaddress area blank. Close the dialog box by clicking on OK.

4. Right-click on the Department Web Page field once again to bring up the shortcut menu and then choose Hyperlink. An additional portion of the menu opens. It reveals the Display Text data entry area (see Figure 16.2). Enter "Department Page" in the Display Text area. Click on a location outside the area to close the menu. The words you entered appear in the field, highlighted and underlined.

5. In the Author field, enter your name.

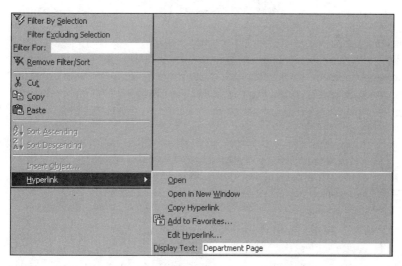

Figure 16.2   The Display Text area on the shortcut menu.

6. In the Most Recent Update field, enter today's date.

7. Close the form.

How HTML Works

HTML is not a programming language per se. Rather, it is a set of commands that instruct your browser how to display text, graphics, tables, frames, and more esoteric file formats within a Web page. When you create a Web page, you're writing HTML commands in a universal format that all browsers understand (at least most of the commands, because Microsoft and Netscape keep trying to outdo one another with special extension commands that sometimes aren't processed on the opposing browser).

HTML commands don't include program structures, such as if...then constructs (as a result, people don't think of it as a programming language). Instead, the HTML commands (commonly called *tags*) tell browsers what text to make boldfaced, what to make italicized, what to make a header, where to end a paragraph, where to insert an image, and so on. The tags look like this:

```
<HTML>
<HEAD>
<TITLE>This is the title of your page</TITLE>
</HEAD>
<BODY>
This is the body of your page, and your logo goes here:
<IMG SRC="mylogo.gif">
</BODY>
</HTML>
```

The tags can be upper- or lowercase (it doesn't matter to the browser), and the browser rewraps text according to the size of your browser. Of course, the preceding Web page is a very simplistic example, but it conveys the idea.

 To see and review the HTML source code underneath a Web page, click on View|Source on the menu bar of your browser. Doing so comes in especially handy when you're troubleshooting a published Web page that isn't performing as expected.

Because HTML marks up ordinary text, and because there are tags that you can use to create tables, the creators of Access 97 (and most other modern applications) have incorporated the ability to export documents in HTML format. One common use for this ability is in conjunction with databases and order forms.

Publishing For The Web

After you've created a database in Access 97, you can use the Publish To The Web Wizard to automatically build a complete Web page that references the database from your Web site. To start the wizard, use the File|Save As HTML menu choice. As it states on the first screen (shown in Figure 16.3), you can create Web pages from datasheets, forms, and reports, and each page is one Web page on your Web site. Notice on the first screen there is a grayed out choice that indicates you can use the wizard to modify previously created Web publication profiles (the process you are going through creates a publication profile: the set of choices you make is one). Except for that, the first screen is information only.

Task 3 Publishing the Department Web Page table and form as HTML.

1. With the test database open, choose File|Save As HTML on the menu bar. The first screen of the Publish To The Web Wizard opens.

2. Click on the Next button. The second screen opens (shown in Figure 16.4). Five tabs are available: Tables, Queries, Forms, Reports, and All Objects. The Tables tab is selected by default.

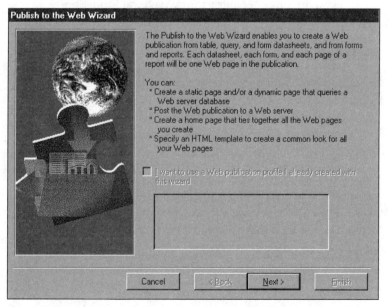

Figure 16.3 The first screen of the Publish To The Web Wizard.

3. On the Tables tab, click on DWP to select the DWP table for export.

4. Click on the Forms tab and then click on the DWP form to select it for export. Notice that if you were in a hurry and wanted to select all objects, you could use the Select All and Deselect All buttons with any of the tabs. Click on the Next button.

5. On the third screen of the wizard (shown in Figure 16.5), you have the opportunity to enter an HTML template file, which allows you to maintain a consistent look on all your pages. Leave that text box blank, and skip to the next screen by clicking on the Next button.

6. On the fourth screen (shown in Figure 16.6), you can save your objects in one of three ways. The first is Static HTML, which is read-only. The other two are Dynamic HTX/IDC (Microsoft Internet Information Server) and Dynamic ASP (Microsoft Active Server Pages). Both of these file formats can query and output from your database—as long as they are on IIS or Personal Web Server (PWS) Web servers (both IIS and PWS are Microsoft Web servers). You can also choose to use a variety of different formats depending on the object. Select Static HTML, and click on the Next button.

7. On the fifth screen (shown in Figure 16.7), you specify the location to which you want to publish your Web pages. I've chosen a local directory, but you can also use this screen to set up a Web Publishing Specification, which allows you to publish to an online location. Enter a convenient local directory (you can use the Browse button to find one, if you like), and click on the Next button.

8. On the sixth screen, your only options are whether to create a home page (first page) for your Web pages, and, if so, the name you'd like to give it. Notice that Microsoft uses the name "default" rather than "index", which is the more common and standard name for first pages. Leave this option unchecked, and click on Next.

9. On the seventh screen (shown in Figure 16.8), you can save the answers to your questions for easy republishing later, with a name of your choice. Check the Yes, I Want To Save Wizard Answers To A Web Publication Profile box and then enter the name "DWP Publication Specification". Click on Finish to finish the process.

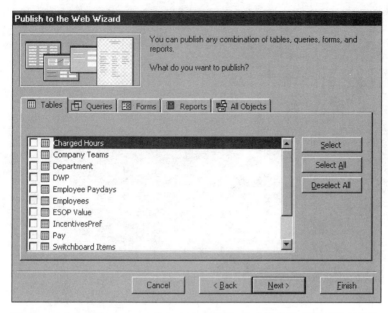

Figure 16.4   The second screen of the Publish To The Web Wizard.

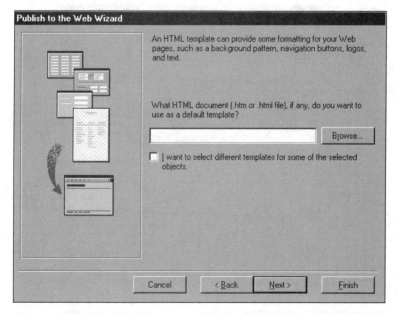

Figure 16.5   The third screen of the Publish To The Web Wizard.

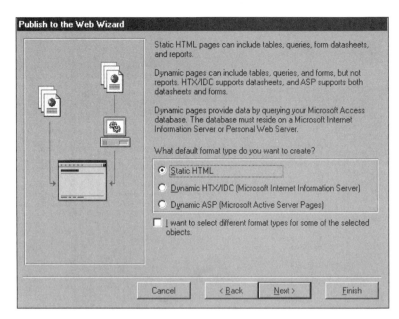

Figure 16.6 The fourth screen of the Publish To The Web Wizard.

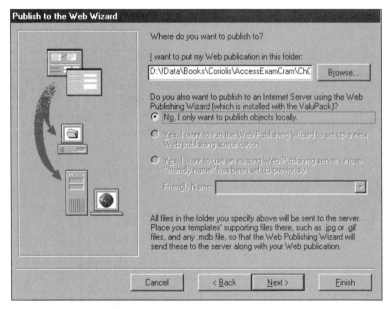

Figure 16.7 The fifth screen of the Publish To The Web Wizard.

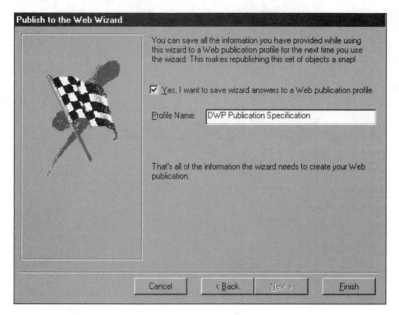

Figure 16.8   The seventh screen of the Publish To The Web Wizard.

When you've finished Task 3, open your Internet Explorer (IE) browser, and take a look at the HTML files that Access 97 has created. They'll be stored in the directory you chose, one file for the table's datasheet and one file for the form's datasheet. Both of them look very similar in IE, like the one shown in Figure 16.9 (the DWP_1.html file).

Building Order Forms With Dynamic ASP

HTML contains specialized tags for creating forms in a Web page as well as tags for creating form elements, such as text fields, memo fields (called *text areas*), radio buttons, checkboxes, drop-down or selection boxes, and even hidden fields. You can also use tags to create the ubiquitous Submit and Reset buttons.

Access 97 allows you to create forms that work with your database and Web site—using a wizard, naturally. Just keep in mind that there are several requirements for using databases with your Web site, especially when you use ASP or Microsoft's Internet Database Connector (IDC). For example, to run ASP:

➤ You need to be running Windows NT as well as IIS 3 or PWS.

➤ The database must be ODBC compliant (ODBC stands for Open Database Connectivity, a standard for database connections). Access 97 is ODBC compliant, as are many popular desktop database programs.

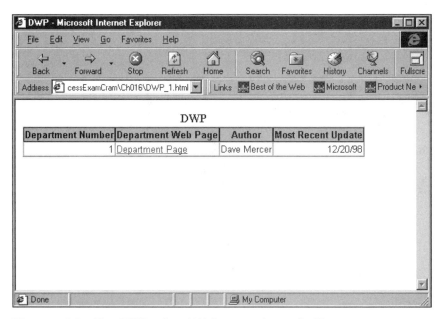

Figure 16.9 The DWP_1.html Web page shown in IE.

➤ The Microsoft Access Desktop Driver must be installed on the Web server.

➤ You need to either copy the database to the Web server or define its network location in the ODBC Data Source definition.

➤ You must define the data source and ensure that users can log onto it.

➤ Supporting *.asp files must have the proper permissions (such as execute or execute script) so they can run.

Task 4   Publishing the Department Web Page form as ASP.

1. With the Test database open, choose File|Save As HTML on the menu bar. The first screen of the Publish To The Web Wizard opens. Notice that the specification you created in Task 3 is now available for use, rather than grayed out.

2. Click on the Next button. The second screen opens with the Tables tab selected by default. Click on the Form tabs and then click on the DWP form to select it for export. Click on the Next button.

3. On the third screen of the wizard, leave the text box blank, and go to the next screen by clicking on the Next button.

4. On the fourth screen, select Dynamic ASP, and click on the Next button (at this point, the path of the wizard deviates from the previous one for creating static HTML).

5. On the fifth screen (shown in Figure 16.10), you specify the Data Source Name, User Name (Optional), and Password (Optional). If you're going to set a username and password for the database, you must fill in the two optional fields. For this task, enter "DWP" as the Data Source Name, and leave the optional fields blank.

6. In the bottom two text areas of the screen, you can enter the Server URL (tells the page where the ASP files are stored on the server) and the Session Timeout (min) parameter (tells the page how long Access 97 waits for a reply). Leave them both blank, and click on Next.

7. On the sixth screen, enter the same directory you used in Task 3 and then click on Next.

8. On the seventh screen, check the Home Page option, and change the name to Index. Click on Next.

9. On the eighth screen, check the Yes box and then enter "DWP" as the ASP Publication Specification. Click on Finish to finish the process.

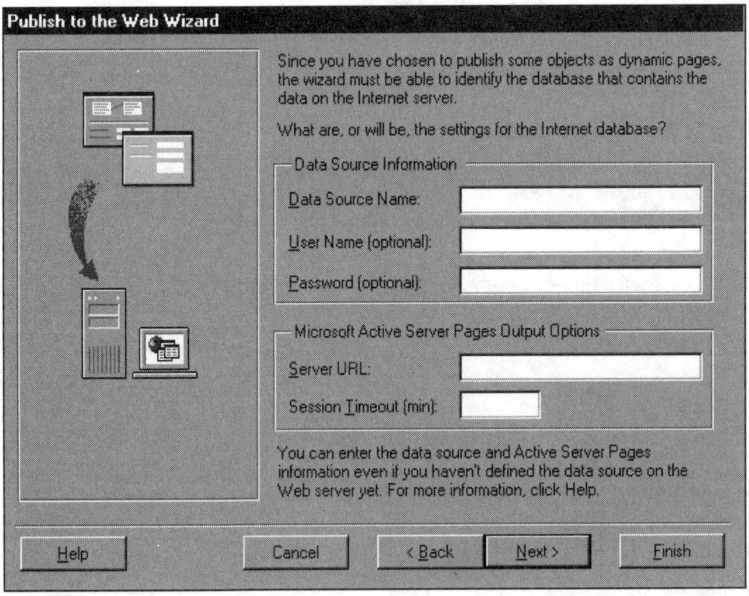

Figure 16.10 Inserting the data.

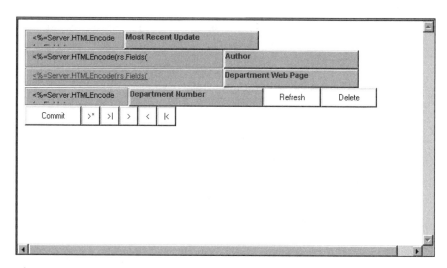

Figure 16.11 The ASP form that Access 97 built.

After finishing your form, look at the DWP_1alx.asp file. Even if you're not running any servers on your machine, you should be able to view the file and what it looks like in IE. Ours (shown in Figure 16.11) came out with some of the code showing in the fields, but you can clearly see what Access 97 builds.

For a better idea of what's going on behind the scenes, examine the code. Here's a portion of the HTML file that shows the code for one of the field objects on the form, the Most Recent Update field:

```
<object ID="Most_Recent_Update"
CLASSID="CLSID:8BD21D10-EC42-11CE-9E0D-00AA006002F3"
STYLE="TOP:121;LEFT:234;WIDTH:147;
HEIGHT:27;TABINDEX:3;ZINDEX:0;" width="144" height="27">
  <param name="Value"
value="<%=Server.HTMLEncode(rs.Fields("Most Recent
Update").Value)%>">
  <param name="BackStyle" value="1">
  <param name="BackColor" value="12632256">
  <param name="BorderStyle" value="1">
  <param name="BorderColor" value="12632256">
  <param name="ForeColor" value="0">
  <param name="FontHeight" value="160">
  <param name="FontName" value="Arial">
  <param name="Size" value="3822;702">
  <param name="SpecialEffect" value="3">
  <param name="VariousPropertyBits" value="2894088219"><%If Not
IsNull(rs.Fields("Most Recent Update").Value) Then%><%End If%>
</object>
```

The Web is the global communications and commerce medium of the 21st century, combining the telephone, computer, TV, radio, print, and networked media into one. Despite the hype about HTML and Web pages, database applications will bring the Web to life, and no modern database application can afford not to include Web functionality.

Access 97 allows you to create hyperlink fields and hyperlinks for the Web and other Office 97 objects, as well as support your Web site with order forms and reports. Much of this functionality is automated, enabling you to concentrate on designing an efficient database, not coding HTML.

Practice Exercises

Exercise 1

> You've been asked to produce a weekly report on the company
> intranet. It's just a static report and no queries are necessary, so
> you can produce it as static HTML. Although you get the data
> from the database weekly and know how to code HTML by hand,
> you decide to do things the easy way and have Access 97 produce
> the report directly for you.
>
> Create a report named DWP that lists the current Department Web
> Pages.
>
> Export the report as static HTML with the name Current Company
> Webs.
>
> Save a publication specification for the report with the name Static
> DWP Report.

Answer To Exercise 1

To create a new report in Access 97, use the Report Wizard. In the Database
window of the Test database, click on the New button with the Reports tab
selected. When the dialog box opens, choose Report Wizard and then choose
the DWP table from the drop-down list. Use the defaults for the remaining
screens.

To create a static HTML version of the report, from the Database window,
choose File|Save As HTML on the menu bar. On the second screen, click on
the Reports tab, and select the DWP report you just created for export as
HTML.

Use the defaults for the rest of the screens, except when picking a location to
publish your report. Choose a convenient directory and then proceed through
the rest of the screens until asked what to name the report. Name the report
Static DWP Report and then finish the wizard.

Exercise 2

The company has recently updated servers, and, unfortunately, all the employees' personal Web pages have changed. Rather than continue to store them as a list on paper, you decide that there are enough of them to warrant producing a new table for storing them in the Test database.

Create a table in the Test database to store personal Web page URLs.

Include the following fields: Employee Number (Number, Long Integer, Indexed Yes with no duplicates, primary key), URL (Hyperlink), and Most Recent Update (Date).

Save the table with the name Personal Web Pages.

Enter the employee numbers and URLs (make them up) for the first six employees of the company.

Use today's date as the Most Recent Update date.

Use their first and last names as Display Text for their links in the database.

Answer To Exercise 2

To create a new table in the Test database, click on the New button in the Database window with the Tables tab selected. Choose Design View in the New Table dialog box, and click on OK.

Enter the field names and their data types in the first three rows of the Design View grid. Make the Employee Number field a primary key by clicking on the Primary Key button on the Table Design toolbar. Save the table as Personal Web Pages.

Enter the employee data by entering six records, one for each of the first six employees in the company. Make up their URLs by entering "www.first-lastname.com" for each employee, where you substitute their names for "first-lastname". Enter today's date in the Most Recent Update field. Enter the employees' first and last names as Display Text by right-clicking on the URLs after you've entered them; doing so brings up the shortcut menu and the Display Text entry area.

Exercise 3

You now would like to publish the directory of Employee Personal Web Pages on the company intranet. You decide to publish them as a datasheet using dynamic HTML.

Create a form that shows the personal Web page links for company employees.

Export the form as dynamic HTML.

Save the form with the name Personal Web Pages ASP.

Answer To Exercise 3

To create a new form in Access 97, use the Form Wizard. In the Database window of the Test database, click on the New button with the Forms tab selected. When the dialog box opens, choose Form Wizard and then choose the Personal Web Pages table from the drop-down list. Use the defaults for the remaining screens.

To create a dynamic HTML version of the form, from the Database window, choose File|Save As HTML on the menu bar. On the second screen, click on the Forms tab, and select the Personal Web Pages form you just created for export as dynamic HTML. On the fifth screen, enter "test" as the Data Source Name, but leave the rest of the fields empty.

Use the defaults for the rest of the screens, except when picking a location to publish your form. Choose a convenient directory and then proceed through the rest of the screens until asked what to name the form. Name the form Personal Web Pages ASP and then finish the wizard.

Need To Know More?

 Klander, Lars and Dave Mercer. *Access 2000 Developer's Black Book*, The Coriolis Group, Scottsdale, AZ, 1999. ISBN 1-57610-349-8. Chapters 30 and 31 have a very nice description of how to use the tools in Access 2000 for Web development.

 Litwin, Paul, Ken Getz, and Mike Gilbert. *Access 97 Developer's Handbook*, Sybex Inc., San Francisco, CA, 1997. ISBN 0-7821-1941-7. Chapter 23 contains complete information about using Access 97 to publish to the Web.

 Viescas, John L. *Running Microsoft Access 97*, Microsoft Press, Redmond, WA, 1997. ISBN 1-57231-323-4. Chapter 10 offers some information about exporting forms and reports to the Web.

 www.e4free.com
The Access Web Publishing page has more information and examples of the text files that show how Access 97 wizards publish to the Web.

Sample Test

This set of practice exercises is slightly different from the test you'll actually take, in that the tasks are performed as though you are creating an application. We do this so you can have an example database to work from. For the exam, on the other hand, the example database and components are already there for you. Another difference is that here, short phrases outline the exercises at the beginning of each one.

The sample database you're constructing is for tracking parents and their children for a day-care center. It is based on the parents (the customers) who have one or more children enrolled at the center. It also tracks several attributes of the parents and the children.

Practice Exercises

Exercise 1   Design Your Database

> Review the requirements for tracking.
>
> Decide what tables you'll build and what their relationships are.
>
> Decide what forms you'll need.
>
> Decide what queries you'll need.
>
> Decide what reports you need to produce.

Exercise 2   Create A New Blank Database

> Create a new blank database.
>
> Name it customers.mdb.

Exercise 3   Create A Table And Fields

> Create a table.
>
> Build a Text field named Parent ID, four characters long, Required, Indexed (Duplicates OK).
>
> Build a Text field named Parent Name, 30 characters long, Required, Indexed (Duplicates OK).
>
> Build a Number field named Total Children, General Number format, zero decimal places.
>
> Build a Text field named Description, and use the default properties.
>
> Make the Parent ID and Parent Name fields a composite primary key.
>
> Save the table with the name Parents.
>
> Close the table.

Exercise 4   Enter Data In The Parents Table

Open the table in Normal view.

Expand the datasheet display of the fields Total Children and Description.

Enter the following data:

Parent ID	Parent Name	Total Children	Description
0001	Jack Smith	1	Married
0002	Joyce Smith	2	Married
0001	Irene Brown	3	Single
0002	George Gonzalez	5	Married
0003	Mary Gonzalez	5	Married
0001	Emily Johnson	1	Single
0003	Peter White	3	Married
0004	Elisabeth White	2	Married
0005	John Oman	7	Married
0002	Lucy Durn	4	Single
0006	Pat Jackson	1	Single

Save and exit the table.

Exercise 5   Configure Access 97 Datasheet Options

Open Options.

Change the default background color of datasheets to Aqua.

Change the default length for Text fields to 40.

Close Options.

Exercise 6 Change The Database Toolbar Settings

Open Toolbar Customization.

Open Toolbar Properties.

Configure the Database toolbar so it cannot be moved from its location.

Close Toolbar Properties.

Close Toolbar Customization.

Exercise 7 Navigate The Database

Open the Parents table in Datasheet view.

Open the Find function.

Find the first married parent record.

Find the next married parent record.

Close the Find function.

Close the table datasheet.

Exercise 8 Create A Table For Children

Create a table.

Build an AutoNumber field named Child ID, Indexed (No Duplicates).

Build a second and third field with the same characteristics as the Parent ID and Parent Name fields of the Parents table.

Build a Number field named IQ Score, General Number format, zero decimal places, Required (Duplicates OK).

Build a Text field named Activities, 20 characters long.

Build a Text field named Description using the default properties.

Make Child ID a primary key.

Save the table with the name Children.

Exit the table.

Exercise 9   Create A Relationship Between Tables

Open the Relationships window.

Create a relationship between the tables Parents and Children.

Use the Parent ID field and the Parent Name field to establish the relationship.

Enforce referential integrity.

Close the Relationships window.

Exercise 10   Examine Join Types

Open the Relationships window.

Open the Edit Relationship window.

Examine Join Types.

Close the Edit Relationship window.

Close the Relationships window.

Exercise 11   Modify A Datasheet And Sort Records

Open the Parents table datasheet.

Size the columns to Best Fit.

Sort the records by Parent Name (ascending) and Total Children (descending).

Apply the filter to the records.

Save the table with the filter.

Exercise 12   Create A Lookup Table

Create a new table.

Build a Text field named Parent Name using the default properties.

Name the table Parent Name. Do not set a primary key.

Open the Parent Name table in Normal mode.

Enter the values "Smith", "Jackson", and "Brown" in the Parent Name field.

Close the Parent Name table.

Exercise 13   Add The Lookup Table To Another Table

Open the Parents table in Design view.

Change the Parent Name field Display Control property to List Box.

Use the Parent Name table as the Row Source.

Save the table.

Exit Design view.

Exercise 14   Set A Default Value

Open the Parents table in Design view.

Set a default value of 1 for the Total Children field.

Save the Parents table.

Open the Parents table in Normal mode, and examine the effects of your work.

Close the table.

Exercise 15   Create A Query To Retrieve Parents By Name

Create a query.

Use the Simple Query Wizard.

Use the Parents table as the source of the query.

Use the defaults for the rest of the query, but have the wizard open it for modification.

Make the query retrieve parents whose last name is Smith.

Run the query.

Save the query.

Close the query.

Exercise 16   View And Change SQL In A Query

Open the Parents query.

Display the SQL in the query.

Change "Smith" to "Jackson" in the SQL.

Save the query.

Run the query.

Leave the query open.

Exercise 17   Create A Calculated Field In A Query

Switch the Parents query to Design view.

In an empty column, enter "Potential Children:[Total Children]*1.1" (without the quotation marks).

Save the query.

Leave it open.

Exercise 18   Add A Joined Table To The Parents Query

Switch the Parents query to Design view.

Display the Show Table dialog box.

Add the Children table to the query.

Add the IQ Score, Activities, and Description fields to the query.

Save the query.

Close the query.

Exercise 19   Create A Crosstab Query

Create a query.

Use the Crosstab Query Wizard.

Use the Parents table as the source.

Use Parent Name for the row headings.

Use Description for the column headings.

Use the sum of Total Children for the intersecting values.

Use defaults for the rest of your choices.

Leave the query open.

Exercise 20   Change Row And Column Headings In The Crosstab Query

Switch the Crosstab query to Design view.

Change the Parent Name field to a column heading.

Change the Description field to a row heading.

Save the query.

Close the query.

Exercise 21   Create A Form

Create a form.

Use the Form Wizard.

Use the Parents table as the source.

Place all the fields from the Parents table on the form.

Use the defaults for the rest of your choices, but have the wizard open the form for modification.

Leave the form open.

Exercise 22   Change A Lookup Field

Use the shortcut menu to change the Parent Name control on the Parents form.

Change the control to Text Box.

Open the properties sheet of the Parent Name control.

Build a query for the row source of the control.

Use the Parent Name table as the source for the query.

Use the Parent Name field in the query.

Save the query.

Close the query.

Close the properties sheet.

Save the form.

Close the form.

Exercise 23   Create A Form In Design View

Create a form using Design view.

Use the Parents table as the source.

Use all available fields on the form.

Arrange the controls so that they are the same size, the same distance from each other, and wide enough to let users easily read the labels.

Save the form as Parents1.

Leave it open.

Exercise 24   Add Special Effects And Colors To A Form

Select all controls on the Parents1 form.

Make the labels appear to protrude from the screen.

Change the background color to aqua.

Save the form.

Leave the form open but minimize it.

Exercise 25   Add A Subform To A Form

Create a form.

Use the Form Wizard.

Use the Children table as the source.

Add all the fields from the Children table to the form.

Use the defaults for the rest of your choices.

Close the form.

Maximize the Parents1 form.

Draw a subform object on the Parents1 form.

Make the new Children form display as the subform for the Parents1 form.

Close the Parents1 form.

Exercise 26   Create A Calculated Field On A Form

> Open the Children form in Design view.
>
> Draw a label with the caption "Potential IQ Score" in the upper right-hand area of the form.
>
> Draw a Text Box control beneath the label.
>
> Enter an expression in the Text Box control that makes it display a number 1.5 times larger than IQ Score for each record.
>
> Save the form.
>
> Leave the form open.

Exercise 27   Change The Format Property Of A Control

> Open the properties sheet of the calculated field.
>
> Change the Decimal Places property to 2.
>
> Exit the properties sheet.
>
> Save the form.
>
> Close the form.

Exercise 28   Create A Switchboard Form

> Create a Switchboard form.
>
> Use the Switchboard Manager.
>
> In the Text area of the first switchboard item, type "Enter parents".
>
> Place the Parents form in the Command area.
>
> Close the Switchboard Manager.

Exercise 29   Add An Item To A Switchboard Form

Open the Switchboard Manager.

Add an item to the Switchboard form.

In the Text area, type "Enter children".

In the Command area, enter the Parents1 form.

Close the Switchboard Manager.

Exercise 30   Add A Date Control To A Switchboard Form

Open the Switchboard form.

Draw a text box on the lower left-hand side.

Enter "Date" in the caption of the label for the text box.

Place the label above the text box.

Make the Text Box control display the current date.

Save the form.

Close the form.

Exercise 31   Create A Report That Lists Parents

Create a report.

Use the Report Wizard.

Use the Parents table as the source for the report.

Add all the fields to the report.

Sort the records in ascending order on Parent Name and then Parent ID.

Name the report Parents.

Close the report.

Exercise 32   Add A Subreport To A Report

Open the Parents report in Design View.

Draw a subreport object in the Detail section.

Make the subreport with the Subform/Subreport Wizard.

Use the Children table as the source for the subreport.

Link the reports with the Parent ID and Parent Name fields.

Use the default name for the subreport.

Close the report.

Exercise 33   Add A Summary Control To A Subreport

Open the Children report in Design view.

Add a Text Box control to the Report Header area of the report.

Make the label read "Total IQ Score = ".

Make the Text Box control sum the IQ Score field.

Save the report.

Exercise 34   Add A Page Break To A Report

Add a page break to the Detail section of the Parents report.

Reduce the width of the Parents report to six inches.

Save the report.

Close the report.

Exercise 35   Add A Picture To A Report

Open the Parents report in Design view.

Draw a frame for an image on the report in the Report Header section.

Add the clipart image Houses.wmf to the report. You'll find it in the Clipart folder under MSOffice.

Save the report.

Close the report.

Exercise 36   Add A Hyperlink Field To A Table

Open the Parents table in Design view.

Add a hyperlink field named Home Page.

Save the table.

Close the table.

Exercise 37   Enter Hyperlink Data In A Table

Open the Parents table in Normal mode.

Enter the hyperlink "www.e4free.com/parent0001".

Close the table.

Exercise 38   Export A Report As Static HTML

Export the Parents report.

Use the Publish To The Web Wizard.

Export the report as Static HTML.

Do not save a publication profile.

Exercise 39   Create An AutoExec Macro

Create a new macro.

Insert the OpenForm action.

Cause it to open the Switchboard form.

Save it with the name AutoExec.

Close the macro.

Exercise 40   Put A Macro In A Command Button

Create a new macro.

Insert the OpenReport action.

Make it open the Parents report in Print Preview mode.

Save the macro with the name Parents Report, and close it.

Open the Parents form in Design view.

Draw a command button.

Make the button activate the macro when someone clicks on it.

Save the form.

Close the form.

Exercise 41   Import An Access 97 Database Table

Close the customers database.

Create a new blank database.

Name the new database customers1.mdb.

Import the Parents table to the customers1 database.

Close the new database.

Exercise 42   Export Data To A Spreadsheet

Open the customers database.

Export the Parents table.

Use Microsoft Excel 97 as the export format.

Use the defaults for the rest of your choices.

Export to the current directory.

Exercise 43   Create A Conditional Macro

Create a macro in the customers database.

Name it IQCorrect.

Place it in the Children1 form in the Total IQ field, in the OnExit event.

Make it activate when the Total IQ value is greater than 999.

Save and close the Children1 form.

Exercise 44   Export A Table As A Comma-Delimited File

Export the Children table.

Use the comma-delimited format.

Use the defaults for the rest of your choices.

Export to the current directory.

Exercise 45   Set And Unset A Database Password

Set a password of your choice on the customers database.

Unset the password on the customers database.

Exercise 46   Create A Database Replica

Create a replica of the customers database.

Create a backup copy during the process.

Place it in the current directory.

Exercise 47   Split A Database Into Front And Back Ends

Create a front end and a back end for the customers database.

Use the default back-end name for the back end.

Exercise 48   Optimize A Database

Analyze the performance of the customers database.

Use the Performance Analyzer.

Analyze all the objects in the database.

Examine the results for actions you should take.

Answers To
Sample Test

This chapter contains the answers to the sample test in Chapter 17.

Exercise 1   Design Your Database

You need to track parents, children, and statistics that are relevant for them, including IQ scores, favorite activities, names, addresses, and so on. For the sake of brevity, we won't enter all the data you'd ordinarily track.

For this exercise, you'll need at least two tables: one for the parents and one that tracks the children for each parent or couple. The relationship between the two is one-to-many.

At least one data entry form is required. It should have a master form and a subform so that users can populate both the parent and child tables with data. You'll also want a form that lets users request reports by pushing a button. To decide what queries you'll need, you need to decide what reports you must produce. How many queries you'll need depends upon what reports you want to write, so you need to determine what reports you want to produce first. If you are tracking parents and their children, it is logical that you would want to have a report that shows detail and summary records by parent or couple.

Based on your determination of reporting requirements, you can build a query that pulls records based on parent or couple, or one that pulls all records, depending on what the user wants to see at the time.

Exercise 2   Create A New Blank Database

Click on File|New Database. In the New dialog box, the Blank Database icon should be selected by default. Click on OK. The File New Database dialog box opens.

A default file name should be selected in the File Name area. Name the database customers.mdb and then create it by clicking on the Create button.

Exercise 3   Create A Table And Fields

In the Database window of the Customers database, make sure the Tables tab is selected (it should be, by default) and then click on the New button. The New Table dialog box should open. Choose Design View from the list and then click on OK. The Table Design window appears.

In the first field, enter the field name "Parent ID". Tab to the Data Type area. The Text data type should appear by default. In the Field Properties area at the bottom of the screen, change the length of the field to four characters, change the Required property to Yes, and change the Indexed property to Yes (Duplicates OK).

Click on the second field row, and enter the field name "Parent Name". Tab to the Data Type area. The Text data type should appear by default. In the Field

Properties area, change the length of the field from 50 characters to 30, change the Required property from No to Yes, and change the Indexed property to Yes (Duplicates OK).

For the third field, enter the name "Total Children". Make the data type Number, change the Format property to General Number, and make the Decimal Places property zero.

In the fourth field, enter the name "Description". Tab to the Data Type area. The Text data type should appear by default. Leave the Field Properties as they are.

Click on the gray box to the left of the Parent ID field and then Shift+click on the Parent Name field to select both the fields. Click on the Primary Key button to make them both the primary key for the table (a composite primary key).

Save the table with the name Parents by choosing File|Save As/Export on the menu bar and then entering the name of the table.

Close the table by clicking on the Exit button.

Exercise 4   Enter Data In The Parents Table

Click on the Open button in the Database window (with the Tables tab selected).

The datasheet appears (in Normal view). To expand the datasheet display of the Total Children and Description fields a little, click on and drag the cursor between the field boundaries at the header of each field.

To enter data, put the focus on the first field (the focus should be there by default) and then type away.

The data is saved automatically, so all you need to do is click on the Exit button to exit the table.

Exercise 5   Configure Access 97 Datasheet Options

Choose Tools|Options on the menu bar. The Options dialog box opens.

Select the Datasheet tab. Change the default color for the background of datasheets to Aqua.

Select the Tables/Queries tab. Change the default length for Text fields to 40.

Click on OK to close the Options dialog box.

Exercise 6   Change The Database Toolbar Settings

Choose View|Toolbars|Customize on the menu bar. The Customize dialog box appears, with the Database toolbar selected by default.

Click on the Properties button. The Toolbar Properties dialog box appears.

Deselect the Allow Moving property by clicking on the checkbox.

Close the Toolbar Properties dialog box by clicking on the Close button.

Close the Customize dialog box by clicking on the Close button.

Exercise 7   Navigate The Database

In the Database window, with the Tables tab and the Parents table selected, click on the Open button. The Parents table datasheet opens.

Click on one of the fields. Click on the Find button on the toolbar. The Find In Field dialog box opens.

Enter "Married" in the Find What text area. Click on the Search Only Current Field checkbox to deselect it, so all fields are searched. Click on the Find First button. The first record with a married parent is found, and the word *Married* is highlighted.

Click on the Find Next button. The next record with the word *Married* is found.

Close the Find In Field dialog box by clicking on the Exit button.

Close the table datasheet by clicking on the Exit button.

Exercise 8   Create A Table For Children

In the Database window of the Customers database, make sure the Tables tab is selected and then click on the New button. The New Table dialog box opens. Choose Design View from the list and then click on OK. The Table Design window appears.

In the first field, enter the field name "Child ID". Tab to the Data Type area. The Text data type should appear by default. Change the data type to AutoNumber. In the Field Properties area at the bottom of the screen, change the Indexed property to Yes (No Duplicates).

In the second and third field rows, enter the primary key fields from the Parents table: Parent ID and Parent Name. Use the default data type of Text. Set the Required field property to Yes and Indexed to Yes (Duplicates OK).

Click on the fourth field row and then enter the field name "IQ Score". Tab to the Data Type area, and change the data type to Number. In the Field Properties area, change the format to General Number, the Decimal Places to zero, the Required property to Yes, and Indexed to Yes (Duplicates OK).

For the fifth field, enter "Activities". Make the data type Text with a length of 20.

In the sixth field, enter "Description". Tab to the Data Type area. The Text data type should appear by default. Leave the Field Properties as they are.

Make the first field a primary key by selecting the field and then clicking on the Primary Key button.

Save the table with the name "Children" by choosing File|Save As/Export on the menu bar and then entering the table name.

Close the table by clicking on the Exit button.

Exercise 9   Create A Relationship Between Tables

Click on the Relationships button on the Database toolbar. The Relationships window appears, with the Show Table dialog box open.

In the Relationships window, add the Parents and Children tables to the window. Close the Show Table dialog box.

Click on and drag the Parent ID field of the Parents table to the Children table. A smaller dialog box, also named Relationships, appears, with the Parent ID fields from both tables displayed on both sides. Click on the second field rows, and select Parent Name from the list of fields available.

Click on the Enforce Referential Integrity checkbox and then click on the Create button. The box closes, and one-to-many join lines appear.

Save and close the Relationships window by clicking on the Exit button.

Exercise 10   Examine Join Types

Open the Relationship window by clicking on the Relationships button.

Right-click on one of the join lines. A shortcut menu appears. Choose Edit Relationship on the shortcut menu.

Click on the Join Type button in the Edit Relationship dialog box. The first join type should be selected by default. Notice the other join types you can select if desired.

Click on OK to close the Edit Relationship dialog box and OK again to close the Relationship dialog boxes.

Exercise 11   Modify A Datasheet And Sort Records

Open the Parents table datasheet by clicking on the Open button in the Database window.

Place the cursor between the lines that separate field headings. It turns into a black cross. Double-click on the cursor. The columns size themselves automatically to fit the data and heading.

Sort the records by Parent Name (ascending) and by Total Children (descending) by choosing Records|Filter|Advanced Filter/Sort. A query grid appears. Put all the fields in the query, click on the Sort row of the Parent Name field, and choose Ascending from the drop-down menu. Do the same for the Total Children field, except choose Descending for the sort order.

Click on the Apply Filter button to apply the filter to the records.

Click on the Save button to save the table with the filter.

Exercise 12   Create A Lookup Table

In the Database window with the Tables tab selected, click on the New button. Choose Design View in the New Table dialog box.

Enter the name "Parent Name" in the first field row. Press Tab to go to the Data Type area, but leave the default Text with 40 characters for the data type.

Choose File|Save As/Export on the menu bar. In the Save As dialog box, enter the name "Parent Name" and then click on OK to save the table. Click on No when Access 97 asks if you want to designate a primary key.

Click on the View button.

Enter the values "Smith", "Jackson", and "Brown" in the table.

Close the table.

Exercise 13   Add The Lookup Table To Another Table

Open the Parents table in Design view.

Click on the Parent Name field. Go to the Field Properties area and then click on the Lookup tab.

Change the Display Control property from Text Box to List Box by clicking on the area and then choosing List Box from the drop-down list.

Choose Parent Name from the drop-down list in the Row Source area. Leave the rest of the defaults as they are.

Save the table.

Close the table.

Exercise 14   Set A Default Value

Open the Parents table in Design view by clicking on the View button on the Tables toolbar.

Click on the Total Children field row and then click on the Field Properties Default Value area. Enter "1" to set a default value of 1 for the field.

Save the table.

Click on the View button to switch to Normal mode. Notice that the place-holder record has a default value of 1 in the Total Children field.

Close the table.

Exercise 15   Create A Query To Retrieve Parents By Name

In the Database window with the Queries tab selected, click on the New button.

Choose Simple Query Wizard in the New Query dialog box.

When the wizard's first screen opens, choose Table:Parents as the source and then add all fields to the query by clicking on the double-arrowed button that points towards the Selected Fields box. Click on Next to go to the next screen.

Use the defaults for the rest of the screens, but select Modify The Query Design on the last screen.

In Design view, add the criterion "*Smith" to the Parent Name column (note the use of the wildcard).

Run the query by clicking on the Run button. The results should contain only records that have Smith in the Parent Name field.

Save the query by clicking on the Save button.

Close the query by clicking on the Exit button.

Exercise 16   View And Change SQL In A Query

Open the Parents query in the Database window by clicking on the Queries tab and then selecting the Parents query.

Display the SQL View by choosing View|SQL View on the menu bar.

Change the word *Smith* to *Jackson* in SQL view. Change back to Design view by clicking on View|Design View on the menu bar.

Save the query by clicking on the Save button on the Query Design toolbar.

Run it by clicking on the Run button on the toolbar.

Leave the query open.

Exercise 17   Create A Calculated Field In A Query

In the Parents query, change to Design view by clicking on the View button.

In an empty column header (first one on the right), enter "Potential Children:[Total Children]*1.1" (without the quotation marks).

Save the query by clicking on the Save button.

Leave it open.

Exercise 18   Add A Joined Table To The Parents Query

Click on the View button to change to Design view in the Parents query.

Choose Query|Show Table to display the Show Table dialog box and then select the Children table from the list.

Click on the Add button to add the Children table to the query. The joins should automatically appear. Close the Show Table dialog box.

Double-click on the IQ Score, Activities, and Description fields to add them to the query.

Save the query by clicking on the Save button.

Close it by clicking on the Exit button.

Exercise 19   Create A Crosstab Query

In the Database window with the Queries tab selected, click on the New button. The New Query dialog box opens.

Choose the Crosstab Query Wizard and then click on OK.

On the first screen of the wizard, choose Parents as the source table for the query. Click on Next.

On the next screen, select Parent Name for the row headings and then add it to the Selected Fields area. Click on Next.

On the next screen, select Description for the column headings and then click on Next.

On the next screen, select Total Children and then choose Sum as the function to apply. Click on Next.

On the last screen, leave the defaults as they are and then click on Finish. The query opens, showing the total number of children that each parent has by the type of relationship they have.

Leave the query open.

Exercise 20   Change Row And Column Headings In The Crosstab Query

Click on the View button to switch to Design view.

Click on the Crosstab row of the Parent Name field and then change it from a row heading to a column heading.

Click on the Crosstab row of the Description field and then change it from a column heading to a row heading.

Save the query by clicking on the Save button.

Close the query by clicking on the Exit button.

Exercise 21   Create A Form

In the Database window with the Forms tab selected, click on New.

In the New Form dialog box, choose Form Wizard from the list.

Select the Parents table from the drop-down list and then click on OK.

On the first screen of the wizard, add all fields to the Selected Fields area.

Use the defaults for the rest of the screens, except select Modify The Form's Design on the last screen. Click on Finish. The form opens in Design view.

Leave the form open.

Exercise 22   Change A Lookup Field

Right-click on the Parent Name control and then select Change To on the shortcut menu.

Select Text Box from the choices available, and exit the Properties sheet.

Change the field back to a Combo Box by performing the same procedure.

Right-click on the Parent Name text box and then select Properties on the shortcut menu.

Click on the Row Source area and then click on the Build button. The SQL Statement:Query Builder opens.

Add the Parent Name table to the query and then close the Show Table dialog box.

Double-click on the Parent Name field to add it to the query.

Save the query. Close it.

Close the Properties sheet.

Save the form, and close the form.

Exercise 23   Create A Form In Design View

In the Database window with Forms selected, click on the New button.

In the New Form dialog box, choose Design View, choose the Parents table, and then click on OK. A blank form opens.

Choose View|Field List on the menu bar. Click on and drag all the fields from Parents onto the blank form. Right-click on the Parent Name field, and change it to Text Box from List Box.

To arrange all the controls so that they are the same size, the same distance from each other, and wide enough to let users easily read the labels, click on each field, drag it until it is wide enough, and then choose Format|Align or Format|Size on the menu bar.

Save the form as Parents1 by choosing File|Save As/Export on the menu bar, entering the name when the Save As dialog box opens, and then clicking on Save.

Leave the form open.

Exercise 24   Add Special Effects And Colors To A Form

Click on and Shift+click on the label controls to select them all.

Right-click on the label controls to open the shortcut menu. Choose Special Effect and then make the labels appear to protrude from the screen.

Choose Fill/Back Color and then choose an aqua color.

Save the form by clicking on the Save button on the Form Design toolbar.

Leave it open, but minimize it by clicking on the Minimize button.

Exercise 25   Add A Subform To A Form

In the Database window with the Forms tab selected, click on the New button.

In the New Form dialog box, select Form Wizard.

Select the Children table and then click on OK.

On the first screen of the Form Wizard, add all the fields from the Children table to the Selected Fields area.

Use the defaults for the rest of the screen's choices. The default name for the form should be Children. The form should open on your screen.

Close the Children form.

Maximize the Parents1 form.

If necessary, open the Toolbox by clicking on View|Toolbox on the menu bar. Make sure the Wizard button is depressed on the Toolbox. Click on the Subform/Subreport button on the Toolbox and then draw the outline of the subform under the existing fields and labels.

The Subform/Subreport Wizard opens. On the first screen, choose the Forms radio button and then select the Children form from the drop-down list. Click on Next. On the next screen, choose the Define My Own radio button. From the left-hand list, choose Parent ID; then, do the same from the right-hand list. Go to the next row and then select Parent Name from the left-hand list; then do the same from the right-hand list. Click on Next. On the last screen of the wizard, leave the default name for the control (Children) and then click on the Finish button. Arrange the controls to lend a pleasing appearance to the form and then save the form.

Close the Parents1 form.

Exercise 26   Create A Calculated Field On A Form

Open the Children form in Design view by clicking on the Design button in the Database window with the Forms tab selected and the Children form selected.

Display the Toolbox by clicking on View|Toolbox on the menu bar. Click on the Label button and then draw a label on the form in the upper right-hand area of the form. Enter "Potential IQ Score" for the caption of the label by clicking twice on the label until text editing is possible.

Click on the Text Box button on the Toolbox. Draw another control below the label. Delete the extra label that appears next to the new control.

Right-click on the Text Box control to open the property sheet via the shortcut menu. Enter "Potential IQ Score" as the Name property of the text box. Click on the Control Source property and then click on the Build button to start the Expression Builder. Click on the equal sign and then double-click on the IQ Score field (from the bottom-middle list). Enter "*01.5". The expression should read as follows: "=[IQ Score]*01.5". Click on OK to close the Expression Builder and then exit the property sheet.

Save the form.

Leave the form open.

Exercise 27   Change The Format Property
Of A Control

Right-click on the calculated field to open the properties sheet.

Click on the Format property and then select General Number from the drop-down list. Click on the Decimal Places property and then select 2.

Exit the properties sheet by clicking on the Exit button.

Save the form.

Close the form.

Exercise 28   Create A Switchboard Form

In the Database window, choose Tools|Add-Ins|Switchboard Manager.

Access 97 sets up the wizards and searches your current database to find any existing switchboard forms. If it finds none, it asks if you'd like to create one. Click on Yes. The Switchboard Manager dialog box opens, and the default Main Switchboard is created. In addition, a table called Switchboard Items that contains data about the main Switchboard form is created. Click on the Edit button. The Edit Switchboard Page dialog box opens.

Click on New. The Edit Switchboard Item dialog box opens. In the box labeled Text, type "Enter parents".

In the box labeled Command, choose Open Form In Edit Mode from the drop-down list. In the box labeled Form, choose Parents from the drop-down list. Close the Edit Switchboard Item dialog box and the Edit Switchboard Page dialog box.

Close the Switchboard Manager.

Exercise 29   Add An Item To A Switchboard Form

In the Database window, choose Tools|Add-Ins|Switchboard Manager. The Switchboard Manager dialog box opens.

Click on the Edit button. The Edit Switchboard Page dialog box opens. Click on New. The Edit Switchboard Item dialog box opens.

In the box labeled Text, type "Enter children".

In the box labeled Command, choose Open Form In Edit Mode from the drop-down list. In the box labeled Form, choose Parents1 from the drop-down list. Close the Edit Switchboard Item dialog box and the Edit Switchboard Page dialog box.

Close the Switchboard Manager.

Exercise 30 Add A Date Control To A Switchboard Form

In the Database window with the Forms tab selected, open the Switchboard form in Design view by clicking on the Design button.

If necessary, display the Toolbox by clicking on View|Toolbox on the menu bar. Click on the Text Box tool and then draw a text box on the lower left-hand side of the Switchboard form.

Arrange the label so it is above the text box and then enter "Date" for the caption of the label.

Right-click on the text box and then open the properties sheet. Click on the Control Source area and then click on the Build button to start the Expression Builder. Double-click on Functions|Built-In Functions and then double-click on the Date function. The Date function should appear in the top window as follows: "=Date()". Click on OK to close the Expression Builder and put the function in the Control Source property.

Save the form.

Close the form.

Exercise 31 Create A Report That Lists Parents

In the Database window with the Reports tab selected, click on the New button.

In the New Report dialog box, choose Report Wizard from the displayed list.

Choose Parents from the drop-down list and then click on OK.

On the first screen of the Report Wizard, add all the fields to the Selected Fields area by clicking on the double-arrow button that points to the right. Click on Next. Leave the defaults on the next screen and then click on Next.

On the next screen, choose Parent Name from the drop-down list as the first field to sort by. Choose Parent ID as the second field to sort by. Use ascending order for both fields. Click on Next. Use the defaults for the rest of the screens.

The report should be named Parents by default.

Close the report.

Exercise 32   Add A Subreport To A Report

Switch the Parents report to Design view by clicking on the View button on the Report Design toolbar.

Display the Toolbox if necessary by clicking on View|Toolbox on the menu bar. Click on the Subform/Subreport button and then draw a rectangular area for the subreport in the Detail section of the report.

The Subform/Subreport Wizard opens. Use the default selection on the first screen and then click on Next.

On the second screen, make sure the table named Children is selected and then add all the fields to the Selected Fields area. Click on Next.

On the next screen, choose Define My Own and then select the Parent ID and Parent Name fields from both sides as the fields to link the tables. Click on Next.

On the last screen, use the default name of the subreport and then click on Finish.

Close the report.

Exercise 33   Add A Summary Control To A Subreport

Open the Children subreport in Design view by clicking on Design in the Database window with the Reports tab selected and the Children subreport selected.

In the Report Header area, add a text box by clicking on the Text Box tool on the Toolbox and then drawing the text box with your mouse.

Click on the label that appears with the text box and then change the caption to "Total IQ Score =".

Right-click on the text box and then open the properties sheet. Click on the Control Source area and then click on the Build button to open the Expression Builder. Click on the equal sign to put an equal sign in your expression and then double-click on Functions|Built-In Functions. Scroll down until you reach the Sum function and then double-click on that. The Sum function appears in your expression. Click on "<<expr>>" in the expression to highlight it and then click on the Children subreport in the bottom-left-hand list. Double-click on the IQ Score field in the bottom-center list to enter it into the expression in place of "<<expr>>". Your expression should now read as follows: "=Sum([IQ Score])". Click on OK to place the expression in the Control Source area of the control. Exit the properties sheet. Arrange the controls on the report in an appealing way.

Save the report.

Exercise 34   Add A Page Break To A Report

In the Detail section of the Parents report, add a page break by clicking on the page break tool and then clicking on the Detail section. Make sure the page break is at the bottom of the section.

Shrink the width of the report to six inches by putting the cursor on the right edge of the report until it turns into a black cross. Then, drag the edge of the report to the left until it hits the six-inch mark.

Save the report.

Close the report.

Exercise 35   Add A Picture To A Report

In the Database window with the Reports tab selected and the Parents report selected, click on the Design button.

Display the Toolbox by clicking on View|Toolbox on the menu bar. Click on the Image tool on the Toolbox, and draw a frame for your picture in the Report Header section.

When the Insert Picture dialog box opens, find the Clipart folder (it should be under MSOffice). Choose the file named Houses.wmf. Either double-click on the file or click on it and then click on OK. The file appears in the image frame. Arrange the frame to lend a pleasing appearance to your report.

Save the report.

Close the report.

Exercise 36   Add A Hyperlink Field To A Table

In the Database window with the Parents table selected, click on Design.

In the first field name area that is open, enter "Home Page". Tab to the Data Type area and then select Hyperlink from the drop-down menu.

Save the table.

Close the table.

Exercise 37   Enter Hyperlink Data In A Table

Open the Parents table in Normal mode by clicking on the Open button in the Database window with the Tables tab and the Parents table selected.

In the first record for the parent with an ID number of 0001, enter the hyperlink "www.e4free.com/parent0001".

Close the table by clicking on the Exit button.

Exercise 38   Export A Report As Static HTML

With the Parents report selected in the Database window, choose File|Save As HTML on the menu bar.

The Publish To The Web Wizard opens. Click on Next. On the next screen, select the Reports tab and then choose the Parents report. Click on Next and then click on Next again. Choose Static HTML.

Click on Next. Publish the report to the default location. Click on Next. Use the defaults for the remaining screens and then click on Finish. Don't save your work as a publication profile.

Exercise 39   Create An AutoExec Macro

In the Database window with the Macros tab selected, click on New to begin a new macro.

Click on the first Action area and then choose OpenForm from the drop-down list.

Click on the Action Arguments Form Name area and then choose Switchboard from the drop-down list. Leave the other arguments as defaults.

Click on the Save button on the Macro Design toolbar. Enter the name "AutoExec" when the Save As dialog box opens and then click on OK.

Close the macro.

Exercise 40   Put A Macro In A Command Button

In the Database window with the Macros tab selected, click on the New button.

Click on the first Action area and then choose OpenReport from the drop-down list.

Click on the Action Arguments Report Name area and then choose Parents from the drop-down list. Click on the View area and then choose Print Preview from the drop-down list. Leave the other arguments as defaults.

Click on the Save button on the Macro Design toolbar. Enter the name "Parents Report" and then click on OK. Exit the macro.

In the Database window with the Forms tab selected and the Parents form selected, click on the Design button.

On the Parents form, draw a command button using the Command Button tool on the Toolbox (with the Wizards tool deselected). Right-click on the command button to open the properties sheet. Enter the caption "Preview Parents Report" in the Caption property.

Scroll down the properties sheet to the OnClick event. Enter the name of your macro (Parents Report) in the OnClick event. Exit the properties sheet. Resize the command button and then rearrange the controls as necessary to provide a pleasing look to the form.

Save the form.

Close the form.

Exercise 41   Import An Access 97 Database Table

Close the Customers database.

Choose File|New Database on the menu bar. The New dialog box opens with the Blank Database template selected by default. Click on OK.

The File New Database dialog box opens. Name the new database customers1.mdb. Click on the Create button.

The new database appears. Click on File|Get External Data|Import on the menu bar. The Import dialog box opens. Select the customers1 database. Click on the Import button. The Import Objects dialog box opens with the Tables tab selected by default. Select the Parents table and then click on OK. The Database window of the customers1 database should now contain the Parents table and all its data.

Close the customers1 database.

Exercise 42   Export Data To A Spreadsheet

Open the customers database by choosing File on the menu bar and (after closing the switchboard) then selecting customers from the list at the bottom of the drop-down menu.

Select the Parents table in the Database window (the Tables tab should be selected by default). Choose File|Save As/Export on the menu bar. The Save As dialog box opens. The radio button for To An External File Or Database should be selected by default. Click on the OK button.

The Save Table dialog box opens. In the Save As Type area, select the Microsoft Excel 97 (*.xls) file type. Click on the Export button. The dialog box closes.

The Parents table is exported to a spreadsheet format and saved in the current directory. If you want to verify that this has happened, launch Excel and then open the Parents.xls file from the current directory (but you shouldn't do this during the test, of course).

Exercise 43   Create A Conditional Macro

In the database window with the Macros tab selected, click on the New button to start a new macro.

Click on View|Conditions to display the Conditions column.

Enter "[Total IQ]>999" in the Conditions column.

Click in the Action column, and choose MsgBox from the available actions in the drop-down list.

In the Action Arguments section at the bottom, enter "Are you sure Total IQ is Correct?" in the Message area. Leave the other arguments as they are.

Save the macro as IQCorrect.

Close the macro.

Select the Forms tab in the Database window, and select the Children1 form.

Click on the Design button to open the Children1 form in Design view.

Right-click the Total IQ field, and open the Properties sheet via the shortcut menu.

Click on the Events tab on the Properties sheet. In the OnExit event, type the name of the macro you just created (IQCorrect).

Exit the Properties sheet.

Save the form.

Close the form.

Exercise 44   Export A Table As A Comma-Delimited File

Choose the Children table in the Database window and then click on File|Save As/Export. The Save As dialog box opens. Maintain the default radio button setting to Export To An External File Or Database and then click on OK. The Save Table dialog box opens. Maintain the default file name that Access 97 has chosen and then change the file type (in the Save As Type area) to Text. Click on Export. The Export Wizard opens.

The first screen offers you a choice of Delimited or Fixed Width. Choose Delimited (it should be selected by default). Click on Next. Comma is the delimited character Access 97 has chosen by default.

Click on Next. The last screen offers you the option of choosing another name or directory for your file, but leave it as is. Click on Finish.

Exercise 45   Set And Unset A Database Password

With the Database window open, choose Tools|Security|Set Database Password on the menu bar. The Set Database Password dialog box opens. Enter a password and then enter it again to confirm it. Click on OK to finish the process.

Choose Tools|Security|Unset Database Password on the menu bar. Enter the password and then click on OK to unset it.

Exercise 46   Create A Database Replica

With the Customers database open, choose Tools|Replication|Create Replica on the menu bar. Click on Yes when asked if you want to proceed with closing the database.

Click on Yes when asked if you want to create a backup copy of your database.

Select the location for your database in the next dialog box. Use the current directory.

Exercise 47   Split A Database Into Front And Back Ends

With the Customers database open, split it into a front end and back end by clicking on Tools|Add-Ins|Database Splitter. Click on Split Database. The Create Back-End Database dialog box opens.

Use the default back-end name that Access 97 has selected and then click on Split to effect the action.

Exercise 48   Optimize A Database

In the Database window of the Customers database, choose Tools| Analyze|Performance.

The Performance Analyzer dialog box opens. Click on the All tab to display all the objects in the database and then click on the Select All button to select all the objects. Click on the OK button. The finished analysis is displayed in another dialog box, which is also labeled Performance Analyzer.

Any actions you should take appear here, although you should review them carefully before carrying them out.

What's On The Companion Disk?

The companion disk contains the Access databases needed to follow all tasks and steps discussed in the book. These files are compressed in a zip format.

See the readme file located on the disk for more information about using these files.

Software Requirements:

➤ Access 97

➤ WinZip or other file compression program

Hardware Requirements:

➤ Platform—Intel and compatible 486/66

➤ Microsoft Windows 95, Windows 98, or Windows NT

➤ 8MB of RAM minimum (16MB preferred)

Glossary

· ·

Aggregate functions   Summary, count, and other functions that operate on groups of data rather than individual values.

Atomic data   Data values that cannot be broken down further for any useful purpose. For example, a seven-digit phone number.

Attribute   Synonymous with fields in a table, attributes refer to properties of an entity. For example, the first name of a person is an attribute of the entity person.

Bound   An object bound to a table or query affects and interacts with the data in that table or query, whereas an unbound object may serve as an interface component not related to a table or query.

Calculated control   An unbound control containing an expression that evaluates to a value.

Cardinality   The quality of a relationship between entities. For example one-to-many, many-to-many, and one-to-one. When expressed as high or low, refers to the number of records in one or another table on either end of the relationship.

Cartesian product   The sum of two or more numbers, referring to the number of resulting records when two or more tables are joined.

Client/server   A computing model defining the relationship between various applications, how they communicate, and what roles each application plays.

Comma-delimited   When exporting text data, field data values separated by commas is a standard format, called comma-delimited. Data can also be delimited by other characters, such as the tab.

Concatenation   The "adding" of one string to another.

Configuration   The way options are set for your database.

Constraint   Limiting factor defined by database rules affecting how records are processed and updated/deleted.

Control   All objects on forms and reports are controls, whether they are fields, labels, radio buttons, and so on.

Crosstab   Data display method showing values intersected by two measures.

Data dictionary   Compilation of data within a database or as a result of a systems analysis, for the purpose of documenting construction and enhancing maintainability.

Data dimension   The domain of an attribute being measured. For example, all the valid phone numbers of a given area constitute the domain, and measurement along that domain is considered travel along that dimension.

Data source   When a database application is made available on a network, it must have a name to be accessed by, and it is then called a data source.

Data type   The characteristics that define a given data value. For example, number, text, and date.

Database application   A database constructed to perform a specialized function, as opposed to a database program from which database applications can be designed and constructed.

Default value   A value that appears when the control it is embedded in is opened. Typically used to ensure a valid value is present in a field, even when the user doesn't enter one.

Entity-relationship   Data model relating entities according to their relationship with other entities.

Expression Builder   A tool that can be used to simplify the creation of expressions as well as helping to ensure correct syntax.

Field properties   Objects in an Access 97 database have properties, and fields have properties like any other object. Among the properties of a field are the format and the data type.

Flat-file   Data model retaining one record for every entry in every applicable table.

Flat-file database   A database consisting of one table with all the data repeated for every record.

Focus   Similar to the cursor in word processing, focus indicates which field is active and may be affected by your keystrokes.

Foreign key   The name for a primary key field that is being used to link a table to the table where the primary key originates.

Header and footer   Reports have sections called headers and footers that can be specified by the entire report, the page, or where individual groups of data change. These sections are useful for inserting data specific to the entire report or by the page, or summarizing data from groups.

Index   Extra data consisting of presorted values that speed searches. Index fields help a database perform searches more quickly but can slow data entry and update.

Input mask   Format enforcer for data entry, an input mask ensures that data is entered in a particular sequence.

Interpolation   Assignment of values by averaging the values of the nearest neighbors.

Join   There are several join types, each indicating how records from one table are related to the records in another table in a relational database. Linking Access 97 supports Object Linking and Embedding (OLE), and data from other applications can be linked into an Access database.

Logical AND   A method of specifying two or more criteria that must both be satisfied in order to retrieve a particular item of data.

Logical OR   A method of specifying two criteria in which one or the other must be present to retrieve a particular item of data.

Mandatory field   A field where data is required before the user can update the record.

Menu bar   The menu bar (or the top-line menu) contains commands as words. These commands can also be executed by key combinations (noted next to the menu choice).

Middleware   Software that facilitates communication, navigation, and analysis of back-end and front-end applications.

Mission critical   Applications considered crucial to the ability of an organization to survive and operate.

Navigation   The act of traversing menu choices, wizard screens, toolbar functions, and so on while you design and build applications, or use a program.

Normalization Technique for reducing data redundancy and error in relational databases.

Null value The absence of data, rather than a zero or space. Null values can mean a variety of things, such as the data is missing or there is no data for that field.

Object oriented A programming term that refers to the practice of viewing all components in the program as entities containing their own data and properties that affect the way they interact.

One-to-many A relationship between tables in which the parent table (the one side) has many corresponding values in the child table (the many side).

Parent-child relationship Hierarchical data model showing entities related to one another as "parents" and "children."

Primary key Unique, non-repeating data values expressly created for relating tables to one another.

Process engineering The discipline of defining, measuring, and improving work functions in organizations.

Project management Time-based management technique for planning and executing projects.

Properties sheet Revealed by a right-click and a shortcut menu, Properties sheets give you access to an object's properties, allowing you to set them as well as insert expressions, macros, and modules.

QBE Query By Example is the graphical interface for designing queries Access 97 presents to the user by default.

Record locking A method for ensuring that only one user at a time can access a particular record.

Recordset A set of records resulting from a query.

Referential integrity A method of ensuring that for every child record there is a corresponding parent record.

Relation Another name for a table.

Reverse engineering The process of determining the objects required in a database and the data that must be present, by starting with the end products and working backwards.

Scalability Ability of an application or system to scale, or add users and required processing and communications power as requirements increase.

SQL   Structured Query Language is an English language (sort of) programming language for databases. It is actually quite easy to learn and understand, and Access 97 queries are formatted in it. You can see the SQL behind the queries you create by choosing View|SQL View on the menu bar. Storage Format File format in which data is stored.

Switchboard   A specialized form that controls the actions of several other forms, reports, and so on. Generally serves as the beginning form in an Access application.

Systems analysis   Analytical approach to the study of complex systems, usually business systems. Closely related to process engineering.

Toolbar   A toolbar contains buttons, drop-down lists, and occasionally menu choices. There are several toolbars in Access 97, for designing forms, tables, queries, and so on. Toolbars frequently contain many of the same commands as the menu and each other.

Unbound   An unbound object may serve as an interface component not related to a table or query, whereas an object bound to a table or query affects and interacts with the data in that table or query.

Validation rule   Criteria specifying the domain (or range) and type of data that can be entered in a particular field.

Wildcard   Character that can be used to replace missing characters, frequently used as part of the criteria in a query.

Wizard   Pre-built function in Access that simplifies the performance of a relatively complex or commonly used procedure.

Index

CORIOLIS HELP CENTER

Here at The Coriolis Group, we strive to provide the finest customer service in the technical education industry. We're committed to helping you reach your certification goals by assisting you in the following areas.

Talk to the Authors

We'd like to hear from you! Please refer to the "How to Use This Book" section in the "Introduction" of every Exam Cram guide for our authors' individual email addresses.

Web Page Information

The Certification Insider Press Web page provides a host of valuable information that's only a click away. For information in the following areas, please visit us at:

www.coriolis.com/cip/default.cfm

- Titles and other products
- Book content updates
- Roadmap to Certification Success guide
- New Adaptive Testing changes
- New Exam Cram Live! seminars
- New Certified Crammer Society details
- Sample chapters and tables of content
- Manuscript solicitation
- Special programs and events

Contact Us by Email

Important addresses you may use to reach us at The Coriolis Group.

eci@coriolis.com

To subscribe to our FREE, bi-monthly on-line newsletter, *Exam Cram Insider*. Keep up to date with the certification scene. Included in each *Insider* are certification articles, program updates, new exam information, hints and tips, sample chapters, and more.

techsupport@coriolis.com

For technical questions and problems with CD-ROMs. Products broken, battered, or blown-up? Just need some installation advice? Contact us here.

ccs@coriolis.com

To obtain membership information for the *Certified Crammer Society*, an exclusive club for the certified professional. Get in on members-only discounts, special information, expert advice, contests, cool prizes, and free stuff for the certified professional. Membership is FREE. Contact us and get enrolled today!

cipq@coriolis.com

For book content questions and feedback about our titles, drop us a line. This is the good, the bad, and the questions address. Our customers are the best judges of our products. Let us know what you like, what we could do better, or what question you may have about any content. Testimonials are always welcome here, and if you send us a story about how an Exam Cram guide has helped you ace a test, we'll give you an official Certification Insider Press T-shirt.

custserv@coriolis.com

For solutions to problems concerning an order for any of our products. Our staff will promptly and courteously address the problem. Taking the exams is difficult enough. We want to make acquiring our study guides as easy as possible.

Book Orders & Shipping Information

orders@coriolis.com

To place an order by email or to check on the status of an order already placed.

coriolis.com/bookstore/default.cfm

To place an order through our on-line bookstore.

1.800.410.0192

To place an order by phone or to check on an order already placed.

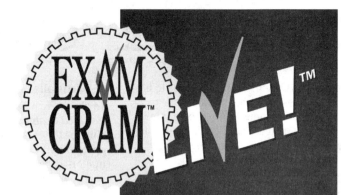

CERTIFIED CRAMMER SOCIETY

PHI SLAMMA CRAMMA

breed apart, a cut above the rest—a true professional. Highly skilled and superbly trained, certified IT professionals are unquestionably the world's most elite computer experts. In an effort to appropriately recognize this privileged crowd, The Coriolis Group is proud to introduce the Certified Crammer Society. If you are a certified IT professional, it is also our pleasure to invite you to become a Certified Crammer Society member.

Membership is free to all certified professionals and benefits include a membership kit that contains your official membership card and official Certified Crammer Society blue denim ball cap emblazoned with the Certified Crammer Society crest— proudly displaying the Crammer motto "Phi Slamma Cramma"—and featuring a genuine leather bill. The kit also includes your password to the Certified Crammers-Only Website containing monthly discreet messages designed to provide you with advance notification about certification testing information, special book excerpts, and inside industry news not found anywhere else; monthly Crammers-Only discounts on selected Coriolis titles; *Ask the Series Editor* Q and A column; cool contests with great prizes; and more.

GUIDELINES FOR MEMBERSHIP

Registration is free to professionals certified in Microsoft, A+, or Oracle DBA. Coming soon: Sun Java, Novell, and Cisco. Send or email your contact information and proof of your certification (test scores, membership card, or official letter) to:

Certified Crammer Society Membership Chairperson
THE CORIOLIS GROUP, LLC
14455 North Hayden Road, Suite 220, Scottsdale, Arizona 85260-6949
Fax: 602.483.0193 • Email: ccs@coriolis.com

APPLICATION

Name:

Address:

Society Alias:

Choose a secret code name to correspond with us and other Crammer Society members. Please use no more than eight characters.

Email:

Got Bugs
in Your
Access/VB
Apps?

Not Anymore!

Microsoft SQL Server • Access • Visual Basic • Outlook • Accounting Systems • VBA

ACCESS OFFICE VB ADVISOR
for Microsoft Enterprise Database & Web Solutions

FEBRUARY 1999

WWW.ADVISOR.COM

Make the ADO Transition Now 6
ADO is flexible and powerful, but be prepared—the conversion process for Access and Visual Basic is not as easy as it appears.

SQL Server 7.0 Database Management 18
...use the new Data Transformation Services to transfer data from Access, Excel, Oracle, and SQL Server.

Visual Basic Accounting Systems: Source Code Included 24
...needs one. Not only do you get the VB Source Code, you also get developer tools and support.

Access Performance Tips 36
...make Access faster with these five code techniques.

Manipulate the Windows API with Visual Basic 44
Use this code to display device information in your VB applications, and learn how to create class modules to encapsulate the functionality of the Windows API for easier use.

Store Your VBA Subprocedures and Functions in Access 54
Develop applications faster and easier using a procedure library database.

Outlook Forms Customization 60
...meet specific business needs and generate automatic e-mail reminders with these techniques.

SQL Server 7.0 Import Export Transform

SPLAT!

ADVISOR Tips 74
• Year 2000 On-the-Fly
• Modal About Boxes
• Validate Two Controls Display Query Results
• Close the Form
• Faster Zero-Length String
• Year 2000 Fix
• Numbers Only Please
• Auto-Adjust Text menu

Ask ADVISOR 12
• Override Access Record Sources
• Access as a Back End to IIS

Volume / Number 2
JOB4 99 C0H07 35 UK£2 50
ADVISOR MEDIA, Inc.

Satisfaction Guaranteed
If, for any reason, you are ever dissatisfied with *Access-Office-VB Advisor*, just let us know. You'll receive a full refund on all unmailed issues remaining in your subscription, no questions asked.